BC

BEYOND INSIGHT

Deep Rhymes, Deeper Reasons

SUMNER L. SHAPIRO, M.D.

INTERNATIONAL UNIVERSITIES PRESS, INC.
New York

Library of Congress Cataloging in Publication Data

Shapiro, Sumner L
    Beyond insight.

    1. Psychoanalysis—Cases, clinical reports, statistics.
I. Title.
RC504.S48   616.8'917'0926   78-70233
ISBN 0-8236-0498-5

Manufactured in the United States of America

Contents

To all who helped,
inspired, and sacrificed

Preface

During the final days of 1976 my first book, *Moment of Insight*, appeared. Its introduction disclosed the several motives that inspired it. Of them, foremost was a wish to coax the layman, with me, back behind my couch, to eavesdrop ethically, and thus observe in operation the uniquely meticulous psychoanalytic method, the one for which I myself had been trained.

Equally important was the desire to make persuasive yet dignified response to myriad proponents of innovational schools of therapy that were daily springing up in our midst, and to do so in an instructive yet maximally palatable manner—to wit, through the anecdotal approach.

Accordingly, combing through my memory, I selected a handful of provocative stories from my practice, then, disguising identities, conversationalized, fictionalized, and dramatized the facts as I felt best befit their narrative rendition.

Then I waited—waited to learn how successful I was in the fulfillment of those ambitions. Results were varied, as varied as the readers themselves. Results somewhat difficult initially to assess. Results which are, it is to be hoped, still incomplete—should my first-born thrive and flesh out to attain its life expectancy.

I found people surprisingly shy. Apparently I intimidated them. Often they demurred rather than express an opinion, let

v

alone develop or expand upon it, or, if they dared to venture one, quite frequently it was condensed into a quick cliché: "Delightful." "Interesting." "Most instructive!"

No few, when pushed, admitted that they would have opted for more intricate and complex plots. Longer histories. Psychodynamics. Sure they could handle them! Others voiced disappointment that they hadn't found new recipes to guide them through their own life problems. Some belabored me with "buzz" words from particular persuasions to which they felt allegiance—schools at deviance with mine—and tried to corner me to reinterpret data—using their acceptable phenomenologies instead of psychoanalytic.

One former patient wrote me in distress. The book! She couldn't understand it, but many others volunteered that it had moved them. Some to tears ... and puzzling to me was the number who reported that repeatedly they had gone back to re-examine it for further comprehension or to search out darker messages—despite my having tried so hard to keep it crystalline.

Straightforward.

And there were those who urged on me increased participation. They most enjoyed those parts in which I was my most obtrusive, active, vocal. Out beyond the wainscot.

Chacun à son gout!

But the great bulk, the preponderance of criticism, inclined so favorably, in truth, that I felt no compunction whatever about promulgating more material—even prior to the publication by colleagues of reviews, which at last did supervene.

It would be overweening to single out the best or to quote them. Suffice it that, in sum, they much encouraged me with "nihil obstats."

Thus a second collection.

Behind its writing again are the major impulsions that generated the first: the wish to ply anew that threefold effort.

No less than with the former, the stories I have chosen are my children and my darlings, hence are destined to labor under the inevitable burdens we impose on second siblings, yet are blessed by that compensatory and unfailing parental blindspot that denies their imperfections.

Those, perforce, must be evaluated now by you and Time.

Res Ipsa Loquitur; E Pluribus Unum; Alas, Poor Yorick; and especially *Whodonit* will please those readers who asked of me lengthier renditions with more complex structure. In them, I have purposely embellished on the "deeper reasons" underlying, as it were, the "deeper rhymes." As is true of all the stories, they too enjoy their dénouements—their "ahas" of the analytic moment. But comprising warp and woof of richness and detail, they weave "beyond" the simple insight, and allow the "ethical eavesdropper" rare peeks into the dynamics and genetics of the symptomatologies presented.

The others, shorter, provocative, puckish here and there, and even inspirational, will, I hope, constrain those students for whom brevity remains "the soul of wit," to repeat their pithy praise.

Finally, also amply found should be compliance with the wish that I emerge, soliloquize, and margin-gloss with my philosophies. After all, to bask in growing confidence and sing his message out must be the staunch prerogative of any one so knighted "author" for a second time—with what success depending obviously on verdicts of yourselves, the critics, and, Time.

1

Res Ipsa Loquitur

Barney didn't sit as I did. He was still standing there before me when I looked up.

He reached into his shirt pocket and from it produced a folded square of paper. Twice he unhinged and flattened out its halves, then slid it forward across my desk top allowing me to notice newsprint on the back. As I reached to pick up the sheet, Barney's face broke into a grin. Square, strong yellow peasant teeth looking like kernels on a corn cob, began to show through the parting of his lips, and bridging the gap created thereby stood a slender string of saliva. When he said, "Pitchers, 'Doc,'" it popped.

"De're worth ten hunnert words."

Bad luck that he'd begun that colloquy with an explosive labial; helplessly I watched a droplet sail across a sunlit arch, then felt it on my cheek.

"I tore dat from 'a *Chronicle*," he said. "Here take a peek." His jack o' lantern smile became a husky laugh.

"Ha, ha, ha, ha."

His chuckle whetted my curiosity, but what I beheld was

macabre, not humorous. "What's the joke?" I asked. I didn't anticipate how seconds later I would be joining in his merriment as well.

It was a cartoon frame, showing a wizened skeleton, a spectre, moribund, with fifteen-twenty intravenous tubes and pipes, either pumping vital substance in or draining toxins off.

As it lay, in military garb, its right arm was cocked in a Nazi-style salute, and belted with a cummerbund inscribed with "El Caudillo's" name, the wraith appeared to speak these lines: "Old soldiers never die."

Sound funny yet? Francisco's death lampooned?

Do you remember how the world, day after day, monitored Franco's final gasps? And how science strove so desperately to save that leader's life?

To me it seemed a horrible tableau—with little cause for mirth. Why had he clipped it out? But, once I had angled it just right and had another look from presbyopic depths—why, I was chuckling too.

Its humor lay within a set of interlocking clues that fitted on each other like a telescoping tube. The story of Barney—and his psychotherapy, and his bizarre experiences—and the basis of our title, *Res Ipsa Loquitur*.

* * *

He asked me to "shrink" him.

Ulcers.

His first had burrowed somewhat unobtrusively into his stomach's lesser curvature. Spontaneously, it healed somehow. The second, by far the more impertinent and stubborn, dug a niche and stayed.

"Duodenal," a surgeon called it, and, as if taking personal umbrage at that dirty epithet, the lesion responded with a pyrotechnic splash. Positively rainbowesque: bright red-orange vomitus, green-tinged bile, then tar-black inky stools.

Understandably those volcanics scared the "livin' Jesus" out of Barney and humbled him sufficiently to hat-in-hand him to my door.

Now, is that an intimation that only such an extremity would budge him?

IT IS!

My new patient was a very basic, earthy type. "Man with a hoe." No foolishness. He was of that stock depicted by The Bard as "plain blunt men," with precious little tolerance for gossamer or quintessential frills.

I mean, he held no brief for treatments of any kind—but surgery as an alternative? No way! He would do almost anything to spare himself the knife.

And I probably should dwell on that. The man was ossified. This brash and bullish character would whimper at the contemplation, which, far more than quests for insight propelled him into therapy.

Just so!

"What choice I got?" he whined. Either I talk wid you 'n' get my head shrunk or the sawbones cuts me up. He'll take my stomach out," then, grinning ear to ear:

"Ya think my knob's too big? What other size ya got?"

The "knob," perpetuating his vernacular, now that he had mentioned it, actually was rather small and, being prematurely bald and almost perfectly spherical, it much reminded me of a basketball, except for lacking seams, and sporting twinning tufts of crisp black hair stuck out above his ears.

In freshman anthropology I had studied heads like his. They went with "mesomorphs," the so-called "muscle men," the type more geared to move about rather than brood and think—to impulse, not reflect. Such was their leit motif. No harm to be reminded, but it would be best for me to wait and see if Barney fit that mold.

He did.

And what a tale his was.

Runyonesque! Right from start right:

Chicago-born with two kid sisters and three kid brothers, and fatherless suddenly at the age of ten, ready or not, Barney was installed as instant head of that assemblage. He had survival thrust upon him.

Street Arab. Dead-end kid. He devised a style that inured him but kept him taut betides, enough to form a tough outer pellicle despite his inner warmth. An armadillo, soft as mush within but cased in skins of mail. Much bristle and much brass.

Do I convey the image? Barney could have modelled for that poster of the driver of a ten-ton truck who stops to let a kitten cross the street, or of the bruising wrestler weeping at a haiku verse (while doing needlepoint).

Down deep, his heart was good.

I could see that as he elaborated the solicitudes he felt about his younger sibs and Mom. I felt it through his humorous attempts to tickle me, and "honest Injun," I wasn't putting on when I chortled at his personal revision on the ten commandments:

"Cast yer bread onna water an watch it come back soggy!" or his real show-stopper, "Share 'n' share alone!" Nor was I patronizing in laughing at his cornball joke about getting his diploma from "Skroo U—the college of hard knocks."

I liked him immediately, which reaction sad to say, was not a universal one among his ilk.

People were too cowed by his "M.O." He withered his wife. His kids gave him wide berth, and his partner, secretary, clients, hirelings all, hopped and skipped and jumped to his command like toadies with St. Vitus dance.

Down to a man. Every last one of them, with a single exception.

Guess who!

His mom!

Godzilla Barney, all two hundred twenty pounds of him, the big and beefy champion, crusher, knee-knocker—to his tiny, fragile mother had remained her baby boy. Really!

Barney had a mother problem. Plain as that.

Herself? To me she sounded like incarnate "Mammy Yokum," diminutive but durable and feisty. She had a ring through Barney's nose and didn't hesitate to pull it.

His nuchal albatross!

In fact, the more we talked, the more I came to understand how pivotal a point she occupied in Barney's gastro-psychic flux.

She seemed a primum mobile in the chain of events that opened up his valves of HCL. See if you disagree:

Only scant weeks before his bleeding episode, Mother had winged westward from the Windy City. After a day or two, Barney's guts started a symphony of borborygmi. Bumped and ground, consumed their mucus, eroded, and bled their poor hearts out.

Hating to see her baby suffer, "Mammy" pitched right in and without realizing it, by attempting to nurse him back to health, came within a trace of killing her boy. He couldn't take her because his every flatulence and eructation made her gasp— worse yet, reminded her about her own complaints, her aches, her pains, her woes.

And once she'd started, her every organ system would report. Her bunions and her joints, her sacroiliac, digestion, and those dizzy spells, the chronic lack of sleep, until Barney, ailing or not, would be obliged to make some lame excuse to "split the scene" somehow.

Together, Barney and I literally spent hours, in which he

inveighed against the woman and how she was destroying him, in the midst of which tirade, on cue, her yearly visitation. It was May after all; bags and baggage, she arrived once more.

But she could stay only a week. Seven days. Mercifully finite span. A man could stand on one hand for seven days if he put his mind to it, my patient thought. How so?

He countenanced and he indulged her, tolling out the hours, the minutes up to flight departure time.

Until, how did Burns put it? About the best laid plans? Of mice and men and moms?

On the eve of Mother's leave-taking, bleary-eyed and runny-nosed, she checked her temperature and found 104. She had the Asian Flu!

Barney was livid. Apoplectic. He could not sit to talk. He paced to and fro within my tiny "surgery" shouting, "The rotten bitch! She hasta catch it in L.A.! Why not Chicago? It got bugs—Aaaagh! 'At's jus' my rotten luck. She's suppos'a be onna plane tomorra a.m. an' she's layin' sick in bed!

"Jesus Chris'.

"Ya know somet'in? Wailin' all day long. She don't shut her trap long enough to ketch her breath. A hunnert four degrees! She'll need a goddam month; fer cryin' out!

"Ya know somet'in else? I got it figgered out da reason I almos' blew my 'kishkis.' It's cause I was expectin' her. Chris', what I gotta do?"

Barney burped.

I watched him peel out and swallow down a gelusil. For half a minute the room was strikingly quiet, then he struck up the chorus once again.

"Ya think dat I'm a 'hyperchondiak?' Ya otta hear my Maw. How many bones we got, fifty-five or six? She hurts in every one of 'em 'n' joints 'n' hinges too. She's a catasterphy—jus' one big goddam' ache."

"No way to tune her out?" I managed against his barrage. He heard.

"Ya kiddin, 'Doc?' I really wish she'd croak!"

Then, pausing to catch his breath, or possibly to ponder what I'd asked him, or more than likely to use the hiatus for proper dramatic effect, Barney reached into his vest pocket. From its recess he produced another foil-wrapped tablet, only larger than the one before. Plain view, he bit it in half, stippling his lower lip and chin with white powder flecks.

Boyishly as if he had just finished a purloined sugar doughnut, he eyed me askance then placed the second half upon the tip of his tongue, maneuvered it into position, and loudly crumbled and ground it to a paste between his molars. Swallowing hard, hand to mouth, he stiffened and allowed himself the luxury of a belch.

"A-a-a-a-ah—Excuse it 'Doc'—A-a-ah—'at feels better. Yeah! She'll bury me, da bitch. Look, *I try to tune 'er static out* excep' she plays it 'stereo.' It catches me both sides, outside 'n' in."

Another belch.

"Besides, she's indestructible. So what she's fulla piles, 'n' kidney stones 'n' hysterecomies? She's had em all. Lumbago 'n' varicose stuff everywhere. I wish she'd cash her chips. I do! I wish she'd pack it in."

Oh he was raking her alright, his aged parent, except that I knew (and most certainly he knew that I knew) that much of what he rhapsodized was tongue-in-cheek. Showman! He loved to stir his audience. Once he had caught its ear, momentum carried him along. He would rise to greater heights:

"Ya talk French 'Doc?' Ya pally-voo? Ya promise this is 'enter-noo?' I groused about 'er to a pal—dis guy who knowsa mob. He says he'll get a contract out fer jus' five hunnert clams. He says he knows dis 'finger man' so's she c'n be erased. Ya

hear me 'Doc?' Ya listenin'? A contrac' on my Maw, 'n' I'd be
ridda her! Fer keeps!''

A hefty enough curse, it was. Pretty salty talk, and power-
ful too, because no sooner had he punctuated the paenult and
the ultima when the telephone rang.

Since my calls are screened, without knowing who was in
trouble I did sense something urgent and I was right. On the
line? Barney's wife. She urged him to hurry home. His mom
was "really bad"—she had had a heart attack!

*   *   *

Barney blanched.

He jumped up from his seat so quickly that his jacket
pocket caught a corner of the desk. Up-ending it, he spilled my
ashtray to the floor and managed to tear loose his seams. He
mumbled an apology of sorts, but left me with the mess of butts
and match sticks and was gone.

He sped home recklessly.

On seeing her son arrive, Mother sat bolt upright. She slid
out of bed and, arms extended, shuffling, zombied up to him.
Like Karloff doing Frankenstein. Clutched his shirt front and
cravat, turned purple, and collapsed at his feet.

Almost as if she'd overheard and was accomodating him.
She croaked. That's right. She simply "upped" and "died!''

His fateful hateful words!

Had he said "*Drop dead twice?*" Well, once would have to
do. An era was at end. Her curtain had rung down.

*   *   *

Ah yes—except for one small hook: the fact that these
days dying isn't what it used to be. Once upon a time they would

hold a mirror to your mouth to see if moisture formed. Or touched your cornea to check if you still blinked, or palped your wrist to catch a pulse, or listened to your chest. Remember?

When you could die with a certificate? Just once. Effectively and neat.

That's all passé.

It's different now: Today death is computerized. They plug you into the nearest wall outlet. Transistors take over. One bank beats your heart; another pumps your lungs. Siphons flush your kidneys, and they feed your veins by tubes. And every vital tick is monitored on screens. Microscopic scrutiny by nursing engineers.

We are at a point, so to speak, where longevity is tied to kilowatts and paying power bills, and, somewhere in the process, needing a philosopher instead of a mortician to see when we are ready for that ride across the Styx.

That is how it unfolded for Barney's Mom. They rushed her to the hospital and connected her. Transfused fresh blood and breathed her souped-up air. Bladder rinsed, colon laundered, she was oscillated at 100 cps with a dozen coaxial cables, pipes, wires, cords, tubes transforming her into a polyethlene queen. Arachne! Lying metamorphosed in a spider web of silver, copper skeins—direct and alternate.

No sunset passed without a visit from her child. Yet, Barney could do no more than stand and stare, eyes wide, himself as much in limbo as his mom.

Then it resolved.

Sunday. Evening.

The hospital—outside the I.C.U. Mother's internist.

In his hand her chart. Its metal binder folded back, the front revealed a set of graphs. Three flat red lines without a peak or trough. Unbroken by relief.

The doctor pursed his lips. His head rocked side to side,

until, eye-contacting Barney, he pulled from his pocket a thick, stubby, old-fashioned fountain pen and with it tapped the topmost sheets of the record emphatically, "clack, clack, clack."

And exploiting his prerogatives, sotto voce muttered, "No. This isn't good! This isn't good at all. No, not at all. Not good!"

"What's 'at suppos'a mean?" Barney broke in, assuming correctly that the soliloquy was at least partly meant as a duet.

"That Mother, face it son ... 'clack, clack, clack,'" the loosely anchored papers echoed, "is just about a vegetable. There isn't any hope. Now I don't want to influence your thoughts, but have a look yourself. You see this evidence?"

Barney quipped, "'at stuff is Greek ta me."

"Well, just look at these tracings. Flat. All flat. No. Her time has come, I'd say."

"Her 'time' fer what, you'd say?"

"For hard decisions. Very hard indeed!"

"Spit it!" Barney rasped. "Ya wanna cut da juice?"

"Er, ... well, crudely put ... er, yes. It's a question whether any valuable purpose can be served.—And you're the next of kin. It's really up to you."

Barney blinked. He swallowed hard. He burped. "Bowed by the weight of centuries" he tilted toward the wall. "A look of ages in his face," and "on his back, the burden of"— a choice. He simply had to think.

But drained and powerless. How many years before had some other physician snipped and tied the line through which she'd fed *him* life? Was this poetic justice? A way to return the compliment, only in reverse? One hundred eighty out?

Topsy-turvy world!

Hysteron and proteron.

An infant being asked to disumbilicate its mom?

His fons et origo?

Barney mumbled, "Pull da goddam plug? Oh Christ. I gotta think."

But there, alas, was a substantial part of the poor fellow's problem. He was a mesomorph. More geared to move about. Besides, the shock regressed him, back back back through all phylogeny, back to something close to protoplasmic jelly. He could feel it in his spine.

Could an amoeba think?

At length, "I gotta walk," he said.

And pushing his way between Hippocrates and the I.C.U. nurse, hardly aware of the former's clapping him upon his shoulder, he impulsed through the passageway.

Weaving along beside the canvas-padded gurneys, he stopped to slug down a shot of ice cold water from the white porcelain dispenser in its wall cut-out, wiping a drop across his temple. Then past the room marked "Doctor's Lounge," past "Central Supply," past the waiting room, all the way to EXIT, where, obedient to body type, he bolted through and gained the stairwell, up.

But here the record falters. Nor is there hope of resurrecting Barney's cerebrations as he climbed. I surmise a potpourri of childhood scenes, Chicago streets, kid brothers, sisters, mother and her gripes—pictures flashing, pulsing, jumbled, a cascade right to the roof.

Where Barney stepped outside.

In the void, dark and impressionless, cool night air allowed some small composure to return. "A vegetable," he whispered. "Like spinach? Rhubarb? Broccoli? Oh shit! Uv alla rotten luck!"

Two hairy hands reached out to the waist-high parapet. Ten stubby fingers ran along its upper surface, delicately—something like a blind man reading Braille. Seeking answers. To some riddle. From the stucco and cement. He tried to sort it out; he really tried.

And periodically, behind him, from the elevator housing came a "clunk, clunk, clunk." Somewhere in the entrails of the building, like a giant yo-yo, up and down, and dimly dawning on him a resentment, of a paradox. The power to maintain that car in service and the wish to stint its use and kill his mom.

Ten seconds more Barney scanned the heavens, counting stars. Ten he spent eyeing the traffic in the streets below. Ten he paced along the rooftop gravel, scuffing it beneath his thick-soled shoes. Then, abruptly, he descended the stairs, retraced his steps to I.C.U., found the executioner, and told him, "O.K. Turn her off!"

*   *   *

During the ensuing three weeks, the visits of relatives, trips to the airport, funeral arrangements, and the thousand other odds and ends in need of tidying when someone's mother dies virtually upstaged the psychotherapy.

Despite my wishing otherwise, our pattern was considerably undone. Yet Barney brushed off my concern. I need not fret, he said. He had "no time to worry on" himself. Luckily a surge of extra "oomph" was speeding him along. Seeing all "them relics" of his past proved buoying—made him feel heroic; he could skip "a coupla sessions, no sweat."

He did. But gave me the willies all the same, because he seemed *too* glib, *too* cool. To my interrogation, always came his answer that he had no regrets, remorse, or second thoughts.

"I hear da way ya caution me 'bout aftershocks, 'n' I unnanstan' how it's later when it hits—cause, so to speak, I was her 'murderer'; dat much psychology I know, but toss dat theory out. It jus' don' work wid me. Ya see how good I look? No pains, no stomach aches!''

I smiled. Why argue with success? Nonetheless I warned him about excessive confidence. He'd have to mourn her loss. I said, "It's not quite over Barney. Don't count chickens; watch your step. You know, mothers are special. All your life, only one. And somehow or other, I can promise you'll be at least a year digesting her death, especially how it came about. So walk on eggshells, will you?''

He wagged his head slightly protruding his lower lip. I continued: "Look, it's normal to be depressed when you lose something or someone close to you; one way or another, all of us react. A person may have nightmares; many just go around slowed up, sulking, 'down in the dumps.' You're a different kind of fella. I mean you *could* have little crying spells or flashbacks, but chances are your nervousness will hit your guts the way it always has. Or then again, considering your style, talking with your muscles, so to speak, you might dramatize her death, act it out, relive it—charade it—follow me?''

"Charades? Naw. I dunno dat game. Oh, once I seen it on T.V., but Doc don't lose no sleep. I'm right on top a' things. I run da whole damm funeral. I done a super job. Ya shoulda seen me go, da hearse 'n' alla caterin', 'n' flowers, everythin'. Oh yeah, I really done it good.

"It's true ya only get one Maw.''

Barney creased his forehead. He ran the back of his rough hand across his brow as if to smooth it, then, in a follow-through, slid his palm and fingers down along his cheek. Reversing direction, he crossed them over the bridge of his nose, rubbing his eyes, back and forth, and back again.

His face flushed but I saw no tear.

"Yeah, dat funeral. I hate them creepy things ... ya know, it jus' could be you got a point about her death upsettin' me. Dis real weird thing happened. I sorta blew my mind. It wasn't addin' two plus two 'n' pushin' out a four. Listen. You know I'm punkchooal. My wife? She's somet'in else. I mean on the mornin' of the funeral, which ain't supposa' be no Miss America beauty pagean', I'm fussin' 'n' screamin' at her to shake a leg a-cause we're runnin' pretty late 'n' then, while I'm drivin' all uv a sudden I see dis red light on my dash? 'Fer Jesus' sake!' It's flashin' out at me! So I says, 'Edna, lookit that. Ya took so goddam long I got no battery. It isn' chargin' up. We're gonna hafta stop.'

"Ya see I figger it's my fanbelt broke er maybe da generator's onna fritz 'n' if I'm in any kinda luck it c'n get fixed up fast, so I pulls into this gas station 'n' I nabs this kid 'n' tells him, 'Mac, hey, over here. Ya gotta help me quick. I'm buryin' my ma', 'n' I tells him about da funeral 'n' all 'n' so he runs inna garage 'n' in a minute he starts wheelin' out some kinda octopus machine 'at's got a hunnert wires 'n' clips, 'n' he starts 'tachin' 'em together unnaneath my hood.

" 'Start 'er up,' he says, 'n' 'Turn 'er off again,' 'n' stands there, scratchin' on his knob like it don't make no sense.

"How could it, all 'em tangled lines—jus' like a spider web? 'n' I'm really sweatin' then, 'n' checkin' on my watch, jus' when it zaps me onna head.

"A thunner bolt—for Jesus' sake—'A *flashin' light*,' I says. I'm ridin' wid my han' brake on. I never kicked 'er off. 'At's what's been signalin'.

"No wonna he can' find what's wrong. It ain't da battery.

"But here's da funny part. I stands there like I'm hypno-tize', jus' starin' at 'em wires. As if I los' my voice, I can't say '*turn 'er off*!'

"Ya think 'ats funny, Doc?"

*   *   *

Well, in due course I pointed out to Barney that he had fulfilled my prophecy. I felt he understood; more so when together we discussed how running with his hand brake set could also be an "acting out," as if preconscious reluctance for the task he was obliged to perform had dictated his mistake.

His grasp of that much encouraged my daring to introduce him to still more advanced theory, and so, with fingers crossed, I spoke a little about ambivalence, with all its pros and cons. That concept might help much with his mourning.

Perhaps for the first time in all Barney's long checkered career someone honored him by attempting a formal teaching exercise. He reacted like Molière's *Bourgeois Gentilhomme*, exuberantly. Remember how the latter thrilled to find he could learn "prose" so quickly and so easily?

It flattered Barney's vanity. Then, like a kid with a new toy, suddenly "ambivalence" was everywhere for him. He found it in relations with his wife, his kids, his partner. His Janus-headed playmate lurked behind every bush and rock.

Everywhere!

Even with me.

With his mother's death, tongue-in-cheek, Barney proclaimed himself legally to be an orphan. Between the lines of that lament I read his asking that the mentor whom he had adopted as a parent surrogate return the favor and adopt him equally. Only fair.

And with the dubious distinction of the teacher-pet relationship, predictably, there emanated equal measures of hostility and love.

The latter came out subtly. Barney tweaked me. Gently. He tested my authority and skills. Take for instance the story of the juniper outside my office and the palos verdes wall surrounding it.

Like so many other Californians I enjoy puttering about

my premises after hours. Week-ends, holidays, and rest assured, with a practice in my home, no minor change nor major goes unnoticed. Only the meekest fail to mention when the carpet is replaced, the woodwork gets repainted, or another plant or shrub has been interred.

Generally, if a patient suspects that his physician performed the job himself, there is a halo hung above the workmanship and the shiny armored knight who did it, however amateur its crafting. But Barney, no wise meek on this subject found, I felt, a perfect way to chide me, consistent with the nether side of love.

He pointed to the baby evergreen standing in the fresh-turned earth.

"Dat pine tree's gonna choke. Ya shouldna' stuck 'er there. Maybe I gotta learn ya, Doc. Ya got it too hemmed in. You'll see. It's gonna die. An' soon."

"Cocky, arrogant," I mused. Of course he could be right. It was within the drip line of a towering pepper and a eucalyptus tree, but die or not, what crossed my mind was his preoccupation with that subject and another death, which, silently I filed under the rubric of his mother's. Her demise, and thinking how, when it might be appropriate, I'd point that out to him, I let him carry on.

"It needs more 'libinsroom.' Ya stranguletin' it. An' while we're onna subjec', lookit here."

His chin jerked toward the wall.

"Ya shoulda' dressed dis post. Ya see dese stones? They shoulda' closed it round. Ya make a cuff like dis. It's more perfessional." And bending over the low parapet that ringed the juniper, he cupped his hairy hands about the four-by-four to show me what he meant. He had a point. I told him so. Nor was I fool enough to joust with Barney on construction. He knew his work quite well. But what about that post? Was *that* an "acting out?" Did it pertain to death? To mother? Or to me?

*   *   *

About a two-hour drive south of Los Angeles, extending twenty miles inland and an equal length along the coast lies the old Santa Margarita Ranch. During World War II and the Korean Crisis, that four hundred square mile area was given to the government—or preempted by it. Renamed "Camp Pendleton," it became the west coast counterpart of Parris Island and Camp Lejeune. Marines, along its lengthy stretch of sand, were schooled in storming beaches and landing maneuvers as befit old-fashioned kinds of wars.

With peace secured and the antiquation of LST's and running, rifle-high, through waist-deep waters, came louder and louder clamorings from lobbyists in Sacramento for the civilian reclamation of that frontage strip. Developers, including Barney, understandably maintained an active interest in any chance to get their fingers in said pie. Therefore, when my patient told me that Major Brittle had invited him and his business associate, along with a group of other gentlemen, to drop down to San Clemente for a look, I could not sensibly deny his request that he be excused from our appointed meeting that morning.

"If there's no other time," I muttered, unenthusiastically.

"Naw dere ain't. This Brittle don't fool around. 'Eleven hundred hours,' whatever dat means," Barney chuckled. "So I either buck da CMC, or take it out on you."

And on a schedule calculated to accomplish that rendezvous Barney and his partner headed out. My patient drove. His long-time friend, unused to early rising, exploited their understanding, and napped peacefully as their business vehicle wended south.

Traffic was sparse. The day was fine and clear. Periodic glimpses of the ocean displayed its graceful arching back, its brilliant points of light, its pleasant azure blue. Off Laguna Barney saw a school of whales lazily migrating down toward Baja California. He stopped a minute, watching silently, then inched back into the road and picked up speed.

At "ten hundred-thirty hours," a road sign indicated the San Onofre exit, the rear gate of the base. He knew to turn just there, and did, spotting the sentry post, then slowing down, nudged his passenger awake.

"Hey Steve, get up. We're here! We gotta get a pass. Ya got da papers in yer case?" His partner nodded. Sleepily he produced the necessary, which, when shown to the fierce yet baby-faced marine, won for them both a smartly executed PFC salute and wave, and a windshield decal granting entrance.

The military road was narrower than the highway. It curved and rose and fell as it proceeded east and south. Speed limits were clearly strung at intervals, yet Barney set himself a somewhat rapid pace. Steve warned him to slow down.

At the first tent camp, Las Pulgas, the lane abruptly narrowed and as it did so, unexpectedly, from a dip within it, a military vehicle—peep, jeep, or semi, loomed dramatically in front of them—too close.

Steve, now wide awake, called out. Barney fought the steering wheel to gain some clearance—which he managed by a whisker as the truck slipped past them and was gone.

"You're driving much too fast," said Steve. "We're gonna make it. Slow 'er down."

And at Camp Horno, unaccountably my patient ran a stop. He apologized but didn't offer more until after they arrived.

At the B.O.Q.

In front of it were parked two military vehicles. The engines of both were running. At the wheel of one, rigid, alert, sat a spit-and-polish USMC corporal, and behind him, three rather pudgy bespectacled mufti-clad middle-aged civilians who were chatting amicably. In the second vehicle, a single gentleman was seated. Its pilot, a Marine Corps Major, on seeing the new arrivals, jumped out and instantly materialized before them. Extending both his hands, to left and right, he simultaneously grasped those of the new arrivals.

"Major Brittle! You must be Ambler and you're Smith, I take it. I suggest we leave at once. Come on aboard. I'll drive," and glancing at his time-piece, large as a muffin on his wrist, and fair-choked with buttons, dials, barometers, and weather vanes, he went on, "It's just eleven hundred hours. Fifteen minutes to the beach, and fifteen minutes back should leave us half an hour. That's just enough. Be here in time for lunch. Cut out!" With which he tucked a swagger stick smartly beneath his right axilla and climbed into his jeep.

On his "ahead" signal the tiny convoy started.

During the ride the Major thawed. Little by little, Steve, Barney's associate drew out of him much cherished reminiscences of World War Two. The Corps had glory then. "Semper fi." It was a proud career. But what the hell! Just twelve more months and he'd be able to retire, half-pay and severance. He might move to L.A. Of course he'd look Steve up.

Even with the thaw, however, one could clearly feel resentments. Bad show to sacrifice that beach strip. Fie upon marinas! Tennis clubs and condominiums! That was what was wrong with our country. Too much pampering and self-indulgence. Twenty years, and eight of combat and a purple heart. That taught you values properly.

Why do I dwell on this? Because Barney, who ordinarily would have been so vocative, sat silent and glum. Steve did not comment on it, but I later learned how puzzled he had been at his buddy's passive grunts and condescending "yups," particularly where his baby, land development, was being so impugned—so wanting him as spokesman. No, that did not make much sense. Not yet.

And when they "hit the beach" and both groups reassembled, and the others were so full of life—reliving days at Normandy and their own military coups, and one portly gentleman, fiftyish, "invaded Normandy," and another "did Dieppe"—Barney who had been in combat at Dunkirk, much out of character, seemed pensive and aloof, refusing to join in.

And when, in order to view the seascape and the contour of the cove of a prospective seabreak, Brittle led the animated pack up a gentle rise, Barney remained below, sitting on a rock.

Brittle shouted down to him that Anacapa could be seen from there; it was that clear, and "ordered" him on up, but as Barney made to do his bidding, his right leg buckled, and threw him to the ground.

"It musta gone to sleep," he fumbled, rubbing it vigorously, "or else I tripped. Don' wait on me. I see enough from here."

Except that two hours later, descending the short wooden stairway from the officers mess at B.O.Q., down to the parking lot, it gave again and but for the hand rail at his side, Barney might have tumbled to the pavement below.

"Martinis," he grumbled. "Chris, I shouldna' drunk so much. You drive us Steve. Come on, let's go."

How did I come to learn in such detail the incident at Pendleton? Only through persistence and what Brittle might have called, "direct assault."

And much later.

I felt I had to, because several times on his descent into my sunken chamber, Barney's foot flopped as it hit the bottom steps, and nearly sent him reeling. This he "figgered prob'ly was a 'tack of the art'ritis" from which he had suffered on and off the past few years.

"But I didn' wanna squawk about it—'n' you know the reason better'n' anyone. Cause yer gonna think it's jus' how ya perdickted from ya books, da way ya warned me it would happen."

I interrupted, "You mean because your mother had lumbago?"

"Yeh, dat's it. Right on! Course my wife claims I been drinkin' much too heavy, gainin' weight besides. Except I ain't. Da drink I mean. I hardly touch a' stuff. Ya think it's on account I pulled my mother's plug?"

"I think we ought to get your leg examined, for a start. You ought to see your doctor."

"Ain't you one?" asked Barney, sheepishly.

"I am."

"So why'ncha fix da leg jus' like ya done da ulcer?"

"If I thought I could I'd prob'ly have a try ... but Barney," I prepared my explanation, "this feels different, or at least I can't be sure without some tests."

"I'd let *you* do 'em," Barney shuffled.

"No, I can't. You would need a good neurologist perhaps."

"Like who?"

"I could help you find one, but why not ask your family physician."

"Well, suppose he wan'sa operate on me?"

"We should cross just one bridge at a time, like adults. You agree?"

"I got no choice, I guess," said Barney, and I smiled to let him know that he was wholly right.

After Barney left, I had the distinct impression he must have been much more worried than he had admitted. I mulled the ancient saw, the caveat, which we psychiatrists do so well to remember, that neuroses and psychoses don't confer immortality. A patient also catches colds or gets the mumps. Besides anxiety, there is a world of viruses and germs, real ones, deadly too. I questioned restlessly, *could* Barney have some other something, like a toxin or a tumor, something growing slowly, pressing on his cord? *I* then heard the clap of thunder, and just as he did months before, *I* beheld the lightning flash!

A high cord tumor, growing slowly, might account for paresis. The one he'd been denying to himself and me. Son of a gun! Of course! That would explain it. He outwardly projected his awareness—on my pine tree! On my post! He didn't care about their strangling! Barney had been talking of himself!

What a miserable unconscious tactic.

It *was* an "acting out." But what a tangled mess! I tried to tease apart the separate components.

Item:

Barney wanted, in his "orphandom" and in the "transference," to be my good little son. Ergo, he should not complain to me about minor aches and pains the way his mother used to do. He would be more grown up, valiant.

Item:

Barney needed to refute my prediction that he would punish himself somehow for having cursed her first, then for taking such an active part in causing her to "drop dead twice."

Item:

Barney had a history of "knifophobia." He would do anything to obviate the need of surgery, even if it meant denial of his symptoms, all his life.

Item:

By ignoring the messages his body sent him, by refusing them admittance to his mind, he could indeed risk grievous self-punishments through accession of serious illness.

There were other threads of evidence besides: the way he'd run the stop sign at Las Pulgas. And his sitting at the bottom of the hill when Brittle called, and his nearly falling from the wooden stairway as he left the B.O.Q. and the pièce de résistance—*Imputing* to the eucalyptus and pepper tree that "strangulating" squeezing, and the cuffing of the post. The lot of it was all about himself!

A growth around his cord!

Know what?

Scant ten days later I had the sorrowful pleasure of full confirmation of my diagnostic coup. Dr. Potter, the neurosurgeon told the two of us (to me in a report) my patient had a tumor, and it should be cut out, and quickly.

Instantly!

Fair enough.

Or was it? Perversity of fate!

The only hospital nearby equipped to handle such an operation, with a proper I.C.U., was the selfsame hospital where his mother said, "Goodbye!"

* * *

Was it a gargoyle?

No.

Just a very small boy with a wedge-shaped head.

Hydrocephalus?

Beneath his lifeless eyes dark hollows cast a sickly, phthisic aura, and in his hand he held a button, the kind you used to see to ring back-door bells.

Running out of it spun a double set of wires, one to the left connecting with a gong and hammer, and the other to the right, plugged into the wall.

The bell began to ring. Quickly!

How very strange! A sound like that. I'd heard such trills before. He rang it once again. Something was awry. Glancing around, I saw my bedside stand.

My clock. Its large hand perpendicular. The small one perched on three.

I'm dreaming.

Three o'clock.

The telephone—another ring—Aha! But at three a.m.?

Beyond the window casement the sky was midnight blue. With effort I could force against its backdrop the delineation of the ink-black hills where, across the gorge, my distant neighbor's long curving driveway lay outlined by the tiny low-voltage sentinel lamps he had strung along its side.

"Ach! Who in hell?"

Another ring. Penetrating echoes, demanding my response. Destroying dreams.

I fumbled for the instrument. A notebook toppled to the floor. On top of it the *Journal of Psychiatry*. "Hello," at last I cried, as much with curiosity as pique.

"Sorry to disturb you, Doctor, at this hour. It's the Mercy Hospital in Chatsworth. Miss Flaherty, the nurse at I.C.U. O.K. to put her on?"

At the other end of the line a confident but friendly voice repeated that name for me, then went on to say that Dr. Potter who was with *my* (sic!) patient wished to have a word. Might she put me "on hold" until she summoned him?

Potter? I.C.U.? Well, that could refer to only one person and that was Barney.

But to orient myself psychically I fished for the date and time when surgery had taken place. How long ago? Yeah, Ambler. What a character! A guy the textbook said you couldn't treat.

Oh yeah!

Well, I threw out the text and kept the human being. So, we would have to write more books to cover him.

"Inadequate psychological sophistication, lacking formal education," but I'd managed anyhow. Shown Barney something about ulcers, magic thinking, ambivalence, transferance, denial, and most recently about *projection*—with that cursèd tumor on his spine.

"Hi, Potter here!"

"Hi, Dave."

"Regrets about the hour, old buddy. How long has it been since medicine disturbed your forty winks?"

"What's up?"

"It's Ambler. Barney Ambler. You remember him?"

"Of course I do."

"Well, let me fill you in and bring it up to date. I guess I told you how I found an 'olive' growing between C_2 and C_3 compressing his pyramidal tract. It was a neurofibroma. Benign, but causing paresis and footdrop, ipsilateral, recall your anatomy?"

"That much," I responded glumly, waiting.

"Well, I scooped it out and closed him up all right. Routine. 'Skin to skin,' three hours, and I got him here to I.C.U.

okay until tonight. The guy has 'flipped his lid' for sure. He's 'outta' sight!' "

"How do you mean?" I managed.

"He's gone nuts for some damn foolish reason, which is why I thought of you. 'Cause you've been seeing him."

"Dave, tell me what he did exactly. It would help if I could get the picture clearer still."

"Okay, look—you know he's on a Foley, and we did a prophylactic 'trach' to play it safe. Post-op, he spiked a little fever, so I started amphicillin, but tonight he shoved the nurse and pulled both I.V.'s out. He tried to yank his Foley—and the monitors that chart his vital signs 'n' E.K.G.—now, here's the problem. I don't want to sedate him with surgery that close to the brain stem, so I put him in restraints, then thought of you."

"Restraints?" And that's when Potter thought of me? That chafed. It told me where I stood with Potter. Jesus Christ! "Restraints" were catalogued in his computer bank beside my field.

Had we progressed so little? Psychiatry had need of pitchmen! Good PR to sell it to his kind.

Potter. Over the years I had known him only casually. In his specialty he was totally competent—meticulous and reputedly brilliant, but outside of it? Must be that therein hung another tale.

How casually? Well, as neighbors together we had protested the subdivision of a large land tract adjacent to our homes. Our wives shopped the same supermarkets and boutiques. Our children attended the same school. In fact, Dave was in the audience the night I gave the "sex talk" to the sixth grade students—with his son—but that was where it ended. And here was the "bottom line," so to speak, of how little I had managed to impress upon him.

The clock read ten past three. Peripherally I could discern

that the alarm was set for its usual five fifteen. Summoning to mind my schedule for the day, I recalled no less than fourteen patients, dawn to dusk. Bad luck!

Barney shouldn't wait. He couldn't until evening. Was there someone I could shift around to make a space? Or someone I could ask to see him in my stead? No way!

I knew him better by far than any total stranger—and the fact was, he knew me.

So, what to do?

"Dave, you there?" I questioned. "Look, I'm pretty wide-awake right now. Suppose I drop around and have a look tonight? You needn't wait. I'll write a note; tell Miss Flaherty and ask her to let him know I'm coming, and the reason, would you please?"

By three twenty I was washed, shaved, and dressed. Rather than rouse my wife, I scribbled her a couple of lines and laid them on my pillow. In the kitchen, luckily the coffee from the evening meal was still in the thermos decanter on the stove. Lacking its usual hot, pleasant bite, and suffering an acid taste, it went down anyway. I ventured outside.

Yes, I recall my thoughts: It felt heroic; I was buoyed. Say what you will—and I'm the last of the die-hards to disparage the office practice of Psychiatry—but, well, there really is something thrilling in the tangible, the practical, the concrete. A palpable contribution at a time of need.

May I philosophize? I would guess the issue bears somewhat upon contrast—sitting all day long amidst shadows and nuances and the spiderwebs—Psychiatry, Alas! And doubly so, Analysis!

Flashback to internship and to days of doctoring with shots and pills. Push the needle in and blood comes out. It is red and bright and unequivocal! No ambiguity to that!

Momentarily at least, I had a sense of loss.

I missed incisiveness, curves, graphs, threads, needles, nurses' uniforms, smells of phenol, scrubbing in. Just think, to find a focus of pathology, "an olive," and to see it, three-dimensional, and there! And deftly, cleanly to "scoop it out," then put it in a jar. Formaldehyde, where never never more could it haunt anyone again, and wreak its woes.

Begone!

How satisfying!

Are surgeons better off, or do they tire and find *their* work routine?

The car door slammed in place. No ambiguity in that! And as I slid the key into the ignition slot and gave a forthright twist, the engine cracked alive—without ambivalence, without philosophy.

And out into the night.

The city might as well have been the moon. Balboa Boulevard resembled a post-atomic holocaust. It stretched ahead, denuded, deserted, silent. The park, the pale blue incandescent lamps, the empty tennis courts, the grassy mall, and off across the street the golf course driving greens, without a solitary figure playing, waiting, walking—nothing. Totally abandoned. Eerie, ghostly.

Silver bright, the moonshine lit the pavement, the asphalt, buildings—really rather beautiful, sedate. They looked a little like the kind of photographic trick one sees these days in movies to portray an intrapsychic bit, a reminiscence or a glimpse into the layers below the conscious, do you know?

And high above the sidewalks, symmetrical, and spaced at intervals, those selfsame street lamps in obéissance to Euclid. Uprights, perpendiculars, and parallels, receding to a point in paired design, out to infinity and gone, reminded me of vertebrae, columnar, and the backbone—Barney, growths, and tumors of the spine.

A mile away a tiny red tail light moved off into the horizon. I neither gained upon nor lost ground to it. Who, I wondered? On what mission? Was that Potter going home to catch some sleep? A watchman making rounds? Patrol? A Casanova? Could another Don Quixote possibly be out on a mission? At this hour? I mean besides myself?

* * *

The West Hills Motel had shut up for the evening. "No Vacancy" in cursive amber neon spelled that out. The Maitre d' was snoozing in his sheets, and tourists were tucked up in their pillows and their quilts.

I drove on thinking, "Sleep, sleep, knits up the ravell'd sleeve of care".... "Perchance to dream"—yeah! What of mine? I wondered, could that image of a child with hydrocephalus, could that have been in reference to Barney too? Had I been dreaming of him? Likely so. I had heard the telephone and instantly I must have slipped his whole "cassette" right into place, a bit disguised, it's true; but Barney—yes—it fit! The wires, the operation near his head.

So Barney pulled his I.V. out? "A wild man!" Well, I had hunches about that.

* * *

A blinking yellow signal flashed out "Caveat!" Of what? Reflexively I slowed down, then drove on through.

Further north, a night cleaning crew had left two giant buffers and some length of heavy-duty rubber cord lying in the middle of the street outside the Valley Bank. The panel truck into which that apparatus would be wheeled sat angled, open-doored, with two stout wooden planks as ramps along whose length the buffers were to roll.

As I approached, a man in grimy white coveralls emerged, then with him, a buxom woman in a woollen sweater. With western nonchalance he waved me to stop, until, with shoving, the pair of them had urged the heavy buffers up and in the van.

Apparently that did it. They had finished purifying the bank. Antiseptic. Desmudged. Wiped clean. Gone the finger-prints and marmalade left on the countertops, the carpet dust, half sterilized the tellers' window panes and judases through which they spoke. Indeed, a baby could retrieve and suck again upon his lollipop, so lintless the perfection of the floor.

What a paradox! Those two laborers with such big blunderbusses could achieve what luckless Barney could not, nor the doctors, nor the nurses, nor the operating room despite the filtered O.R. air, the caps, the masks, the gowns. The autoclaves. Permanganate and phisohex and surgical technique. The pinnacles of scientific skill.

It's true.

They opened up his theca, only after studious precautions.

And yet, how easily an errant bug strolled in. I mean despite those obstacles, and split himself in twain, then multiplied again, until a million hydraheaded monsters filled his theca up with fomites and debris.

And spiked a fever for him.

Poor Barney!

Less clean than Valley Bank? Good grief!

But violent? No! Microbes won't do that, or pull out intravenouses. Takes more than germs. We should see.

*   *   *

On the corner of Mason and Chatsworth, directly across from the Hospital, courtesy of Sylvan Realty, were offered to the sleeping world the temperature and time:

Three-thirty-nine and fifty-five degrees.

In the parking lot were scattered half a dozen cars. Five clumped close to the entrance by "Emergency." The other, a "Jag," was all alone in the area reserved for "Doctors Only." I pulled beside it wondering—had Potter waited there to talk with me?

At a desk, absorbed in a magazine whose cover sported naked bodies, the gray-uniformed Security at last looked up but did not speak. I started to explain my mission and to ask the way, but noticing an arrow labelled "I.C.U.," unchallenged, followed where it led and then beyond.

The elevators had an innovation. Braille embossings by the buttons for the floors. Good idea! How come it took so long? Third floor, and through the swinging doors.

Voilà!

Shades of 1984!

I had left behind the present and stood in the cabin of a spaceship. Headed where?

Along the walls were panels of black boxes. Each had its window and, across its face, green squiggly wiggly lines in sinusoidal waves, and "bleeps." Trailing out of each came arm-thick insulated cables, coupled massively then diving out of sight beneath the floor.

Coaxials.

Buck Rogers! Dr. Jekyll's lab, at least!

Was any humanoid about? An astronurse? "Hello!"

With some trepidation I entered more deeply into the flying saucer. The inner chamber was a cheerless pit at best. No portholes, not a drape or vase with flowers, nothing showing color, nothing soft. But cots or pads or hammock-like affairs—I should guess some six of them—bolted into place around the room.

They looked like dental chairs extended out, bilaterally flanked with tubular aluminum and little wheels presumably to rotate or depress those lumpy sacks of grain.

Sacks of grain?

Could those be people? Body forms? Good God!

And back behind within her glass enclosure, on a dais of some sort, a stewardess, or nurse, replete with space-suit uniform and stethescope, and coming out to talk to me with papers in her hand?

Orwellian; I cringed.

"You're here for Mr. Ambler? I'm Miss Flaherty. Doctor Potter said you'd come. Please follow me."

I looked to where her finger pointed. A skinny figure lay within a metal frame. One of the flour sacks, except that the creature had some shape I could force upon it. Yes, a neck, a head, and contours like a rump and feet and toes.

It had a face.

But could that be the man I had been treating? Sallow, wasted, sunken-eyed, and two weeks' growth of beard?

Aha! It had a tracheostomy!

And those were wrists!

And manacled!

To either side.

I heard it breathe.

I watched it stir and move.

Yes, it was Barney. But how he had been transformed!

Again I inspected my erst patient. It was Barney. Okay. Where to go from here?

About his wrists were loosely fitted leather thongs. Restraining gauntlets. And haematomata, black, blue, some resolving yellow, older than the rest. They covered his antecubita and dorsa of both hands. His flesh was parchment, and his lips, puffy, dry, were twice, no thrice their normal size.

A gargoyle!

Had I guessed it?

Here was the portrait of a man who had had his brush with death.

*   *   *

In the nursing notes, I read about his progress. Just as Potter said, Barney would have been transferred to a surgical floor by then, except that when he "spiked" a fever and awoke to find himself fitted to a harness of wires and tubes and things, he somehow "grew extremely agitated."

Here, let me quote the chart.

"Patient restless. Visited by wife. Three p.m.: very agitated; asking for his mother; started on amphicillin I.V. Patient belligerent. Dr. Potter called. Six p.m. Pulled I.V. out. On Dr. Potter's orders placed in restraints. Warning staff not to give him injections. Keeps shouting, 'Pull them out of me.' NP consultant to visit prn."

Returning the binder to the nurse, I asked if she thought Barney could be roused enough to talk. She drew the plaited curtain through its ceiling track and separated the three of us from the right half of the room (which seemed unnecessary somehow, considering the states of consciousness around), then bent over him. He shifted; she called his name again, then mentioned mine aloud.

"Barney!"

And what a dreadful turnabout. This man, or what was left of him, who for two score years and some had blanched if "surgery" were even whispered, who paled at dentists, physicals,

even barber chairs, and avoided shots and pills to foolish far
extremes, now, by this triple trick of chance, like Damocles, was
chained beneath the shadow of them all, and in this very room
and hospital in which his mother died. Was this her selfsame
cot? Awaking to find himself strung up within that web?

Arachne!

His dreams full-blown to life?

How weird coincidence! How little Potter knew or fath-
omed. How little Flaherty. Sure, "violent." Indeed! I guessed
his reasons, his intentions in such acts.

Restraints! How little cure they held.

Miss Flaherty kept after him, calling, "Barney, Doctor's
here to see you. Open up your eyes. I'm going to free your hand.
Okay? You put it on your neck and you can talk, alright!"

And as I stood waiting I reflected silently about this
"I.C.U."

It goofed.

For sure.

Men in tip-top physical and emotional condition would
loose their hinges in a place like this—so bleak, austere, so
soundless, sightless, gray. That's right! The astronauts themselves hallucinated when their sensory input was curtailed this
way, just as with fevers, or exhaustion and great fears. And not
so much as a time piece in the room to fix on, or to tell the days
from nights.

"He's more alert. I've shown him how to cap his tracheostomy to speak. I'll leave the two of you alone if you don't
mind."

I squeezed my patient's fist. "Don't try just yet. I want to
fill you in.

"You know what place this is? Mercy Hospital. You're in
the Intensive Care Unit. Am I getting through?"

Beneath my touch his fingers found their way to signal an

affirmative, so I went on. "It's April third and almost four fifteen—in the morning. You lie back and listen. Even if you know the story that I am telling. You just try to clear your head, okay?"

He nodded slightly as he lay there, meaning, "Yes!"

So I repeated to him seriatim all the pertinents, stressing names and dates and hours and days, on purpose, offering, I hoped, an orientation both in time and space. To bring him back from Buck Rogers's world to mine and to the incident for which they had called me—his I.V.

Then he began with effort ... haltingly. He told a story of a "dream," a fever dream he had the night before.

It was a great exertion. I have taken considerable editorial prerogative in its rendition; nonetheless, its essence is a landmark in a couple of careers—his and mine.

Its outline?

Nightmarish. Nine point five or six on Richter nightmare scales—about a spider. Seven, eight big hairy giant legs approaching him as if to squeeze his throat. He had tried to scream. Except the monster had a "zapper," an electric shocker. And it paralyzed and froze him where he stood, then started choking him. That was when he woke.

"And pulled your I.V. out?" I asked him, somewhat gleefully, I guess.

"Dat's what ... dey tell ... me," he replied.

"And are you clear enough to analyze that dream?"

"Ya mean connec' it up?" He struggled, pressing on his neck.

"Or should I sort of shelve it till tomorrow, when you're stronger? I could come ... ."

"Uh uh! I get it ... it's a pretty ... scary deal ... dis goddam place ... uv alla ... rotten luck ... .Yeh, dat dream's ... pretty good ... it's like ya ... warned me 'bout."

"Right on!" I glowed. "But take it easy now. I think your work is done. I want to say my piece."

And believe me, I did. Need I spell it out? Or does it all wash clear? The Romans had a phrase, *Res Ipsa Loquitur*: "The thing speaks for itself."

Yes, Barney's dream told all.

Of course I would enforce, repeat, and underline it for him, and in an expurgated version to Potter, I hoped. Maybe to the world, if I could find a way. And so, rethreading through the corridor, I nodded to Security, and out. Still dark but somewhat cooler. The beacon beamed out five a.m. Still fifty-five degrees. Buoyant, I went sailing down Balboa, home.

I brewed fresh coffee. Brought some to my wife and answered with a wink her question where I had been.

And later, just about, oh, three months later, showed that cartoon frame to her, smiling with a query, "Would you agree this picture's worth 'ten hunnert words,' my dear?"

2
Hang Up

In the southwest corner of the northeast section of our highly industrialized country, there is a tiny village that even today retains its antique appearance. The great waves of urbanization that undulated westward and south swept around it, behind it.

Sabattus.

Eclipsed.

Rinsed once over lightly, but otherwise unchanged.

Its lake, its trees in their shocking autumn foliage, its springs of crystal waters bubbling from the ground, its lush summer greens, its whistling bob whites, its gentle rolling hills, and its single proud summit, Mt. Sabattus, pristine all, remained gloriously immutable since Leif the Lucky walked upon its sod—or Christopher Columbus.

It boasts a church, gray, unpainted, and a nearby little clutch of houses. Most of the others lie dispersed, tangential to their rock-bound farms.

At the junction of two highways there stand a service station and its only store. General merchandise. Windmills churn out the electricity to those hearty residents who live year round in its hefty clime.

In winter, a white silence blankets the town. During summer, spring, and fall, a score of motor cars may weave through its placid streets from dawn to dusk.

Charles Turner had been born about five miles out of town. His father, a stern, redoubtable German, kept pigs, cows, and chickens. To the local inhabitants, he sold milk and eggs. From his vegetable garden came the produce that sustained his family—himself, Mrs. Turner, and three children of whom Charles was youngest.

School lay three miles distant. Every student walked to class both ways. Each day. And when the drifts of snow banked six and seven, sometimes eight feet high, a boy might miss a week of classes. Maybe more.

No matter. All the others did. And teacher too.

"Life creeps in this petty pace from day to day...."[1]

The Turner farmhouse had a genuine fireplace and hearth. A kettle actually hung from an iron hook and brace riveted into the wall. Beneath it the erratic pyrotechnics of crackling snapping fires spit out lively birchwood sparks. They danced in arcs, made crazy-angled ricochets, then died their glowing deaths upon the floor. Cold ash ghosts.

Charles read of Lincoln. He learned how that president's life much paralleled his own—sharing distant hikes to their school houses, the rustic country ambience, the dearth of modern plumbing. Except, the Turners had a faucet in the sink. It ran an ice-cold stream of sparkling fresh water drawn from deep below; and it was potable.

When Mr. Turner shaved, his wife would heat him just a solitary potful on their Franklin stove, the one on which she cooked her meals. As regards other conveniences, the Turners all accommodated to a style euphemistically alluded to as "basic."

[1] Shakespeare, *Macbeth*.

Pay heed, for there a major fret would bruise a youthful mind.

Each evening settled down upon the littlest Turner lad the disquieting awareness that no matter how he coaxed his bladder and his bowel to void themselves before he went to sleep, his biologic rhythms would impel him to go groping through the dark and dreadful back behind the house, toward the hated privy.

It needs further description: A dozen yards beyond the main structure, suitably at the edge of a slight decline, Turner had built his family the only such facility his children would know throughout their formative years.

Eight feet high, with a sloping roof constructed all of knotty pine, the little cubicle perched there like the fabled Toonerville Trolley. Its shiplap and its uprights either through the freeze and thaw of winter, or the torques of ice and snow— or the rough-shod carpentry of its builder—permitted tiny crevices and chinks. Through them whistled spooky draughts and crawled all forms of loathsome insect specimens and legless other things.

A single benchlike plank nailed astride a frame of two-by-fours, with a ragged hole cut into it, offered child or adult wherewithal to adjust himself whereby to be relieved. The door was double-hinged, but one had rusted, fallen off. A grown-up's efforts could close it. Charles could not.

He loathed that place with all his youthful heart. He feared it, and during winter evenings, lying abed, when icy atmospheres would huddle him beneath his heavy eider quilt, his silent prayer, consistently, was but to pass the night with continence. Otherwise, he would be obliged to slip beyond the cozy comforter and out into the frozen air, through the pitchy night, up toward the knoll, into the monstrous maw of that infernal cubicle.

Stench of lime and feces, ammonia, burning acrid fumes. Thoughts of lurking spiders. One could bite his bottom. Worse still, poor baby, for him the rounded aperture was truly large enough to risk his slipping through. Be ever lost in fetid, horrible, amorphous, ill-defined below.

Would any wonder that the youngster pressed his thighs together, squeezed his buttocks tight, and preferred to squirm and dance and wriggle when his bladder filled—in hopes he might avoid, at least till morning, that summons to the privy, to his doom?

Charles's teachers never understood his stomach cramps mid-afternoons, took no notice that throughout twelve years at school he never raised his hand to be excused, not once!

* * *

Ultimately the nice quiet small boy grew into a nice quiet big man. Through a twist of the wheel (which need not concern us) he met and married a well-to-do summer vacationer, a widow, his senior by some years.

At her insistence he was pried out of his childhood haunts, and moved down the coast and inland. To Connecticut, where nepotism ruled; and Charles was made a figurehead within the mega-company commanded by her kin.

He was given an office with a window and a desk and chair and phone. But, fortune did not smile: for Charles, despite his new authority, was swallowed up in gloom.

He did not—could not—produce. Things piled upon his desk without his knowing why.

Embarrassed, Charles's superiors were stuck. A contre-temps. Forth and back between them passed the buck. Proverbial hot yam—until emerged an inspiration, to consult the company psychologist. He gave a TAT, a Wechsler-Bellevue test, but could not "squeeze" from the executive what had compressed and clamped him so together. He suggested interviews of greater depth and breadth, with me.

Contrary to my customary practice, and with some misgiving, I allowed the appointment to be set up by the referring doctor, so, as a double check I felt I needed confirmation from my patient. But—Charles did not telephone.

As time grew shorter, I decided to telephone myself—no luck. I left my message anyhow. On the morning of the day we were to meet, I tried anew to reach him, only to be told, "He says he'll call you back!"

He never did!

Was it thus inappropriate that I should feel annoyance? Not at all! The man seemed impolite and irresponsible at best.

Annoyed indeed, but only for the moment and without rancor. As an analyst one learns to welcome all the clues and use them to diagnostic purpose, not to seek reprisal. So, when Charles actually did appear, I smiled, shook his hand, and noted his apology, stammered out past glowing cheeks and down-turned furtive eyes.

He "should have called," he muttered, but that was pretty much his problem: *fear of telephones*. He dreaded talking on them. Could not force himself to do so irrespective of his tries, at his job.

Aha! A fear of telephones. Of course things piled up on his desk. That would explain it. A "phonophobia," whatever that was! I had never heard of one before. Nor did I realize I would need six months of sessions to flush that symptom out and learn its deeper roots:

Sabattus.

And those early rustic scenes of Turner's life.

How so?

In Charles's home they had no telephone. Nor any in

Sabattus. No, the first he had ever seen was on his trip from Maine, in Boston—and that one, a pay phone. Hard to believe, but true.

Getting warm?

A pay phone, in the city, off the street, in back of a garage, oh, about a dozen yards beyond that structure, at the edge of a slight decline, perched there like the fabled Toonerville Trolley. His virgin instrument, within its "outhouse" booth!

3
Ever Kill Your Kid Brother?

An explosion!

Comets and asteroids went whizzing in all directions. I clawed reflexively, and catching something reined it in.

A sleeve! An arm! My son!

"Lemme go," he wailed, thrashing. "Dad I gotta split. She wants to kill me. Lemme go!"

In an orbit out beyond my reach, his sister idled her engines. Panting, glowering with rage. The veins along her slender little neck appeared dilated, full, and ugly. Even so, for that young lady, beauty lay in store. Clear enough!

For my son? Besides his bullish strength? Handsome, rugged looks. I knew.

Such babies!

Yet what perplexing creatures.

Yes this was how they played.

This is a revised verson of a paper that appeared in 1973. *Psychiat. Quart.*, 47: 203-207.

I wondered if their infant spats inevitably implied all the classic extrapolations. Were they destined to be rivals? Irretrievably? Sister versus brother?

Our books predict it, and so the theory teaches.

"Carolyn!" I yelled. "Come back here. Quickly."

She protested. "Dad, I didn't start it; he did." But her final words were garbled by rebuttal from my son. In *his* version *she* was instigator. And then that battle seesawed till at last, finding the strength to shout them both down, I screamed, "Enough! Go to your rooms. And fast! An hour ago at least I gave you characters your final warnings. Try to act like humans for a while and maybe then I'll open up your cages. Scram!"

"*But, Dad*" (together).

"No you don't. Get moving. No more arbitration!"

And still hopeful that I could patch Nirvana back together, I turned them a deaf ear.

In the basement was the project I had promised to my wife. I intended to complete it but, even as I rounded the corner and descended the stairs, through the ceiling rafters I could hear their soft-shoe shuffle and their "sibling rival song":

Carolyn, in shrill falsetto, singing, "I hate you, brat. You pigface! Now look what *you* got us into, fathead!" ...and her brother's contrapunto, "What did *I* do?"

"What did you do, moron? You stuck your stupid tongue out! Ugh that tongue! *I hate it! I hate you. I wish that you were dead and buried.* There; I said it! *Oh, drop dead!*"

Paul wailed, "Oh yeah! I'll stick it anytime I wanna. 'Nyaah'"—which braying taunt accompanied that "super loathsome" gesture, I surmised.

Fade out, and the world had peace again.

Kids!

What a business!

Well, no way I knew of sweetened life without them. But

wouldn't they ever fathom how their bitter, petty conflagrations, so intense and self-sustaining were the nucleus of the bigger, graver strifes of full-grown men? And of tribes? And nations?

Would it never dawn on them (or on the rest of the world for that matter) how right here in one's very family the basic formula of power struggles might be found?

Here lay the roots of feuds, vendettas, and rebellions—and thinking so, I fell to reminiscing how I had myself been taught that very cosmic lesson, a long, long time before. On a summer evening on a blanket in a meadow out beyond the city and its haze.

Yes.

I remembered:

I'd been fighting with *my* kid brother. Little David with Goliath. It was nothing consequential. Rest assured. Only then *my* father interceded. He philosophized for *me*. Pointing to the heavens, he identified the Dippers, and Orion, and the Evening star; he compared *them* in their orbits to the molecules and atoms of a vast celestial "something"—intimating nesting patterns—which repeat, repeat.

And he spoke about those petty "games" of Love and Hatred that men play. Just a simple innuendo, but enough to dwarf yet forecast to return—on larger scales, the little childhood squabbles and world wars.

And I reflected how his wisdom might have managed puny, foolish foibles—and the problems of the big, bad world they would live in one fine day—when my reverie was ended—by sounds of crunching gravel; I looked out.

Good grief! What rotten timing! That's Bob's car! So he's finished his Dune Buggy, eh? And he's coming by to show it to the kids, and to take them for a ride, he thinks! Oh yeah! Well, not today! Their punishments will stand; they're grounded. I imagined they knew so, in their cells.

Indulgence and exception only weaken moral fiber. Learn the hard way, good for them. Builds stout character, it does.

But, when I finished stomping sternly up the stairs, I was greeted by my wife who was *alone*, smiling innocently, waving farewell sweetly, fondly, to a trio disappearing down the street.

"Honey, *They were grounded!* Didn't they tell you?" And my wife responded volumes with her shrug.

She would never have excused them had she known. Oh no. On discipline, we rarely disagreed.

And I guess I waxed a little sentimental toward their Mom, and the job that we were doing with our brood. And how lucky we had really been so far.

I mean those horrors in the papers, and the tragedies one reads of, why they hadn't touched us—in the main—when again my reverie was broken.

By the phone.

And a voice.

Tantalizingly familiar, though it seemed inside a tunnel, as it kept repeating "Daddy, please come quickly; Paul's hurt badly!"

"Paul? Hurt badly? But *where are you?* Sweetheart! Answer! Can't you hear?"

"Accident ... oh Daddy ... near the park. Ran a stop sign." She hung up. An insanely jumbled message I heard myself recounting to my wife.

* * *

I remember driving. Two automatons watching scenes unfold before us: weird tableaus: See that woman? Standing in her doorway, gawking, craning on her toes? But why? And that knot of children running toward that spot? And that freckled, red-head youngster pointing—to our son! Oh God!

Paul!

Lying crumpled on a bloody blanket in the road.

And Carolyn, shouting at her brother where he lay.

And Bob! Confused and wandering about!

Was it possible a quarter of an hour could set this stage? An ambulance! Had anybody called one yet? "You did? Thank heavens," I responded.

It arrived!

* * *

I was in a room where someone carried on insistantly about insurance and my family physician. I saw silver basins, shining tools, and hypodermics, sheets, and doctors' caps and sterile gowns. And I remember how a pair of strong attendants put Paul gently on the table. White pajamas then appeared, out of nowhere, right on cue, and the high-domed spot burst into brilliant light. Formed a halo for the medic with its rays. Yet, he looked so very youthful, and so calm! And how confident his orders! I stood watching as he washed away the clotted, matted blood.

Detached—removed, until I felt a pressure and I heard: "You are simply not allowed sir. It's our rule. Leave him. Please. Go wait outside. We'll call you when there's news about your son."

And I remember in the foyer, minutes later, something tugging at my arm. Paul's sister, Carolyn, in agony, hanging on those words.

Of course! Guilty girl. Echoes were resounding in her mind, how she'd blurted to her brother, "Oh, *drop dead!" Just because he'd stuck his tongue out!*

Would he die?

And as she kept up her entreaty, "Dad, he will get better, won't he?" It began to dawn on me that her sick, sinking feeling had its core within that guilt. For sure! She was still herself an infant irrespective of her years! And was steeped in magic thinking:

"Honi soit qui mal y pense," I mouthed. Her evil thoughts betokened evil deeds. Just thinking them could do her brother in.

How to help her?

Her?

Ha! Father, heal thyself. You're not immune.

I was also restless, fitful, nervous.

I myself regressed. I kept flexing time to fit my fancy, shuttling back and forth, to the future, to the past.

I revisited that morning, blow by blow: the embroilment with my children. Yes, I chafed. Had I been sterner, stricter, they would *still be locked up safely in their rooms.*

Firmness! Lenient man!

And elsewhere backward to remember the indulgent obstetrician who allowed me in beside him at Paul's birth.

I projected to the future: wending heavy, home; I might have to phone Paul's Grandad with the blackest kind of news.

And I rummaged through the present in attempting to decipher all the noises bouncing 'round. They were full of dreadful portents. Paging someone from the blood bank? Paul need blood?

And I heard the thumping footfalls as the teams of aides and nurses scurried by.

In the archway stood a Florence Nightingale. Nurses and their poker faces! What does wagging of her finger signify! To follow?

Oh, ye gods! Had something happened? Would she tell us? Nurses wear such poker faces!

* * *

So the three of us competed for the narrow filing order in her wake. Lurching past the cubby with its rattling drinking fountain, and around the x-ray unit went our troupe—behind the clerk's reception desk and chair, myself, my wife, then daughter, up to where expressionless, the youthful doctor stood.

"You're Paul's folks?" he asked us, blandly.

"Paul, our son?" I blurted. "Tell me he's alright."

The medic kept on droning from a script, "Brain concussion, I should say. Though the pictures of his skull look pretty good. A week or two I'd get him back to school. Lucky little fella, don't you think?" On the echo of these words our daughter nearly swooned.

"Oh you're Carolyn, his sister? Paul's been asking for you. Says he wants to see you badly. Come on in." Hearing that, she shoved us all aside.

There he was! Alone. Our son.

A tiny, turbaned genie swathed in cloth, lying on the table. At his feet his things. Rolled up, the wreckage of his erstwhile jeans and shirt, frayed grubby sneakers, and his socks. I watched him squinting feebly as we neared.

Poor kid!

Yeah!

Did I say "feebly?" Well, it seemed so. But once he had the spotlight, shall I tell you what transpired?

Would you hope that he was chastened, that he had tasted of remorse, that Nature would allow exception just this once?

Or was it as the stars predicted? Even as my father warned me—when he spoke of Love and Hatred?

While his sister stood there gaping, Paul got up. Balanced on one shaky elbow, he invoked his sibling option: He reared and stuck his tongue out!

4

Roots

Frank was desperate. He had to get his rest. What in hell possessed his wife anyway? So, okay, if she wanted to strip that cabinet. But why at one a.m.? And if it had that many layers of paint on paint, on top of paint, why couldn't she wait till morning? He told her that a can of liquid sandpaper, which she could pick up at the hardware store, would boil it off. Fabulous stuff! Peels it. Washes it away.

"Come on Liz! Come on to bed," he wailed.

"Uh, uh. You go to sleep. I've started and even if I can't get it all done tonight, I've got to get at least a peek at what's really underneath. It's fascinating. Like I'm seeing the history of all the people who ever owned the thing. Someone sure liked green. Heavenly days!"

"Christ's sake," he called. "I can't tune out that sander, Liz. Jesus! What do you hope to find, a Chippendale?"

But his words were just a token at that juncture. Feebler than before, and within scant minutes poor weary warrior, he closed his eyes. Surrendered quite to Morpheus. He had his job. It needed him all perky at his desk by eight a.m.

Not so his wife.

She labored and labored and labored clear through to three o'clock. She *had to see the base.* Compulsive? Single-minded? What the hell. She didn't work. She could sleep late. In fact, the only real commitment she had all day was going to see her analyst, mid-afternoon.

Her analyst? For what?

Hers was a kind of morbid monomania. Ever since her parents had confronted her with her adoption, well, since that very moment she was obsessed with thoughts of tracing out *her roots.*

5

Dance to the Music

She was sixty-five and sad.

Her family had grown into adulthood and peeled off and flown away. In the great big house where once her children had squished sand between their toes, played hide and seek, had sneaked the first delicious furtive puffs of cigarettes and had had their teen-age parties, now alone, she and her aging husband rattled around within it "like drumsticks in a big tin can."

When the sun shone, it seemed to her a whole eternity dragged out its arch across the sky. Nothing filled her daylight void—the vastness and emptiness of time. She felt indeed as if its vacuum had somehow seeped inside her, awaking sympathetic resonance in hollow vital organs.

All drained out.

And awfully, awfully blue.

By night the picture was none improved. True, Marvin would come home. But so close to retirement, he always needed rest. And once the meager meal had been consumed and the half a dozen dishes had been rinsed and set to drip to dryness in the wire rack on the sink, a creeping desperation waited to devour her in their bedroom down the hall.

Marvin's habit invariably curled him in a knot at the far end of the king-size bed their children chipped in to buy them on their fortieth anniversary.

He snored.

A tortured rhythmic anguished snore, all night in cadence of its own.

That really got to her.

If only Marvin cuddled, if he only held her. Admittedly the heyday of the blood had cooled. But why not just a little intimacy? Married all that time to lie like posts? Like rocks?

She'd pass on sex. Thanks anyway! But tenderness at night. Oh God! If only he would hug her as he used to do so many years before.

"How might I help?" I asked.

"It's the music," she replied, sadly swaying her head from side to side. I saw her aging yet still lovely profile and the wrinkles in her neck. "It keeps buzzing through my mind the whole night long."

Without surcease, like an obsession, for hours on end she heard it, as if some phantom organist were playing it through ghostly pipes.

Poor cameo. Poor blue-eyed lady. Poor white-skinned trembling woman. Poor wren. To be thus haunted by the sounds of other worlds and frightened so to verging upon madness and losing hold of things.

That's why she had come to see me, the reason she had called. "It's the music," she repeated. "It won't stop." Nor day, nor night.

But how to tackle music? Where to start? With base or treble clef? With counterpoint? Could she name for me at least the titles of the songs that plagued her so?

"It's just one song," hoarsely she croaked back. And she could not recall its lyrics or its name. Not at all. Well could she hum me several bars? I could recognize them, possibly. "Don't be shy," I urged. "Try to help me help you. Please."

She did.

And do you know what finally she rendered in a shaky voice, tentatively, watching while I fought against a laugh.

"Tum te tum te tum," she quavered, as despite my most heroic efforts I began to chuckle right out loud. Not at her, but at my happy insight. "It's enough," I cried. "I think I've got it. This the tune you're singing?—'Tum te tum te tum?'"

She nodded.

"I think that we have flushed your demon. Your song is titled *Strangers In The Night*."

6

Alas, Poor Yorick!

Pity!

I was spoiling a delicious dinner: linguine in a clam sauce savored with onions and garlic, lightly sautéed in butter and olive oil. Spoiling it, shoveling it down, wine and all, single-mindedly aware that only if I did not dawdle could I shower, shave, dress, and be on the freeway by seven fifteen.

Rush, rush, rush!

Well, by that hour the inbound traffic would be sparse. With any luck I would reach the parking lot just a few minutes late. My group could wait. That was not asking much of them. Rank has its privilege.

My group?

A motley bunch of senior medical students with whom I met weekly at the Neuropsychiatric Institute—deep within its catacombs. The white rats learned their mazes faster in that edifice than this Professor of Psychiatry!

"Don't get lost again," I cautioned myself, reflecting all the while that if the pace imposed on the kids was still the way it used to be, a little breather would not be unwelcome to them, really.

They were four only, yet a mixed bag to say the least. Mixed in their backgrounds and ambitions, and mixed in their tolerance for any subject material not yet amenable to key-punch or computer, let alone their sympathies for the basic psychiatric message: Carlson the would-be surgeon; Stein, who hoped to become an analyst; Taylor, the lone woman of the bunch; and McNulty, the sharpest of the lot, who would join his brother one day, practicing internal medicine.

To me they appeared to typify, by coincidence, even possibly to caricaturize the major persuasions that prevailed out in the broader medical community: Carlson, whom I projected into the image of a scrubbed and polished, clear-eyed, stubborn Scandinavian, would maintain both a psychic and a surgical asepsis. His operating team, his office staff, and even his own person would be keyed to an intolerant, inflexible perfection, but he would be about as cordial to "contaminating" thoughts about the id and ego as to the bugs who tried to penetrate his sterile world. I would trust him totally to take out my appendix, but I would never seek his counsel for a teenage lad who liked to wear his sister's bra and panties.

And Stein? Neurotic Stein? With all his nervous ardor? Brilliant, swift, and very likely shored up by a hundred hours or more of psychotherapy down somewhere in his vita. Him I saw emerging from his training with the prejudice that so tended to deny that men had bodies wrapped around their minds. He would ask me, I suspected, for a recommendation to my Institute, thus explaining his patronizing and protective attitude. As if I needed him to run my interference. Well, a good analyst might help him.

And Taylor? Yes, indeed. Miss Taylor! An utter loss! Was I being chauvinistic? She had no future whatsoever in the healing arts, and worse, had gracelessly displaced some more deserving man. Oh she was beautiful, and smart, but after graduation, was planning to become the second wife and social complement of a world-famous plastic surgeon. She would not even intern.

And finally McNulty. The others called him "Cautious Mac!" Now, *he* was worth my effort. I shall tell you why: He challenged all my theories. Fairly.

Anxiety! Could one map its neural pathways? Or "titrate" man's aggression? Or could Psychiatry furnish him formulas for handling the admittedly functional fractions of ulcers, migraine, or essential hypertension? If not, was he better off to listen to the pharmacologists and detail men who merely treated symptoms? But held a little back, uncommitted as it were?

That I liked.

For their semester, I had outlined a schema calculated to survey the entire field. Now, halfway through, we had skimmed at least the surface of anxiety, hysteria, conversions, phobias, obsessions and compulsions, and by design were leaving for the finale a hasty run through of the psychosomatoses.

Most evenings the students would present case histories of ward patients who characterized one or other of those classifications. However, I had suggested schedule flexibility. That prompted Mac to request a discussion on depression.

He had no particular clinical example in mind, but being aware that his future practice would encounter people afflicted with *it*, had persuaded me to comply.

At the crest of the Mulholland ridge, just where the freeway starts its long smooth curving decline downward into Westwood, I noticed a police car angled across the emergency lane and shoulder. Behind it stood a foreign, low-slung, open-top something. Its driver wore a mask of dejection.

Depression, ha!

I chuckled; a "luck out" anecdote to start my talk—but for the rest? How best to pry the lid off of Pandora's Box? To let emerge the shapes and shrieks and sounds unholy? "Loathèd melancholy! Pride of Cerberus and blackest midnight born." Milton was great, but I could not fill an evening with what I knew of him.

No.

I needed an example from my practice; the students would learn and remember from a tale far better than from any stultifying pedantry, especially after a twelve-hour day like theirs—but, which tale?

And then, as I approached Sunset Boulevard, across the landfill to the right, outlined against the blue-black twilight, I saw the silhouette of a sleeping bulldozer. Trundled for the night, a 'dozer.

A dozing 'dozer. A digging 'dozer. A 'dozer digging holes and moving earth for homes and homes with swimming pools and pools and Dana and Dana and her Dad!

Ah the mind! Its labyrinthine twists!

Instantim!

A whole cassette in place! Names, dates, locales, the affects, moral, all. I had my clinical example, lovely. Relieved, I pressed the pedal underneath my toe, accelerated happily, and hied on south to Westwood.

* * *

"Gentlemen:

"Last week, you remember, McNulty asked for a discussion of depression. He was right to suggest that clinicians in every specialty and subspecialty will find themselves dealing with it, which makes particularly crucial that good doctors recognize and handle it appropriately.

"Mark down the word 'protean.' That is the best one to apply. Know what it means? That its manifestations will present themselves in varied forms and guises.

"The surgeon who performs a hysterectomy or amputates a finger, or the orthopod who puts a star quarterback's ankle in a cast, or the dermatologist wrestling with teenage acne, or the ophthalmologist who recommends the cataract excision, or the gastroenterologist—all, without exception, sooner or later will have to countenance depression in their patients and hope to remove or modify it exactly as one would a virus or bacterium impeding perfect cure.

"I am being flowery I know, possibly attempting with this evening's portrayal something difficult at best, yet totally desirable: That is, to get you interested in the phenomenology of depressions and into a mental frame that will look upon them as a diagnostic challenge and a therapeutic 'must.' To try to get you neither to despair if you detect its presence nor to get depressed yourselves if you discover that there are infinite slips between the textbook management of a 'case' and the actual clinical consummation of healing.

"The story I have chosen will present you with all the important data. There will be 'red herrings' too. I shall run through it quickly then ask you questions. By now I am sure you have learned how much significance I personally attach to that didactic way.

"It is the story of Dana and her depression, and its successful treatment—and of many things besides.

"Listen."

When Dana's father died, everyone feared for her. She was not grieving properly. No, certainly not as a person was

supposed to, considering how sorely she was going to miss him.
All of her life she had worshipped that man.

Openly.

Unabashedly.

No secret there.

Nor had it bothered her one jot when her sophomoric,
long-locked friends wagged fingers or baited her out loud
alluding to their father-daughter love with tales of Oedipus,
Electra, or King Laius.

Not a bit.

She would laugh, toss her head back confidently, fanning
out her luxuriant raven tresses—ruby lips, white teeth flashing—
and candidly admit she was his thrall.

Pray, what was wrong with that?

Her Daddy!

She would ask you.

What harm!

For her "Daddy" cut a notoriously handsome figure. His
was the classic "front of Jove," Hyperion. Besides his bachelor's
in romance languages, he painted. Oils. Breath-taking in their
clarity and strikingly original.

He played the oboe and the cello and the bass dextrously
enough to sit in with the Lower Tujunga Amateur Symphonic
Group, and he wrote poems. Some were clearly inspired by
Dana, even dedicated to her; others, slightly veiled and given to
meandering a little philosophically, nonetheless quite obviously
related to the richness and the beauty of their lives together.

He was ethereal, artistic. He personified charisma, love, but
he never was so lofty as to compromise attentions to his only
child and heir, or so impractical that if a faulty washer had to be
replaced, or trap beneath their antique sink flushed clear, or
leaky roof patched dry, or downspouts freed of leaves, that he
need call for help. Oh no! He was so capable, so rounded, and

so three-dimensional! He was the kind of man referred to as *ein Mensch*.

And their romance—in sooth such title was deserved—attained its early zenith on the day Dana's mother passed away; in rare but no less fatal contretemps with adult chicken pox. Succumbed, and with that awkward timing, assumed thereby a ghostly, pale survival in the mind's eye only of their five-year-old.

Then mummy's crusted, hemorrhagic, puckered scabs, like raisins on her skin, were interspersed with living raisins in the youngster's bowls of breakfast cereals, and equally mixed up with the numbered dots of kiddies' line completion games. The ones both of them had used to play together of a Sunday morning in that great big bed.

A tracery, a phantom, outline parent only who went zig-zag, dot-to-dot or pock to pock—a hollow-bodied, empty-centered, ectoplasmic vision where fuller, vital woman should have been, which happenstance undoubtedly intensified and underscored and disproportionated Nature's balance in said ancient tale of Oedipus.

What next?

The little girl grew up.

Easily she slipped into the role of Daddy's helper and companion. Her dividend thereby was a self-assured precocity. It attracted and surrounded her with a coterie of underlings, but, in the balance, as a handicap, she realized that somewhere, somehow, she would have to pay a price. Such was her Moira, wasn't it?

She graduated high school with honors. Teachers respected her uniqueness and her flair. They called her "sensitive" and "bright." Underneath her photo in the yearbook, "talented" was written, and predicted for her were clever, worthy deeds.

Why not?

Few if any ever saw the detriments of Dana's finer tuning: those sudden bursts of temper and pique—or her capacity for taking lightning umbrage over mere nothings.

In college she elected Music. Two arduous years devotedly she turned in her reports on time, attended all her classes, and was provident pursuing her degree. Then suddenly, to everyone's surprise—no warning—she abandoned all. Returning home, Dana accepted a job as "girl Friday" to a young executive in one of the light industries that stippled the area around her childhood haunts.

In unison her friends sent up a shrill lament. How could she thus abandon her career? Especially for so pedestrian a choice? Really! A company that manufactured hydrochloric acid and chlorine for the control of algae in the walls of swimming pools?

She knew what she was thinking of.

Hennessey. Her boss.

The bachelor. Eligible. Likeable. In charge of distribution of their product all throughout the southwest region of the States.

Nice chap. True, rather pallid in contrast to Dana's incomparable father, but a steady, wholesome man with whom a girl might settle down and raise her kids. "Straight arrow" sort. Imbued with many minor virtues:

Sober. Sweet. Patient. Easy-going. Durable. Uncomplicated. Had his "act together." Did it matter if a tinge of motherliness graced his image? Was that a flaw? Or if he spent his Sundays weeding crabgrass then barbecuing (with a chef's hat and an apron)? Was it a fault to pick up dirty socks and drop them in the hamper, or to coach the Little League, or make a ritual of being home from work by five-fifteen?

"Square?" Well....

Not everyone was obliged to marry "turquoise freaks" or

sandal-slippered liberals! Those "'mildewed ears!'" She would not even date them! No! Dana knew her mind. If Hennessey would have her, she would him—despite the chorus ululations.

And Hennessey? He would! You bet! They did! They married, and then bought a home one block from where her father had raised her—continuing his ambience, extending it. But "could Cordelia wed and love her father all?"

One never learned because, with his demise, a balance gravely shifted. Poor Dana was left dangling, especially, since death was sudden.

Unexpected. Needless. Accidental. A mere age fifty-nine. En route to work. While pausing to adjust the trunk-latch of his classic TR-6. Up-ended by a bicycle, a foolish kid!

A pedal or the handle bar, some metal object caught him squarely in behind the belly of the gastrocnemius, which formed a clot, which loosed an embolus, which slithered to his lung and wedged itself in tight and would not be dislodged, then triggered a pneumonia, a rare resistant strain of some bacterium, which, just as for her Mom, proved no less fatal.

Dad was gone.

* * *

Hennessey arranged the funeral. He was unused to such events, and felt uncomfortable, unsure. Dana's academic emancipation seemed to him to make a priest incongruous, but, in ultimo, considering the expectations of the broader family, he sought one out.

To his mixed surprise and relief his wife accepted that, if rather passively. She was preoccupied, not quite herself. Some troubling thing was turning in her mind. Everyone sensed it; none could define what. Then again she was so unpredictable.

The necessary details were too "commercial" and that

touched her off. She smirked at all the unctions. Repeatedly she snapped at "insincerities" and "sham." In fact, she barely managed simple amenities when earnest well-wishers extended her condolence—and she actually screamed that a "monkey-suited toady" walked her through selection of the casket then persisted in his queries about interring Father in a grave beside his wife's. But, with the ceremony, Dana somewhat steeled herself and stiffened to her task.

Mercifully the weather was clement. A gentle mist shielded the Valley from the sun. Heavy in patches, along the undersides of ledges and the scattering of umbrellas, it formed little condensation droplets. Mourners found excuse to wipe their spectacles and eyes, and Father Diaz took the opportunity to lyricize, alluding to Heaven shedding tears.

Some wept.

But those who did and those who didn't, in a mute consensus wished that Dana would. They shuddered at her poise. She seemed too stiff. That sentiment was whispered back and forth. Between her Aunt Maria even, and her Uncle Frank. And Father Diaz noticed. He had seen such calculated iciness before. At his final benediction, "in nomine," etc., as clay was strewn upon the casket in its pit, he seemed to look directly at poor Dana who responded like a frieze: a frozen, lifeless statue, moving nothing, save her slipper heels in restless alternation in the dampened graveside grass.

Precisely as she held herself all evening, demurring at the kindness and offers from her friends, including Hennessey, who wanted badly to sustain and to protect her once that dreadful day had ended.

It would help to let him cuddle and to hold her. Could she? Would she? Please?

Rejecting nod.

She would be alright. "Don't fuss." Her father had taught

her facts about control. His philosophy could rise to such occasions. He would have countered grief by keeping busy. Dying was a necessary phase of human life. The dangers lay in sentimental "junk." Time heals. If she constructed "schedules" she would manage. Hennessey would see. Her father might have wished for nothing less.

And Dana kept her word: She became compulsively organized about their home. Ritualistically, she set up Mondays to wash and clean. Once worn and scarcely even soiled clothing was flung into the hamper, then combined with the week's dirty linen pile. It she carted to the laundry and heaped upon the shelf by her machine. Then the utility room would hum with interlocking rhythms of the washer-dryer. Each article retrieved, at last, was shaken, ironed, and tucked away in closets or in drawers.

The same intensity attended cleaning and dusting. Ashtrays sitting empty on the countertop were vigorously scrubbed. The carpets took a heavy weekly beating, and the silver was polished to a gleam. She swept her kitchen floor thrice daily. Tiles were stripped, then sealed and buffed and made to shine like new. And in the cupboards every cup and saucer came to life, to sparkle as it seldom had before.

Her Tuesdays she assigned to shopping. And the menus she selected gave her plenty of toil—baking her own pie crusts, making Yorkshire puddings, even homemade salad dressings. Work, work, work!

On Wednesdays, bowling. And accepting tasks of organizing leagues, and getting sitters for the group and picking up the members of her team—all that.

And Thursdays, something else—whatever, just to keep her engines running, straining—every day replete with busy, busy deeds. Full days, no time to think, to feel.

You see?

Bereavement could be managed. Six more months, its leading edge should blunt—she guessed.

Until five-fifteen one bleak wet afternoon, as winter light was waning. Hennessey returning home sung out a loud "Hullo." He found his sweetheart motionless in bed. Blinds drawn. The household deadly silent. The ashtray stuffed with half-smoked filter tips.

The dinner? None was cooking. The breakfast dishes not yet cleared away or even rinsed. "The children?" In response she mumbled something, but would utter no further word to allay her husband's frightened plea, "What gives?"

What gave?

It gave washless Mondays. Tuesdays she stayed home. The Wednesday bowling ceased. On Thursday nothing stirred, nor any day all week. A crisis, prompting Hennessey at last to holler, "Help!" Out loud, to their family physician who said problems such as Dana's went beyond him, so, he scribbled down my number on his pad.

*   *   *

Hennessey's lucid telephonic description of the events that led to his wife's breakdown posed no diagnostic challenge. It was crystal clear that his wife was suffering a reactive depression and one that very likely was much intensified owing to its unusual predisposing factors.

However, the nosologic straight-forwardness was to have no effect upon a therapeutic course. At least for Dana. Not directly.

Uh, uh. She, as the saying goes, was a "reluctant dragon."

In the hierarchy of her desires, irrespective of her misery, trips to a psychiatrist lay at an uncontested nadir. Oh, she was depressed alright, and didn't deny it, but "to surrender" totally, and "throw herself" upon my "mercy"—not on your life!

Actually, I knew that such reluctance, distressing as it may have been for Hennessey, prognosticated well for his wife. Such fight, such *esprit*, indicated that Dana had not given up. That was good; but unless such a thesis could be got across to *him*, results could be disastrous.

I considered saying so, but did not reckon with poor Hennessey's forgivably naïve and sadly desperate suggestions (how despondent he must have been!): to pretend he would "take Dana for a ride," then just "happen by" my office. An aunt of his had been railroaded to a sanitarium that way. Failing that, his back-up ploy: for me to phone his home and make believe I was an erstwhile army buddy, traveling through. He would invite me to dinner, to observe!

Yech!

He hardly even mouthed that scheme before its bottom fell apart. Dana would never swallow it.

Nor I.

"So what then?" he turned to me.

I said, "the truth!"

He did not mind my mild rebuke that starting any therapy dishonestly could only breed mistrust, the last thing patients need.

"And after that?"

I said I was unsure, but, having mulled the matter, I proposed he visit me once or twice to see if I could furnish him a guideline for his dealings with his wife. It was always possible that later she would join him or even change her mind and come along herself.

* * *

Hennessey made an appointment for my next free hour. The unhappy man poured out elaborate detail of Dana's situation. His manner was exceedingly forthright. How accurate her assessment of an "overgrown boyscout!" The pity was though, that the "preparedness" associated with that group was not equipping him for survival in the wilderness of grief.

Yet, the marriage and the overall relationship had many pluses. Hennessey revealed unusual reverence and devotion toward his precious spouse, and she apparently reciprocated.

Somewhat remarkable was the enigmatic fashion in which their mutual love accommodated to her Dad. They formed a strange triumvirate, something of a firmly based tripod whose balance now, with Daddy's "leg" lopped off, was perilously threatened.

I assumed that my "student" would be aware that a true technical cure for his wife demanded no less than literal resurrection of that man. I assumed also that he did not know much about the fundamentals of depression. These I could sketch out, but, in so doing, I should steer clear of the very imminent likelihood that the time and circumstance of Dana's Mother's death, and the characteristics of her subsequent life with Father, undoubtedly added a most undesirable complication to Dana's psychologic growth, and to her potential recovery now.

What more?

Foremost, I felt impelled to assure him all depressions are temporary. That they always do pass. Did he know that? I asked him, hastily adding that I was not overlooking how rough they could be, or how seemingly interminable. And I admitted there were no guarantees either that they would not return.

" ... All of which you probably realized yourself," I ventured, "but, hearing it from an expert can't hurt any. Okay? Now, let me tell you something you may not have known. That underneath every depresson there is always anger. Plenty."

"You're telling me," he broke in. "Dana's not the girl I married anymore. She's ... 'picky.' It doesn't matter what I do. I'm always wrong. I'll give you an example: Last Thursday. I got home. She hadn't started dinner. I suggested, 'Chinese take-out, honey?' and she landed on me. Says I'm 'too accommodating all the time' and was I looking for another 'Merit Badge?' Oh boy, that stung.

"Is that some kind of fault? I mean I tried to be a good guy and she really shot me down."

He paused. Then resuming, "and swears! You know, when I first married her—"

"Hold it, Hennessey," I interrupted. "That's a good example. Before you change the subject, let me make another point. Her anger is not bad. Did you realize that?"

"It isn't bad?"

"No, not at all."

His forehead wrinkled. I was not getting through.

"Well, maybe not for her, but, boy, it's killing me."

"I understand, except you are the healthy one just now. Of course it hurts. Only you have to handle it as if you were a kind of paramedic. Don't take her symptoms personally, or all that much to heart."

"I don't follow you," he started, then shifting his position, he pulled out of an inner jacket pocket a huge pipe whose bowl was carved into a woman's torso, like the masthead of a ship. Rather than charge it with tobacco, he placed it professorially between his teeth and continued to draw air through the stem, watching me and awaiting my explanation.

I continued, "Okay. Picture it like this: If Dana met you in the doorway peppered with spots or if you discovered that she was running a fever you would not go to pieces, would you? Or 'retaliate?' Her anger is a symptom very much like those except that it is abstract.

"It is even a *good* symptom. Shows she is still fighting. You should not let it get to you any more than a paramedic or a doctor would those spots. Okay?"

He shrugged his shoulders and protruded his lower lip, pouting slightly, "I guess."

"Well, let me make it clearer still. Look, haven't you ever heard stories about guys who go home and kick the dog if things went wrong at work?"

"Oh sure! That happens all the time. The dog catches it because he's standing there."

"Right! Okay. Now, let me bring an example still closer to home. Forget Dana for the minute. Did your mother or your sister ever turn into a 'witch' the day before her period?"

He smiled. "You better believe it!"

"And lose her temper or act short?"

He sucked upon his pipe, reflectively, then answered, "My Mother used to natter something terrible, but my Dad said, 'Look the other way.' I think I'm seeing what you mean about being 'clinical' and letting it blow over."

"And you did not take her 'nattering' to heart?"

"Why should I? It wasn't my fault. I was pretty well-behaved. Usually."

"Or personally?"

"Uh, uh. No. Once I got it figured, I mean what was going on. I think I get your message: Dana's moods will pass just like my Mom's. Ignore her, eh?"

"Whoa, now!" I broke in. "I didn't use *that* word. I didn't say 'ignore.' To be a good para-anything, medic, psychiatrist, husband or friend, you don't 'ignore.' Quite the reverse. She needs your empathy, your understanding. Patience. But do not lose perspective either. Look, your wife is hurting. I know you realize that. *Do* pay attention. Try to feel her feelings with her. Share them. Keep in mind that she does not want them either, but until she's ready, they will probably hang around, like they are supposed to. Actually, it is pretty normal to be acting just the way she is. What is going on is part of mourning, only with her it is exaggerated.

"Did you ever hear of Sigmund Freud?"

Hennessey nodded, slowly first, then vigorously to dispel my doubts.

"Know what he said? He compared Dana's kind of behavior to what happens when you run a hand lens along a Turkish carpet. You see a blown-up distortion or a magnification of the patterns, even though the sequences and the relations are still valid. You follow me?"

He continued rhythmically raising and lowering his head only a little more slowly—I imagined with some slight self-satisfaction, and relief—which were suggested further when he angled his pipe and assumed a rather contemplative pose.

"Let me go a bit more into it. Apparently you found that last analogy helpful. I am going to toss out another one of my own manufacture. It could be instructive if you do not extend it too far or take it too literally. Alright?

"Psychiatrists believe that whenever a person gets depressed, somewhere along the line a significant *loss* has taken place. Every time. Dana has lost her Dad. If there were some miracle to restore him, I could guarantee that she would be better. You agree?

"Other people also lose something precious, only it may not be so obvious what it is. They often do not even know themselves. So they do not know what to strive to get back or how to compensate ... in what direction ... just the feeling that something valuable, prized, either concrete or abstract is missing.

"Think you can guess what happens next? *Anger!* Plenty! The human reaction to losing a prized possession is rage. It might even be fury, but, here's the rub: We live in a very civilized society. To express such feelings openly is usually taboo. Forbidden. Even harboring violence and retaliation or revenge makes us guilty.

"Am I clear?"

"Perfectly, so far," he responded, as with a flourish of his hand he invited me to continue.

"Okay, now one more wrinkle: The fantasies come anyway, and when they do, guilt with them. Then something in the mind takes over. It struggles to deny them, to suppress and to control them in order to ease that guilt. To make us feel better. Only the process that I am describing is really far more of a tug-of-war than I can get across by just mentioning it. An awful lot of mental energy is apt to be called upon and consumed. And continues to be.

"Here is the analogy—at least how I picture it—as if people actually had up in their psyches an enormous vat or tank, full of energy to begin with, but one that empties as the energies drain out, as that control is exerted.

"Then when the level is really low, it's as if some sort of gauge or float along the bottom sends out signals saying, 'Hey, it's nearly empty; we're running out of gas!'

"Dana was at that point the day you found her sitting in the dark alone and so drained that she was even unable to answer your simple questions. In fact I think you said she used those very words, that she was 'hollow and all drained out.'"

"Exactly," Hennessey replied, meditatively, moving his chin jerkily up and down, pursing his lips. The memory was fresh enough to hurt him yet.

"Alright. The description fits, but more than that, it hints at what to do.

"Maybe you have even anticipated my next remarks. Two things: either you stop her spending all that energy suppressing the guilty feelings and you allow her to let the angers rage—

now mind you, I do not mean literally to kill the boy who ran her father down, or to blow up the hospital where he died—but to encourage her having those thoughts and talking about them freely, to express them, or, the second thing is ... "

Hennessey interrupted, looking pale and upset. "You want her to express all that?" "Verbally," I repeated. "Even if she takes it out on you. Let the *ideas* flow. Remember 'sticks and stones?' The names she calls will never hurt you. Let it out!"

"Gollymoses!" he said under his breath.

"Do I surprise you?"

"Yeah. No. I mean now that you've explained it. Man alive, have I ever been a chump," he stammered, reddening. "The way I argued with her for saying all those rotten things. Boy, I guess I really blew it."

"Probably, but I doubt that the damage is irreparable. Only let me finish what I was trying to say, Number two ...

"I'm sorry," said Hennessey. "I'll shut up. It's just, well, okay. Please go on."

"The second thing or the other half is from the opposite direction. Besides stopping the outflow of 'gas' you could pour some in the top; replace the losses or, of course, you could do both together."

"Pour it in the top?"

"Right. Fill the tank up. You know what does that? What does it is obviously the reverse of loss; it is *gain*. A gift, an 'ego trip,' an object or (sounds 'schmaltzy'), just plain 'love,' respect, patience."

A broad grin spread across Hennessey's face. "You fill the ol' tank up, eh? That shouldn't be too hard." He chuckled softly, even a bit smugly, picturing, I imagined, some specific contribution he could make to bail his darling out.

I asked to hear his thoughts, but rather than expand upon them he repeated the last bit about the tank one more time, then slowly stood up, tucked his pipe into the front of his jacket, and bent forward reaching into one of its inner pockets for his checkbook. From that he tore a check, and as I watched, in a bold hand, silently, wrote my name, my fee, and his signature across its front. He lay it on my desk.

"You've helped me quite a lot," he said. "I wish I hadn't waited so long to come here. You know, I used to think, I guess like Dana, that you had to be really 'spaced out' or something, or that you fellas just grunted and wouldn't talk. What you told me sounds real useful."

"I could have been quiet. That would not have done the trick. I thought that you should have a formula to go by. But, you don't have to leave so soon. There is still some time."

He waved me off. Apparently he had concocted other plans. He shook my hand and left.

Four weeks later he was on the phone once more.

"Did anything go wrong?" I asked.

"It's me," he muttered glumly. "You'd probably explain it that it's me. *I'm* 'runnin' out of gas.' I guess I need a little pumped into my top."

"For what?"

For what?

After our session together, the young executive, inspired by my words, and in an earnest desire to fulfill Dana in a long-standing yearning, but one that their hand-to-mouth economy would never manage, decided to take the plunge—to build his wife a swimming pool.

With a lot of fancy footwork and by exploiting "connections" at the plant, even if it meant going into hock. That, he figured, was the one "prized object" he could supply. Besides, the idea was a natural. A pool was "family." It was even an investment of sorts. Later down the line he could recoup expenses from the heightened resale value of their home.

And there was a perfect place right outside the kitchen window in their yard. Dana could watch the daily progress while she worked. Ultimately she could supervise the children when they swam. And friends would visit and would use it.

All roads led to Rome. A pool! A really neat idea!

And things went "swimmingly" at first. On schedule. Within the cul-de-sac outside their house arose a Matterhorn of sand. Beside it grew a levée of cement—the Great Wall of China. Eighty-seven sacks. Symmetrical, in double-wrappered skins, then workmen in a tractor. And look at that! So that's the way to do it! A section of their fence got lifted out, then back and forth and back the 'dozer started pushing, digging, deeper, deeper down, with Dana watching every progress, saucer-eyed.

Guess what! Washing dishes, and then cooking, cleaning bit by bit. Humming little strains of music, as before.

How lovely it would be to have a wife again!

And what a stroke of genius Hennessey's had been! Damned right! It was worth the home-improvement mortgage. Bet your life! The way he saw it, through our teamwork, he and I together, we had brought his Dana back to life, which justified the monthly bite.

Only, as suddenly as the miracle had begun it also stopped; toil ceased.

Unannounced.

Abruptly. Not a single workman showed the live-long day. Then the 'dozer stood there, rusting. Rods of half-inch rebore mildewed in their drive, and the sand pile leveled off and rounded by degrees. Dana drifted aimlessly at first, then started frowning as before. Hennessey, bewildered and perplexed felt panic growing in him, enough to holler "Mayday," and to call, because she was becoming unresponsive and withdrawn.

Melancholic. No matter how he tried to pull her out of it,

or get her to "express" and to let him bear the brunt with his new strength.

Instead she postured, hours, staring out the kitchen window at the interrupted digging in the yard. "Catatonic" was his term, and "hypnotized." Even if he shouted to her, she would stand there, gaping at that hole.

Was there nothing we could try? "Quickly?" Hennessey petitioned, searching out an answer in my eyes. "Well, why not finish what they started?" I proposed. "Hey man! You'll see. They will. Because they have to get paid. It's just their style. I explained all that to Dana—if she heard. They've gone off to start another project somewhere else. You know? That's typical of contract labor.

"They abandon something halfway through like ours. It's how they always do it. They'll return. For sure."

"How long has she been waiting up to now?" I wondered. "About two weeks," was his reply. "It is a little longer than I like, except, you know, I thought that she'd be grateful. God, I've plunged us really deep in debt to dig that pool. And I hoped that Dana'd feel that, 'cause I'm worried. I'd've thought she'd see the sacrifice, the way you put it, like a token of my love, to 'fill her up.'"

And even as he spoke those last three words I got a flash. A visit from my darling. Serendipity. The Muse of Insight! I muttered, "Staring out the window, is she, at that hole?"

Distractedly and faintly Hennessey said, "Yes, the whole damn day! That's right."

"Well Hennessey," I chuckled, with self-satisfaction and I guess a trace of smugness, "Listen here! You do exactly as I tell you. Double time! Okay?

"Go home and call the workmen. Bribe them if you have to, and get them on the job—no 'ifs' or 'buts,' and I promise you the miracle you want. Agreed?"

The young man stared at me. "I'll do it if you say so, but how come?"

" 'How come?' 'How come' is that you have a great big cavity sitting in your yard, just halfway dug. What does it measure, twelve by twenty, give or take?"

"I'd say ... "

"And Dana just stands there staring at it all day long? And fumbling with the breakfast dishes, then again at lunch and dinner?"

* * *

At precisely that point I broke off the narrative and surveyed my audience. It was gratifying to see that, despite the lateness of the hour, they seemed to hang on my every word.

"Mr. Carlson, would you care to hazard an opinion as to the missing last sentence in the story?"

Carlson did not respond. He fixed his pale blue eyes upon me. Both the irises were visible as perfect circles underneath the lids. Furrowed, his brow bespoke an anguished concentration, but it could offer little more than the intimations that it was unfair—with nothing tangible that one could snip or saw or suture back together.

Then shook his head.

"Gosh, I donno. No! I'm with Hennessey," at length. "His wife should have realized the sacrifice he had made. She wasn't being reasonable. He could have talked to her, the way he did to you. Did he, about the contract labor? Hell, two weeks isn't long. He could have made it clear."

But Stein broke in, "Christ, John, he couldn't! Don't you see? Dana wouldn't have heard a single word he said. She couldn't 'reason.' That was her problem!"

"So what do *you* suppose I told him, Stein?" I asked my future colleague.

He equivocated.

"It's a really good example. Your story. It hits a lot of points about depression. What you actually told him then? Well, I'm not sure exactly what you said, I mean 'exactly,' but it was probably something about loss and anger and being drained. That part was really clear. Dead center. You mean literally you said just one more sentence and Hennessey was 'cured?'"

"No, not quite," I started to correct him, looking around at the others as well. "I interpreted to Hennessey with just one short sentence why I insisted that he finish the pool and why I 'guaranteed' that Dana would improve if he did so. I had really crawled out on a limb so I must have seen something that Hennessey didn't, but that Dana did.

"Besides, I didn't use the word 'cured!'"

Miss Taylor cut me off: "It's a beautiful story," she said to no one directly, then, leaning forward, she placed both shoes on the floor, and assuming a pose reminisent of Rodin's *Thinker*, spreading her knees and grasping her chin in one hand. Behind, the other found her flank.

"Dana was a woman. Men don't understand us," she reflected. "No, men don't understand us at all, do they?"

Upon those last syllables she leaned back, crossed one silken calf upon the other and half-smirking, started, like a pendulum, tauntingly, to swing the diaphragm of her stethescope back and forth. A little smile curled upon her pretty lips.

"Could you expand your answer, or your question?" I asked, amused, intrigued, wondering whether I had misjudged her after all.

"Dana had some kind of relapse. I think she knew her husband cared, only she couldn't get through to him. He was too ... too ... practical. She wanted to be felt."

"You're very warm," I coaxed her, but having apparently overextended herself with that exploratory salvo, Miss Taylor could not keep to the point. She reiterated that Dana sounded like a "dear." "How much she must have suffered to be married to such a 'pragmatist.'"

I turned to "Cautious Mac."

"Your turn, McNulty. Want to try?"

In his fashion the young man appeared to have been playing the tale's highlights silently through his computer, weighing, sorting, underscoring, combining, all the necessaries as a good diagnostician must. Sifting clues.

"I'd like to run it through another time," he ventured, not surprised when Stein broke in a little shrilly, with a "Jesus Mac, it's not a deposition! We're just speculating; take a shot!"

"Well, okay. You're right. It's not a legal instrument, exactly. These features ... she had only grieved approximately half of the anticipated year. Right? And you stressed that her attachment to her father was unusually strong, owing to his attributes and the premature death of her mother. So she may have needed more than the typical year, but she was gaining with the 'supplies' that Hennessey was pouring in.

"She was a secretary, or a 'Girl Friday' to him earlier, so I imagine she knew about budgets and the like, to respond to Carlson."

Taylor winced and shifted in her seat.

"But when the work was stopped, I guess she lost something again. I don't know what. Anger? Control?"

"You're hitting all around it, all of you, but I want to remind you that there was one specific inspiration I received that gave me insight. Some symbolic thing I managed to decode, which Hennessey had not."

Stein spoke up. "You said that the Muse bit you."

"Right."

"You got an 'insight?'"

"Right."

"You saw something that Dana did too, but Hennessey didn't?"

"Right again. Let me remind you. Hennessey *was* a practical fellow. Just as Miss Taylor says. Dana was not. She was artistic. Like her Dad. She dealt in allegory, symbols—or at least so I imagined. After all, I never actually met or spoke with her. I am assuming from her husband's descriptions, but even so, my guess is that she reacted more to shadow than to substance. I sensed besides that she was unconsciously displacing strong feelings from one object onto another."

Taylor shook her head. "That poor sweet thing. I give up. What did you say? Did the story have a happy ending?"

"It did. So far as I ever found out. Hennessey followed my advice and got the job completed within days, and the last I heard Dana was ticking along like a Swiss watch."

Stein, all smiles, obviously satisfied (and picturing himself as having chosen the winning team right from the start) commented, "It's a great example of how an analyst can be of direct use. Down to earth. I think it was super the way you stepped in and told him what to do. Especially since you weren't actually analyzing Hennessey or Dana. Very instructive! Neat!

"So what did you say?"

"Do you all give up?"

They did.

It was after ten p.m. Time to quit. I had teased and stretched their curiosity to bursting, so I picked up just where I had left it off.

"... and Dana stands there staring at it all day long, fumbling with the breakfast dishes, and then again at lunch and dinner?

"Hennessey, my friend, your wife is not savoring pictures

of your kiddies playing or of poolside frolic, or of entertaining people from your plant. There is only one reflection coming from that pit, so far, and unless you get it finished fast, that is the one that she will ever ascribe to it! Don't you realize what Dana is seeing?

"Until you get it done it is a three-dimensional nightmare come to life—a resurrection of the source of all her grief. That hole is just a king-sized mammoth *grave!*

"Her Father's!"

7

The Noose

Marines have no physicians of their own. Synthetic "Semperfi's" are borrowed from the Navy by the Corps. And in those times of crisis when reservists are called up and given uniforms and told they are military men, despite the fifes and drums and martial filigree, civilian sympathies survive.

I mean, just being "Shanghai'd" for a cruise cannot subvert a man's philosophy or even bend it very much.

And so?

And so, vast boundless chasms yawn between those regular Marines, who volunteered, and tender-hearted medics who have been both drafted and commissioned to their roles—especially psychiatrists.

Accept that. Q.E.D.!

Another thought:

What value in a war amidst bazooka bursts and howitzer reports our interview techniques? Their quintessential frills? Their fine Italian hand where words and themes and plots, with gestures or restraints, depict a human's style, his subtlest subtleties? His way of doing things. And yet I must confess that I

am "hooked." An hour with a man invites sheer artistry. The
process is unique, symphonic to my mind.

Harmonics, overtones, and grace notes—all indicative,
prognostic, blended into one consistent whole, explaining whence
my choice to meet a patient "cold." Without prehistory.

I loathe those cablegrams my colleagues like to write:

"I'm sending you a kid who's hung up on his Mom." Or
"'Survey' this freak out. He's homosexual!" If such be cogent
facts they surface when we talk. Triangulate themselves through
skillful interviews. In contexts of ideas and acts, outspoken or
implied.

Could you imagine a Marine not boasting of his girl or
how much beer he drinks?

"Split" to a sultry afternoon: Korean War. Camp Pendleton. My orders? To assess a consultee referred for an exam. A
dismal, abject youth they plonked across my desk. Head down,
responding not a word to anything I asked.

A sheaf of papers in his fist, emblazoned with a tag. In red,
"PRECAUTIONS—CATATONIC SCHIZ." That emblem now
was gossip on the ward. In harsher worlds outside, it was a
ticking bomb—for him a hangman's noose!

I ought to strategize somehow, to spare him if I could. Re-
interview the lad, not simply sign the forms and tag him thus for
life.

I said, "I know your name. That's it. (I might have been
precise and called him 'PFC.' The biceps of each arm displayed
a single stripe. Small use to mention that. It was so obvious!).
Now, can you tell me more? Like why you're here; what's
wrong?"

The youth made no response; no flicker. Not a twitch.

"I see your record, but I have not studied it. I would rather
learn from you the story it contains, whatever you can say."

I pictured Shakespeare's Lear. The warning from his lips:

"Cordelia, speak again. From nothing nothing comes." Nay better! Mend your speech; "Your fortune hangs on it." I doubted that the lad would profit from those lines, and yet I savored them.

"You find it hard to talk?"

The Sphinx sat motionless.

"It's alright; take your time; then tell me what you can."

I looked across the desk. His scalp—a field of wheat. Its myriad short stalks sprang out of bronzed, white turf. Each perfect golden shaft exactly as the rest, cropped accurately down to contour out his skull, a "flat-top," mowed that week, before he "came aboard."

Despite his hanging head, I saw his pug-shaped nose much seasoned by the sun. His ears, like apricots, parenthesized his face. His eyes, although shut tight, I pictured steely gray.

I gave him eighteen years, and guessed he'd finished High. Excelled in contact sports, and lettered more than once. I fancied that he left a pie-faced girl behind, and to her he wrote notes with misspelled tender words. My hunch said he had sibs, of either sex, one each. His "Mom" spent time on "chores" while "Dad" was "fixing things."

You know my regnant thought? How very trim, this lad! His off-green uniform was pressed and "squared away," presenting knifelike pleats and flawless fields of cloth, a khaki small-knot tie and polished combat boots.

"What thoughts run through your mind? Why can't you let them out? Are you the quiet type that always acts this way? Hey, look! A lot of guys like you have sat across my desk. The only role I play is sorting data out. I hope they made it clear I don't give punishment. I do 'detective work.' I'm not the CIC or any kind of 'cop.'"

Were those the magic words? He winced a bit just then, so I pulled back to wait. Some silence would not hurt. He needed time to think (God only knew of what) as somewhere from *my* past I conjured up a man whose words had taught me much. We called him "Sherlock Holmes" because he had the knack of ferreting out the facts.

He lectured to our class about a problem man with epileptic fits—just when he drove to work. My teacher figured out it was a grove of trees that lay along his route. The shadows of their trunks made flickers on his brain; *they* triggered off the spells.

A diagnostic coup. Inspired detective work. Could I match skills like his?

I checked the boy again. How neat and trim he was ... wait! ... chevrons on his arm. But look, that noose! That tiny loop of thread where *double stripes had been.*

This youth was stripped of rank! *They made him shave* one off. That single thread survived, a token of his dreams. I nodded toward his arm and whispered at his sleeve:

"They 'busted' you? That it?"

He heaved, then with a tearful flood he washed ashore his tale.

Today I can't remember it—the reason for his "bust"— but never shall I forget that errant loop of thread and what it saved him from.

8

Whosoever Is Without Sin

On Thursday afternoon the huge clock atop City Hall said exactly three minutes to four. Already the slanting rays of a feeble winter sunshine, yellow and pale, were yielding to lengthening blue shadows in the streets. Those few pedestrians who had to turn the corner to head up the hill grimaced as they stepped out of the lee of the broad Clinic building and into the icy blast. Their short and quickened paces were acknowledgement of an impending freeze.

Driven by the wind from the east and north, menacing dark patches of nimbus clouds were being blown in. Sparse, and, only occasional at their perimeter, beyond they seemed condensed, heaped up.

I felt uneasy over what the traffic might be like by six o'clock; the conference ended then. And standing meditatively within the casement of the old knee-to-ceiling window, surveying the sky and contemplating problems that a heavy rain would bring, listening to the radiators hiss and bump, dreaming, looking out, I lingered just another moment to rehearse my opening remarks on Chipper's history.

It was a heavy one. Ponderous, alright. Reminiscent of that fast-approaching storm: minor pecadillos first, peripheral and sparse, then driven by some ominous and unseen force, they too had bunched together and precipitated out.

Just like those clouds.

"Blow winds and crack your cheeks! Rage! Blow! You cataracts and hurricanoes."

I would be obliged to tell the whole of it exactly as it was. Sans editing. And pray, why not? Without a doubt its essence was familiar to both the nuns who were to be my audience.

Poor Chipper! Poor baby!

Hellcat!

Yes, tell it as it was, and then, if Faith and Hope and Charity, the heart of which they represented, philosophically, could smile upon him yet, despite its weighty content, and grant permission to the boy to roost again beneath their spreading mantle, why Chipper might be saved.

But, if otherwise, the youngster would be packaged up and sent, first class, to some place on the outskirts of the city. Far beyond their pale and mine.

Chronologically, he had aged enough to graduate to higher levels in the Youth Authority.

Without our Clinic's guidance he would sway to left or right through other influence, and, in the presence of a gang of seasoned criminals, do an apprenticeship of more sophisticated tricks, in no wise therapeutic.

Chipper!

Odd my ambivalence! I'd miss him actually. True! I would. That scamp! Like missing chicken pox or warts. And then, as if to justify said curse, I rubbed my tired eyes and rummaged through a hotch-potch of nostalgic reminiscences: his mischief and his foibles.

Strange what comes to mind: a fragment of philosophy

once whispered to me at a party, by a tipsy Javanese:

"Men went aan alles," I believe he said, with a wink, "zelfs hangen!" Roughly, that a man gets used to anything in time, even to the gallows—"even hanging!"

"Even hanging!"

Then I laughed out loud in recognition of my reason for associating to that phrase. I was remembering how Chipper used to hang, literally, out of the playroom window—second story (oh, there was a fire escape, of course)—or leap from chair to desk then race around the room out into the corridors, me chasing.

Breathless, freckled-faced, with greenish, tartared teeth, ragged make-do clothes—so, so institutional: ill-fitting, State-laundered, sewn, resewn, repatched with gussets to preserve them. For just one more semester.

He acted out his conflicts so transparently, the little pest. He *needed* to be chased and captured. He *wanted* to be held. By anyone, brinksman! He would test the limits, challenge you to love him.

I had been writing something in his chart, sitting in my swivel. Chipper climbed behind it, applied his version of a stranglehold, then ridiculed my dandruff. Some enchanting way to make a first impression!

He plunged me into problems of the overactive child. Hyperkinetics. We had no drugs those days. Just talking. Small wonder I felt doubtful. Could our two wild years of "psychotherapy" have rooted underneath his scalp and damped his frenzy?

Had he learned aught of compromise, delays, or substitutions?

*   *   *

A long, black, official-looking car rounded the corner of Main Street. An important car with gleaming chrome, spotless windows, deep treads in its unworn tires. And, as it slowed and parked eight inches from the curb, exactly parallel, I knew with certainty what next.

Moment of reckoning:

Its driver, trim in his gray uniform, sprang out and opened the rear door. I watched his passengers emerge: two nuns.

Maintaining dignity, and with a grace approaching elegance, they slid their habits, coifs, and selves along the cushioned seat. Despite the gaucherie of that maneuver they emerged unruffled and intact.

The taller, whom I guessed to be the elder, glanced all around the street, then, adjusting the cant of her bifocals, zoomed in on our number. Satisfied, she breathed a message to the man, who touched a finger to his temple. A salute; then climbed back in his vehicle and eased it into Main Street, as the ladies, individuated, next regrouped into a unit—an ebony amalgam, which like liquid flowed along the sidewalk to our stairs and scaled them.

In the foyer, just beyond the narrow vestibule, we introduced ourselves, the senior, Agatha, Therese, her junior, and finally myself. My chief had not arrived. Then down the long and dimly lighted corridor back to the library.

I felt at sixes and at sevens. How should I chat with nuns? Ought I avoid religion? What then? Talk politics or sports? Could I tell jokes? I had but one conviction, to avoid discussion of our "case" before the "boss" appeared. He seldom kept folks waiting. But how to fill this hiatus?

I lamented that the room had grown dark, and fumbled for the light switch. Damned stroboscopic flicker! Then I condemned discomforts of the straight-backed arm-rest chairs, the kind we took our notes on.

Tut for my awkwardness! It worsened with their silence. I sensed that I was staring.

Did sisters at the convent prize conformity in aspect? To fit some tacit image? Was there a code of dress to cover every article of clothing? Even glasses?

Agatha's were silver-rimmed. Small octagons. Quite clerical. Precisely what one pictures for a nun. Multiple diopters. Thickened lenses that both minified her eyes and made them bright and piercing. Yet, being blue and clear, they blended an intelligence with kindness. Her skin was absolutely flawless. Its pallor underneath those ghastly incandescent bulbs gave contrast to her habit. And her lips, the merest meagre lines that contoured each word spoken.

And Therese? A complementary shadow. A muted, minor melody augmenting and enhancing.

Both of them, so disciplined, controlled, so proper, that foolish as it sounds, their simple presence made me restless. I felt sinful and impure, intimidated by just standing there so near them.

Had Chipper? Living with them?

Would Chipper? Back among them?

Could he draw fresh strength from Scripture, and quit tossing them those curve balls? Then you know my train of thought? The paradox. The paradox of asking—as I knew I surely would—that these fragile, porcelain figurines admit into their hushed and finely structured universe a wild bull like Chipper! He had nearly wrecked their china shop already. If only one could promise—be oracular, prophetic—would he cast more stones, or "cool it"?

That reverie was broken. At five minutes after four Dr. Wunderkind arrived.

His actual physical appearance was anticipated by the sound of animated conversation with a colleague just outside the door.

Cracked open to admit his leading foot, and to reveal his hand on the knob, it rendered us a captive audience to every word he said.

No, nothing really private, but enough to document his rebel's reputation: feisty, independent sage.

It would seem that following our meeting, another had been scheduled. Board of Directors. His presence was requested. Only he reneged. He said a storm was brewing, and despite the indiscretion, he decided he would "fly." Made his mind up. "Take it or leave it!"

I knew why.

Dr. Wunderkind had just completed building for his family a rambling, ten-room ranch house, twenty miles distant. Its basement had been flooding. When he pushed on through the doorway, I was terse with introductions.

So too he: a single crisp rejoinder as he picked up Chipper's chart.

"Ach, Till Eulenspiegel!"

I launched my peroration.

Without interruption, nay, without so much as the susurrus of the Sisters' cloth, a cough, or clearing of a throat, by half past five, I had reviewed, in depth, the salient features of my patient's checkered past.

I touched upon his mother's antenatal sprees, her pregnancy, his birth, his subsequent adoption—and rejection—and I documented, link-on-link, the anchor chain Fate wound around his neck. Poor kid—the luckless, passive victim!

Then, I chronicled the youngster's contrecoup: I really waxed dynamic. He was taking *active steps*, I said, to strike back at his Moira. That was how I saw his capers. All those "merry pranks" were sheer retaliation.

Still I had my obligations: to catalogue the lot. So, joyless but unflinching, I surveyed the wild parade: how twice he fired the convent, his countless bold elopements, with joy rides in their car, and how he had been recaptured; and the thefts and his prevarications! Nor did I gloss the *meisterstück*—the time he bit the sister on her knee, infecting her patella!

I let the record speak.

Let the Quality of Mercy be not strained. I pled for reinstatement! One last chance. To show what therapy had wrought upon his soul. I sat, attendant on their judgment.

But first, my Chief should air his wisdom. We focused on him, waiting.

Dr. Wunderkind did not blink. He kept on reading, flipping pages of the chart. Those titubations of his head I took as approbation, and the drumming of his fingers, on the desktop, restlessness, impatience.

"Tap. Tap. Tap."

By now, a gentle rain was falling. In half an hour that drizzle would be sleet, then snow. Poor boss! Oh I could read his mind: to race home. Get it done. Finish fast with Chipper, then speed off. He deplored procrastination.

My mentor was one of those rare incisive dynamos who take shortcuts to everything—even rules—and always pushed the limits. Never dawdled. Not him. Even driving. Storm or no. Floor it! I would not be surprised if he was not stopped that night as had happened twice before. He was not reckless, but impatient.

Remember Raskolnikov? Described by Dostoievsky? The student who had reasoned so persuasively that laws should flex to fit the person? That was Dr. Wunderkind, and wasn't that a kick? That traces of a Chipper could be found in *him*? Who headed this big clinic?

Would the sisters recognize that and react?

Return an adverse verdict?

I heard the doctor's monotone break in:

"Good job! A history like this! It really is a rough one! Like spinning wool from wisps of spider webs. No substance. All fragments. I'll tell you how I see it: Chipper needed love. And parents. Parents for controls. He got a great big zero. Next to nothing. In his superego I see huge and gaping holes. A conscience should have grown there. Gossamer. Just pieces!

"Two years ago I almost balked on his admission, but look here: real gains. He's 'taken in' his doctor. Learned *his* values. He can tolerate frustration, talk instead of act. And postpone. That's great!

"He's growing. Learning right from wrong. Slowly bit by bit. You sense it? I'm sure he should stay on, at least another year, or two ... which means returning to your school. That's better far than jail. You buy it?

I did.

Ten to six. The sands of time were running.

The nuns?

At last they broke *their* silence. They explained that no decision could be reached without more consultation with their Board. Over the week-end. Then they asked a spate of keen and searching questions. Varied, technical, considerably brief, at first, then focused on one target. Bull's eye! What risk that Chipper would set fire to the convent? Was he still a "pyro?"

His other pranks were bearable. But before the school would readmit him it might ask one "guarantee." No more fires. Ever! Could we promise them that much? To which I heard my teacher (ichor in his tone):

"Come on! We promise nothing. We're not Gods! You ought to know that. All too well. Uh, uh. No! Humans always fool you. Always will. Take Chipper back, but cross yourselves! And cross your fingers. He's the best he's ever been so far, since he was born. You've got to. If you don't the State will ruin him in jail. I've seen that happen time and time again. But don't expect clairvoyance. Not from us. Nor for the likes of mortal man!''

He smiled and clamped the chart shut on his thigh.

His own spectacles, also silver-rimmed, but circular, slid down an inch along his nose, and rested at its ridgeline where I thought it had been broken. I watched him eye the weather out of doors.

Upon the window panes and mullions hail was beating. Darkness of the night already settled in. We heard the sounds of horns and autos starting, straining, stopping, and of buses inching through the traffic snarls uphill.

"No, not for *man's* behavior," he reechoed. "You can count with certainty on absolutely *no one* in *this* world. Not even on *you nuns*, not even *me*!''

They said they'd think it over.

* * *

We had a horrible blizzard Friday. Nobody in the entire city got to work, but by Monday things were back to normal. When I arrived at the Clinic, I met Dr. W. in the foyer. He was smiling.

He asked if I had heard the news, but without awaiting my reply, he further qualified the question.

On their verdict about Chipper, and about the "ticket?" With a funny, sheepish, puzzling kind of grin. "They took young Eulenspiegel back. You're going to save him."

"But the ticket, did they catch you speeding home?" "Who me? Not me! Their chauffeur got it. 'Drunken driving!'"

* * *

And the boy? He stayed in treatment. Two more years. And he behaved. Far better than expected. The last I heard of him he had petitioned to become a priest.

9

E Pluribus Unum

Straight as a surveyor's transit line, extending east and west along the thirty-second parallel, about an hour's auto ride due south of San Diego, separating Mexico and the United States, lies La Frontera.

Running on, that boundary later zig-zags. Wiggles like a rattlesnake across the State of Texas, ultimately plunging into waters of the Gulf, but, back before those sinuosities, like sentinels at either end, there stand the border towns, Tijuana, and her sister Mexicali.

Spot them on a map, then note how, thrusting down, into the blue Pacific, there intrudes the rugged, little-known peninsula called Baja California—an enchanted land.

For me to visit Baja always has been tantamount to stepping through a looking glass. Few travelogues have done it justice. Photographs could never reproduce its charms. How could they capture its essence, its aroma? Listen to these names: La Paz. Cabo San Lucas. Mulege. Loreto. San Quintín.

Need more?

Consider then that if you swung an arc whose radius was

one day's journey out of brash Los Angeles—its hustle and its smog, its din, its buildings blown from glass—down into Baja, where the blacktop pavement ends, you would pinpoint, a still tiny, antiquated, telephoneless fishing village: San Felipe.

Approach it! You will encounter vistas set in prehistoric times: miles and miles and miles of virginal sand beaches, touched alone by arid, lifeless lands and azure skies. Beaches from whose shoals no human yet has launched an outboard motor. From whose dunes no frisbee ever sailed. Beaches so pristine in glory that upon them, it would seem, no biped has ever trod.

Could it intrigue you?

For a sojourn if you wished to get away?

* * *

I met George at the airport. By pure coincidence, just as I, he had emplaned his wife and kids to visit relatives back East. Flippantly, we teased one another about the perils of our temporary bachelorhood, then agreed to dine together in the Skydome Lounge.

There, between the croutons of a Caesar salad and a wedge of apple pie, he told me how he wished to slip away. To weekend. Anywhere at all, so long as it was quiet. That was when I mentioned Shangri-la.

I was going into isolation. South to San Felipe. To read a bit and polish up a story. If real solitude was what he wanted, I would be pleased to have him tag along.

Poor obstetrician! How little bait it took!

"Sounds like paradise," he muttered, then he grabbed the check and paid.

Allow me to portray the man before you meet him further. George is kind. Humane. And filled with boundless energies as well. In fact, I used to puzzle whence he drew such zeal—delivering kids at three and four a.m., then racing to his office, seeing patients, operating, always making rounds—consistently so "band-box" fresh besides.

I asked him once in passing, "Hey, George, what's your secret? If I'm kept up all night I look like hell; you glow! And what about your whiskers? Don't they sprout the way mine do?"

I can see him laughing. Jowls jiggling. "Of course," he chuckled, "but I keep four razors! I'm like 'Minnesota Fats.' I thrive on image. One's at home; one's in my car. I shave while driving. I've got one that's in the locker at the hospital, and one I leave at work."

He theorized that the ordeal of childbirth could be lightened for the leading actress if he dressed to lend her his support. I appreciated that. It seemed empathic, yet my sixth and seventh senses cautioned "caveat," because George never called in psychiatric consultation for his patients, even an eclamptic who became psychotic on a Sunday. That struck me rather odd, although the fact is hereabouts our medicos are rather polarized: three groups:

Some are pro, respectful, sympathetic, never hesitate to make referrals. Others? Suspicious, think we try to wash men's minds. A communistic plot. In between, a small group, uncommitted. Skeptical, but mostly laissez-faire. That is where I felt George belonged.

I wondered if a weekend spent together would enlighten or antagonize him.

Mind, I never beat a drum or proselytize. Not directly. Oh, indirectly sure. I try to lead my life as an example—"to love and to work." If anybody notices, that's fine, which does not mean I am skittish about humor, insights, funny slips of colleagues' tongues or pens.

Like teasing George for instance ... about the paper he had

picked to decorate his office. It was Trichomonas! A blown-up
mural of its microscopic form! It really was! Flagella! Cysto-
somes! The works!

He played it straight the day I told him. "Trichomonas?
That's a yeast—an ob's *bread* and *butter*! Why not do it tribute
on my walls?"

We laughed together heartily, but at that line, psycholog-
izing stopped.

* * *

The monotony of the San Diego Freeway got to both of us.
Small talk, local politics, and sports. We tried a classical music
station, but its signal faded as we left Los Angeles behind. Our
inland route avoided all the coastal cities. I grew a trifle restless,
wondering if I should frankly speak my mind.

Upon it lay a question.

Technical. About obstetrics. George could answer. I should
ask him so that I might weave the data into what I had brought
along to write once we arrived, except to pose it could have led
us into controversy. Maybe to the DMZ itself.

At the town of San Ysidro, the last stop before crossing
over, we agreed to fill the tank and take a coffee break. "It's
now or never," I exclaimed and started in.

"George, will you be honest with me?"

"Sure," he smiled "Who's the luckless girl?"

"No, really. I'm not kidding. Look, I've got you as a kind
of captive. This once you can't run. There's no one on a table
full-dilated. If I start, you'll have to hear me out, okay?"

"You sound a little cloak-and-dagger, Doctor. What's the
deal? I promise not to go. Where would I?" Still smiling.

"I have a question. For a story I'm attempting, but I
hesitate to ask it. You know why? I'm afraid that it'll get us into

conflicts—philosophically, about my practice—and I'm really here to have a pleasant time, the same as you."

"I promise to behave. What's on your mind?"

"A term."

"A term?"

"A name I can't remember. You would know it. Interrupt me if it starts my talking shop too much."

"Bet your duff I will! Lay on!"

Upon the formica tabletop before us the waitress plonked two heavy mugs half-filled with light brown coffee. Against their porcelain white, the liquid looked both weak and sickly pale. Beside them, with unnecessary splendor, she arranged forks, knives, spoons, two napkins in their rings, a tumbler full of ice and water—which I drained at once to get it filled again.

"What it boils down to, George, is the possibility, or better yet, the likelihood of a woman's having twins by different men."

"How do you mean?" he asked, half rotating his chair and running his palm across the stubble starting from his chin.

"Look," I answered, "I understand about identical twins. One ovum splits in two. And about fraternal. That's when separate eggs are fertilized. But, what if a woman had a lover whom she saw in the morning and afterward her husband later that same day? Could she have twins by different men?"

George nodded up and down. "It's happened. The name you're looking for is 'hyperfecundation.'"

"'Hyperfecundation?'"

"Yup. That's what it's called. Been written up."

"I'm glad I asked. I never heard of the term before."

"You probably don't keep up. I've seen at least half a dozen papers here and there. It doesn't happen often, but it can. I hope this isn't personal," he grinned. "Why did you want to know?"

"I thought you'd never ask!"

With a smirk I slid the check out from underneath the sugar bowl and added, "That's the basis of the story I brought along. I'd like to try it out on you, but, as I've said, you're captured, so say 'uncle' and I'll quit. Okay?"

George shrugged.

*   *   *

Having never before driven a Seville, I deemed it wise to acquaint myself first with all the knobs and buttons. Forget the windshield wipers; but the horn and dimmer switch could come in handy. "Quite the set of horses. What's it go for anyway?" I asked.

George told me, and I whistled low and long. "I'll give it every courtesy. You want to get it extra coverage for the other side?"

"No, the way you've talked of San Felipe I don't think we'll see another car till we return. You're right. It cost a bundle, but I've earned it. I put eighty hours a week in at my work. Sometimes more! Staggering the amount of money that I handle. But expenses are high too—nurses, office rent, equipment, and malpractice. It's a goddamn treadmill. Running all the time. I do a lot of unpaid stuff besides. Do I sound guilty, Sigmund?"

I kept silent.

Purposely.

Machiavellian, my scheme.

Into its slot I slid the silver key. Fuel and air were mixing nicely in the carburator and with prodding from my toe the panther leapt ahead.

"I'll say my piece before you get all caught up in your story," he continued. "I'd really like to hear it; what the hell? Why not? But I think that I can read between its lines. You're sort of skittish about how I view your practice, so I'm gonna clear the air. Okay? In the main, I favor what I know of Freud and his disciples and of all his contributions, but you do attract an awful lot of 'kooks,' and the thing that really frosts me is your fee. Analysis, I mean five visits weekly, is for millionaires, the rich and superrich. Alone. Oh, sure I know about your clinics—and the waiting lists that run a mile or two in length. But where can my colleagues send a person who needs you but is penniless besides?"

I burst out laughing!

"Hey, I wasn't kidding! That's my beef. I'm sorry. I don't see the humor," he replied with feeling.

"George," I croaked, "I really set you up. The story that I'm writing gives the perfect answer. Just sit back and listen. You can talk tomorrow. All day long."

We crossed through customs, then with the big car properly positioned on that east-west transit line I expected few distractions. However, I had to do a preface to the preface. There was method in my madness, rest assured:

"Did you ever hear of the book Robert Lindner wrote— *The Fifty Minute Hour*? They made a movie from it, *Pressure Point*, and a television series.

"Its title has survived as our calling card. Every *fifty* minutes, we take a break of ten. That practice dates back to Freud. He must have stretched his legs or gone to get cigars. Maybe he had to savor what he had listened to, to let it sink in more. Anyway, that work and break routine has become our trademark. Isn't that *metonymy* or *pars pro toto*? Come to think of it, *you* say '*the praevia* in room 13.' Anyhow, as I was spouting, even though that fractionation has been the habit, there is nothing holy that keeps it always so.

"When I first started treating children, we worked teams. My associate would interview the mother. Meantime I had

Junior in with me. We saved the final *quarter hour* for a tête-à-
tête to swap notes.

"A propos ... I've met some dynamos who take no break
whatever. Their offices are hung with double sets of doors—one
to enter, one to leave. That way you don't see the other patient.
Kind of rhythmic and productive, but reminiscent of the
Keystone Cops.

"George, do you remember back in World War Two the
way they swung the hull plates in behind a freighter sliding
down the weighs?"

George nodded. "Yeh, but what's the point?"

"You'll see. My own analyst had a special variation. He
used to put two 'in betweens' together. That gave him twenty
minutes free for tea, or coffee. One chap I knew worked in his
home; he would move his sprinklers back and forth."

A faint smile suggesting amusement and incredulity began
to spread across George's round and handsome face. Whatever
threat had warranted his initial defensiveness was slipping fast
away.

I told him the last guy was a lusty one. The hidden virtue
of his pattern was a chance for "hanky-panky" with his wife.
That broke George up; but I continued:

"What I need to stress is that we're an efficient bunch. We
really try to ply time wisely. I'm the least exception. You'd be
amazed what I can manage in those minutes. But, know what
I'm mostly busy with?

"My nemesis? My dragon?

"Desk-top clutter!

"George, it's like an avalanche! Letters, more insurance
forms, advertisements, fliers. Every kind of pamphlet, junk an
awful lot of it. Much I jettison, unopened."

"Same with me," he sighed.

"Then there are journals. Those I sort. Some I'll riffle on

the spot, like a tachistoscope. Now, here's the message: Have I conveyed the pressure? Busy or not, one spring morning, I suppose between ten-fifty and 11 o'clock, I speed-read an article, but found it had me glued utterly. I couldn't believe what I saw:

"It was a paper written by a prestigious scientist at the University. Research. Unbiased. Measuring the *economic* dividends of psychotherapy."

George started to protest. I kept right on.

"Truly! Chi-squares, sigma, double-blinds, probability, standard deviations, you name it. His results: forty-seven hours of counseling, on the average, mind you, would 'augment a patient's earnings by 19.3%'!

"Think of it! A year of weekly treatment turned a pauper into Croesus!

"It was dynamite! Proof positive that lying on the couch brought better interest than stocks, or bonds, or second mortgages! It was a landmark document. Hey, listen—harking back to your remarks—do you realize that hardly a day goes by without my hearing, 'Yes, I know I need your help, but at those prices we'd be bankrupt in no time! Sure I've got my hang-ups, but why substitute one problem for another?'"

"So I wasn't that far off," George snapped.

"Uh, uh. Impeccable such logic—on the surface, but my experience over the years had suggested the reverse, a reverse I had never seen spelled out in black and white."

"Your experience?" he asked.

"Sure. Hey, look, when you're on the canvas with depression, or anxiety has made you a human pretzel, you don't produce. If psychotherapy unkinks you, *then* you blossom. Put the work out. Bosses notice. You get kudos, bonuses, promotions, raises, bottom line. Your bracket has to rise. I've seen it countless times, but never kept score—that's the preface.

"Now my story":

Across the front seat, George shot a baleful glance. From the corner of my eye, which I dared not remove from the road, I could see the expression of a beagle, weary, sad, and a wrinkled forehead consonant with doubt.

We were passing through winding mountainous terrain. Simple but elegantly beautiful. Loosely piled boulders, ranging from grapefruit- to watermelon-size were strewn everywhere; around each curve, a vista—steaming, baking flatlands far below. I felt remorse about my ignorance of basic geologic facts.

"Just one quickie before you plunge us into it," George muttered. "Is this story true?"

"Scout's honor," I responded, saluting with two fingers to my temple. "Only the names have been changed to protect the innocent."

He snorted. "You're not 'window-dressing' it a bit?"

"I thought you said, 'one question.'" I replied.

"Yeah, shoot!"

"Hey George, you know that I'm a sucker for the well-turned phrase."

"And I'm a 'captive audience.' How far to San ... wherever?"

"Oh, I'd say two hundred miles. I'll let you out to hitch. Someone will pick you up ... although you kind of need a shave."

George beamed. "Here, lemme have that road map. I've never been on this particular stretch before. Kind of wild, but interesting. One peek, then I'll sit back and close my eyes and listen."

"I love it. Every inch," I cried.

I slid the folder out from behind the visor and tossed it in his lap. George studied it. "I really didn't mean to interrupt ... ah, there's Mexicali. Hey! Across the border—Calexico. Do you know something? That's the first time it occurred to me.

"Mexicali and Calexico. They're half-and-half names. Half Mexico. Half California."

"Except it didn't come out even, did it?" I proposed.

"How do you mean?" George asked.

"Try it and you'll see."

"Yeh," he mumbled. "Calexico should be 'Mexifornia' to be precise."

"I hear it used to be until the City Fathers changed it. 'Too suggestive.'"

"Okay. 'Too suggestive?' What's the gag?"

I tried to keep a straight face. "No. Really. Take another look. Do you see those twin towns, San Luis? Right on the border? One north, the other south of it? Okay, now see *Tecate?* Do you see Tecate down in Mexico and its duplicate, Tecate, up above? That's where they had the problem."

"What?"

"Border towns. Sin Cities. Full of brothels, pornos, if you follow. Had to change their names. Used to be Te-Cali up on our side, but underneath was Forni-cate!"

"Oh for Christ's Sake," George guffawed. "You'd better do your script."

* * *

"In the Van Nuys Village Tract, alternate models have the carport on the side instead of in front. Try to visualize it. Picture one with wilting, purple wisteria that needed trimming from the lattice. See it? Lots of gingerbread and kitsch. There's an old pickle barrel, halved, painted red, made into a planter. Plenty of crabgrass. Upturned bicycle and empty trash cans lying on the lawn. Okay, close up on the bedroom.

"In it Lorelei Schultz has just attempted to end her life.

"Time: two-thirty p.m. on a hot, breathless, smoggy afternoon. Within fifteen minutes of the carpool's letting off her kids.

"Place: the queen-sized bed.

"Manner: pills. A fistful of antihistamines, aspirin, proprietary sleeping draughts, and Valium, the last two in the phial.

"As 'attempts' go, it didn't sound too 'serious,' but I didn't complain when my answering service put her call straight through as an 'emergency.' She'd had my number several weeks, but had delayed phoning: 'financial reasons.'

"If she could arrange to get the sitter who lived in their cul-de-sac, she could keep an appointment with me late that afternoon, except she didn't drive the freeways.

"So I plotted her a route by surface streets. Her fumbling with directions and her having me repeat, several times, contributed to a rather unkind image of a dim-wit, to be frank.

"I had overlooked her being fuzzy from the stuff she had consumed. And fantasy went on to conjure me a plump, bedraggled, unattractive middle-aged craft, much gone to barnacles and moss.

"A prejudice for sure. I pictured her a curler-headed witch.

"Well, let me tell you, I have never been so wrong!

"When she stood there in the doorway, George, I gasped.

"I wish I could describe her! I was giddy with one look. Lines of poetry started running through my mind. I thought of Mona Lisa—then I heard myself reciting, 'There's my last Duchess on the wall,' and then, 'Shall I compare thee to a summer's day? Thou art more lovely and more temperate....' "

"A real 'de-icer,' eh?" George rasped.

"I wish I could do her justice. She was alluring, like a magnet. Drawing me. Two sad eyes, the shape of almonds, and their color, set against a perfect olive skin. Inside my thoughts were racing—how 'Beauty's ensign yet was crimson on her lips and in her cheeks and Death's pale flag was not advancéd there....' "

"Jesus Christ!"

"No, Shakespeare. Romeo."

" 'Lay on, McDuff.' "

"Her eyes, mysterious, yet soft, her nose, upturned, freckled, cute. I still can hear her cooing through those pouting, parted lips, 'Hello, I'm Lorelei.' "

"For sure!" George barked.

"A soft, slender, little hand lingered like the kiss of a butterfly on my sleeve, then lighted on my palm. 'I need your help,' she sighed, then drifted toward the couch.

"('Vamp! You keep away from there! We'll do this man to man!') I beckoned toward the chair. She paused and smiled beguilingly, then curled up in its arms.

"Could she have been aware? Or realized that as she had arranged herself, the folds and open buttons of her blouse invited peek-a-boo? And talk of miniskirts! George, I didn't need advanced degrees to clue me that I was in the presence of one of those 'rare and radiant maidens' who by their simply sitting still can turn a fellow's brain to jello. Bones to peanut butter! That gal's beauty would have brought a stone to life. Believe me!

"Lorelei indeed."

"She was well-named!" George managed, with a grunt.

"Quite apt. The legendary sorceress. She would split me on her rocks. I knew the mermaid's tale. The seamen she had wrecked, but I should prove redoubtable. I must watch her every move."

"I'll bet," he winked. "You really spread it thick."

"Quiet, George. There's more. What next? A gold-tipped cigarette. Blue-green paper. Pulled it out of nowhere, and just hung there, waiting, waiting, for Sir Galahad to light it.

"I didn't. So, she did herself, but must have got a sulfur

fume too close to her eye. Two sparkling tears welled up; one overflowed the rim. Zig-zag down her cheek, it dropped upon her skirt.

"The other? It waited for a 'gentleman' to leap across and daub away its hurt. I watched as from her dime-size purse she teased a tissue out, then tended to herself, a corner of it twisted to a point, as fluttering her lids she speared a wee mascara fleck and clucked her tongue at it.

"The nightingale! The hummingbird! How delicate, pe-tite! You know the world 'mignonne?' Poor Magdalen. The batting of your eyelid fans won't dry that dampness up. The weeping didn't stop. It tapped another source."

*   *   *

"Lorelei's saga was relatively straightforward. Nor was Lorelei truly her given name. It was Marie. Marie Renée.

"Her ancestry went back to Canada. Acadia. The haunts of Wadsworth Longfellow's *Evangeline*, the 'Murmuring pines and the hemlocks.' Her father brought the family across when she was very small.

"He had been a miner of asbestos up in Thetford. Underneath Black Lake. A stubborn, proud, intense, uneducated man who used to swear in French that he would sooner 'croak' then wear the recommended face masks. His *grandpère* and his father never used them. '*Zut!*' he used to shout, probably explaining his contracting chronic pulmonary something, which retired him to the States and coughed him to an early grave when Lorelei was five.

"Widow benefits proved hopelessly inadequate for the needs of his bereaved and kids. Literally they went hungry, threadbare, scared. They tasted much of poverty, its pinch, and worse, become demoralized, worn out.

"Lorelei's mother had married young. His death left her still subject to the chemistry of natural desire, except that Scripture, as the lady felt most comfortable with it, committed her to wedlock once only. For all eternity. Her husband would be waiting in another world. And so, she suffered. Martyrdom with all its bitter fruits (she liked to quote the dying Pontiff John—how sweet the termination of his life, his miseries and pain).

"With what results?

"The spongelike mind of Lorelei absorbed. Those vitriolic attitudes on Life. On sex. And money. May I paraphrase it?

"To the widow (hence her children) men were, every one of them, *bêtes noirs* who took advantage. 'Beware, they'll use you! And the merchants! All of them will cheat. They'll rob you deaf and dumb and blind! You always count your pennies in their presence. One short blink and you're undone.' These opinions became the creed of Lorelei as well.

"I was able as I traced the major roots and radicles to construct a theoretic framework. The youngster's libido, which had started out alive and well, perforce obeyed our 'metapsychologic quantum theory.' Damned up, left, it looked for outlets, right. If not through normal cultural expression, then through channels that afforded compromise."

George blinked. "You saying she became 'perverted?' "

"In a sense. But say that phrase with caution; it is so widely disabused. No, only in a sense.

"Lorelei became a morbid *tease*!

"Folks recognized it. Her nickname was the 'tart of Lewiston.' "

"Oregon?" George whistled.

"No, George. Lewiston in Maine. Oregon has a Lewiston too."

He loosed his shoulder strap and shifted in the leather bucket seat.

"I'm probably exaggerating."

"I guess," George said, "but it's kind of interesting. Lemme be sure I've got the picture. Your analysis was that the mother's ... frustrations and bitterness were picked up by the daughter. Jesus! That's unfair."

"You're right. But where could she complain? I mean except to me? Years later. And worse than that, the youngster didn't know. She wasn't aware."

"I get the point," George nodded, "and she was naturally lovely too?"

"I'd say! Of course, I never saw her as a child, but from descriptions she must have been a nubile little lady. A fragrant, floral petal the bees all buzzed around."

"We're going on I take it?" from George. "What are you, a poet?"

"Sometimes, George. I try."

"Proceed."

" ... whose reputation spread across the river up to Brunswick. Down to Bath, to the artist colony in old Ogunquit and across the bridges and into Portland where it met the Navy and was taken out to sea, and left behind a trail of disemboweled heroes, each of whom succumbed in wooing her."

"With one exception."

George asked: "Marlon Brando?"

"Close. Jim Schultz. He made it. He survived. His slipper fit on Cinderella's foot."

"How come?"

"I don't really know. Possibly what spared Prince Charming was his tweedy Boston background. Or his knowledge of asbestos and Black Lake. He had toured that area as well as much of Maine. Technocrat Computing, his employer, had commissioned him to research out a site. Some place where the taxes and the wages would support their setting up an ancillary plant.

"He took a fancy to the country around Auburn, and commuted for a bit, then moved his things to stay up north, but much preoccupied with business, garnered next to nothing of the local gossip, so, in meeting Lorelei, was unapprized of what the buzzings were.

"The fellow was obsessed. He couldn't sleep or eat or concentrate. Like the hero of a Russian novel, he was dizzy with 'brain fever' all of whose surrealistics featured her bulging blouse, the ample graceful curvings of her hips, the blossoms on her tawny cheeks, those deadly calves. To him, this Lorelei was utterly incredible, and made the more so in that she took kindly to his Florsheim shoes. His small-bowled pipe. His wit. His Cantabridgian pedantics. His jackets with their double cutaways behind.

"So he proposed, and six weeks later they were married. In a church. Precisely as his Lorelei had wished.

"I'll keep to basics, George. An instant family ensued. Kids, one, two, three; I'm sure you know; the hardest way in the world to launch young wedded bliss. You can catalog the predictables: infant colics, teethings, brats who slept by day then cried all night, each night. The broken washer, heater, frig. Those ground the couple down.

"Red-eyed, how many times in desperation did they spin around Lake Auburn hoping the engine roll would lull the crew to sleep? Or trundle up the babies with their pacifiers to the Drive-in, and leave halfway through the feature film? Exhausted. Tense.

"Do you know how frequently Jim had to duck out of business conferences and speed on home because Michael stuck his finger in the toaster, or how Tracy swallowed poison he had set for ants?

"I'll gloss it. Take my word that what had started as Nirvana was becoming Hell on earth. Stress. Strain. Short tempers. Weariness and Gloom. Tiny incidents became atomic detonations. Frequent loveless nights.

"Give him his due. Jim tried his level best to manage. Then there was the goddamn budget. If only they had funds to week-end down in Boston, or New York, or shop just once at Portland's finer stores. Lorelei was sick of all those camp-outs. Burgers! Fries! She wanted caviar, but there were doctor bills and endless debts.

"He grew them vegetables out back behind the barn. Lorelei? Resorted to novenas whose fulfillment would have brought a shiny pot of gold—except that nothing happened. Oh yes, the septic tank caved in. And Michael needed orthodontia. When the roof leaked, hubby patched it with old shingles from the shed. Sound like a sinking ship? It was.

"One last resource. Jim's cousin Frank, out West. In his latest letter, that voluble and worthy gentleman had raised the question why the kids didn't make the trek, the East was 'moribund.' Balboa, Davy Crockett, Lewis and Clarke. They had seen the light, followed the sun. 'Come on,' he urged them, 'I can help to get you started. Hasn't Technocrat a branch in Anaheim? So say the word and I'll start looking. Tustin. Orange or Canoga Park. Just tell me when.'

"Can you foresee the rest?"

George smiled. It was not difficult at all.

"Do you know Malibu?" I asked him. "A good friend of mine bought a hillside cottage overlooking the sea. Really nice. All along his driveway there are sycamores. They curve in graceful arches. Twisted limbs that frame pictures of the ocean. Deep, deep blue.

"It's a spanking little picture postcard, the house settled so perfectly within that grove of trees, except for one conspicuous flaw. There's a patch of wild mustard. It's a ragged plant, shapeless, irregular. Full of tics and bugs. I went to see him on a Sunday, and I started thinking about Lorelei.

"Why did I? Was it because she too was beautiful but also had some flaw? Nettles in her life? And if so, what were they? What was the 'ugliness' that had prompted her toward self-destruction? What should I, finally, lay bare among her sycamores?

"Actually, I felt a little guilty that on a day of leisure I had conjured up her face, her form. That is not supposed to happen, technically; yet, somehow it did.

"Oh, I figured out why! First it was the sight of all those skimpy swimming suits. The girls at Malibu. I had visions of my patient clad in a bikini. What a knockout she would be! But, that was only part of it. I knew I had to find that ugly patch of weeds. I followed my ideas, let them flow.

"I scanned them. Try to follow. It's important. Kind of bears out how a guy should use his intuition, and his training. Separates the men from all you foolish boys."

"I'll do the best I can, only I don't see anything unusual in appreciating a woman's beauty. I do it all the time. So you thought up a gorgeous female when you saw all those bikinis. That's a matter of esthetics, not morality," George argued.

"I agree, except I wasn't moralizing. Had I been, I should have missed the crux."

"Which was?"

"Which was the very touchstone of her problem. Hang in, George. I shall try to clarify: In our first session, Lorelei was ripe to talk. The history came pouring out of her. Factually. Details. But it wasn't the *content* of the recitation that mattered so much; it was the *form*. The way she telegraphed her charms.

She came on like Gangbusters. Apparently that was her style. With such an intensity that it got to me. Enough that when I saw other 'charming girls' in bikinis I naturally remembered Lorelei. Only what is appropriate to do at the beach may be inappropriate in the office. Except she couldn't turn it off."

"So?"

"So, if I were your garden variety egotist I would have duped myself into thinking it was me. Big 'shrinkologist' and all. Doctor. Office. Opulence. Prestige—to say nothing of my physique. But, being an analyst, I knew that what she was doing in an initial interview, turning on all that seduction with me, was very apt to be *her customary thing*. With everyone alike, young Lorelei would play the temptress."

"I get your drift. So, were you right?" he asked

"You'll have to wait to see.

"Naïve Easterners. Packed up and left. Good old cousin Frank! He really goofed. Technocrat Computing was in Anaheim alright, but the tract he put them in lay forty miles away. Downtown Van Nuys! His words were 'freeway close.' That meant a second car, which meant a second mortgage and a case of 'Valley Fever' once they had settled in."

"Valley Fever?" from my listener.

"That is my eponym for it. It happens so consistently, I think it deserves a name. Husbands commute to jobs so far away that they come home exhausted. Freeway-weary. Drained. The wife who has been alone all day would like to scream. As consolation to avoid the nervous breakdown, they put in a doughboy or a bigger swimming pool—which escalates the payments, so the guy starts working nights, and weekends! It's a vicious circle."

"Is there a cure?" George asked.

"Well, that's what Lorelei was seeking with her suicidal

gesture; only a dark element was lurking still, I believed. To find it we would have to dig some more.

"At our second encounter, Mrs. America looked drawn and pale as chalk. I said so, and urged her to explain. Her face became a beetlike splotchy red. Then damp, as raindrops started trickling from her eyes.

" 'Some ... thing simply awful to confess.' Those were her words. 'I'd almost rather die.'

"Lorelei shifted where she sat. She blew her nose. From its original position, like a barricade before her, she maneuvered to the side her 'suitcase purse.' This one was enormous, slung from double-buckled broad leather straps.

" 'I'd almost rather die!' resounded.

"Should I mention to her on the heels of such dramatic statements that exposed now was a tantalizing stretch of naked thigh?"

George watched me. I had visions of his holding back his breath.

" 'I'm utterly ashamed. Ashamed,' she re-echoed. 'May I tell you? Is it absolutely safe? If only time would let us turn it backward. Do you know? As rough as things have been with Jim, there's just one day ... ' and then the clutch of tissues garbled what was spit into their folds."

George bent forward. "Didn't you ask her to repeat?"

"I didn't have to. 'It would be the day that ignoramus came to "hype" us on a pool. Imagine, us! That son of a bitch! Oh, excuse my language. But even that's too good for him. That's what he was, that stinking, blue-eyed carrot-top!' "

George broke in. " 'Blue-eyed carrot top?' Is that patois? Canuck? What's it mean?"

"Hush, George. Listen. 'I should have slammed the door right in his goddamn face, except he had the saddest, kindest, bluest eyes. You know? Sort of wild, electric, staring, pitiful, and deep? They penetrated me alright! They must have watched me, every move I made. Tiny pupils. Could he have hypnotized me, do you think?

" 'Never mind. I've gotta tell you. Give me room. I will. I mentioned that we have three kids. I lied. We have five. There are twins!

" 'Fred and Teddy. Born right here. Pure Angelinos. I got on my knees to coax Jim for a baby. That poor boob! He wanted a vasectomy back then. I talked him out of that, I did. No, not account of no religious reasons. "Jim," I said, "one more will bring us luck. You'll see. I'm happy when I'm in a family way. We got the crib 'n' all the baby things."

" 'A pack of rotten, stinkin', filthy, selfish lies! Know why? I hadda trick that dummy sweetheart into thinkin' that a baby, if we had one, would be *his*!

" 'That's when I should'a killed myself. That salesman. Pig! I pitied him. So help me God I did!

" 'I asked him how his business was. If he was sellin' much. "Real terrible," he whimpered, 'n' I saw him mop his brow. So, would he like a coke or wanna sip a beer? Course he could drink it in the shade. I'd kind of sit with him, except that I'm not used to beer 'n' tranquilizers too. Am I supposed to blurt this out? Oh, can't you help me, please?

" 'I'll skip the part that hurts the most. We did it, then and there. He made a fool of me!'

"Lorelei's frame shook. When she paused for breath between sobs, her inspirations were so deep and long I wondered whether she was starting a seizure. At length she set her teeth and through them hissed: 'It's almost four years to the day. Our little baby twins! Fred's exactly like his Dad, but Ted's a carrot top! Blue eyes and orange hair. Just look at me! You see my olive skin, natural dark colored locks? They're just the same as Jim's!

" 'How's that for True Confessions Magazine? I begged him. He never smelled a rat. He never never did! Poor darling! Do you know how hard he's had to work to keep us all alive, and how I've let him down?' She paused again. And wept.

" 'He never did find out?' I questioned.

"Biting the tissue, she shook her head wordlessly, obviously very tense. 'No. But that's the thing of it. He's destined to one day.'

"It was growing dark. 'I wonder,' I said half to myself, yet within earshot 'if I can sum the substance up: your single contretemps with the salesman—just that one time—got you pregnant; you'd been afraid of that possibility, so you made Jim try as well, and both men did. You had fraternal twins, except that one is like your family and the other is like *him*. Now you are afraid that the secret can't be kept much longer. But why end your life, and why just now?'

"Slowly Lorelei confronted me. It's true, I mused, that a face *could* launch a thousand ships. Or two. What beauty!

" 'A carrot top,' she shrieked, 'with wild blue Irish eyes! Oh, damn! Look, I've told it much too fast. The rest, it's building all the time. I can't go anywhere. The PTA. Little League. Wherever I take the twins some jackass can be counted on to ask, "Hey, Schultzie, who's your milkman? You steppin' out on Jim?" And one of these days that trusting goon is gonna get the message; that's what I'm afraid of. Fini! Kaput!' Her finger crossed her neck.

" 'Do you think it likely?' I interjected. 'I mean what appears to have happened is pretty rare, I think. Unless a man is fairly suspicious....'

" 'Kaput!' she interrupted me.

"Well, I could see no way around treatment. Even the course it should take. She had found, I imagined, some catharsis already in having made her 'confession' to me. Now, if I could show her that I merited the deeper, more abiding trust, the kind that time alone can breed, it might be possible to make some confrontations, and eventually to help."

George said, "Back it up! Define that word."

"Which one?"

"Confrontations."

"Alright. I wanted to *confront* her with some selected historic data she had given me. To wit, being fatherless, she probably was disproportionately dominated by her mother who had problems of her own. Mother sounded plaintive, and seductive too, if you read between the lines. Lorelei absorbed her style. Result, she tempted and she teased and at the last moment would dance airily away. Repeatedly.

"I would confront her too with the background poverty that ground them down as kids. But I would also point out that deprivation can be a stimulus as well as a disaster.

"Do you know the saying, 'Poverty is no disgrace, just an awful inconvenience?'

"She forgot it if she'd heard it. Jim did too. It appeared he had potential. That he needed tiding over. Kids do grow up; things pass. Those would be 'confrontations.'

" 'Insights' flow from them. I don't want to get pedantic. Let me carry on. See if I'm not clear. Okay?"

He smiled.

"Okay. Then I would show her how she was overreacting to the reputation, ingrained as it was, of being poor. And how a mother of five kids and a pretty decent wife besides, doesn't suicide as a result of one false step with a 'wandering minstrel.' Even if he did 'flagrante her delictu!' "

"Jesus!" came from my companion, but its tone was clearly bright.

"So, the next step would be to help her break the vicious circle."

"Now you lose me."

"Sure. Possibly I've also tried to shorten it too much."

"Are you kidding? Hey! I don't mean it. I'm getting a lot from listening. Only not that last."

"Lorelei," I said, "was so guilt-ridden that she couldn't keep things up. A big part of her husband's work depended on public relations. If he was to advance at all, he had to entertain. Vendors from here and there. And their families. And take them places with his wife. That's when she would come apart. If she could assuage her guilt, help him indirectly by improvement of her moods, and directly by working for his team instead of against it, going out in public, if he got promoted, earned more money, got vacations, paid the bills...."

"I yield. I yield," George cried.

"I told her the nucleus of those ideas at the close of our second meeting. Then I suggested an appointment later in the week.   •

" 'You name it. I'll be here,' she said, stood up and shouldered her valise. However, instead of moving toward the door she slid the bag again by its long leather straps slowly to the floor. Freed from holding it, her hand found its way, backside to, around her forehead, then, like a cup, over her face, leaving exposed only those eyes.

"More tears. Awkward moment. There I stood a scant six inches from her, gauchely shifting weight from leg to leg, searching for some platitudes to voice, when suddenly, unexpected, Lorelei reached out and clung about my neck.

"Embraced me!

"Hung there limply, molded to my form. Her every contour discernible beneath, her perfumed hair, the olive skin— her all.

"Was it a reflex?

"Was I suddenly decorticate? A laboratory frog, freshpithed? Who moved my arm and voiced my voice for me? And muttered, patting on her fragile backbone.'There, there, there,' then managed, 'Hey, c'mon. You're not a four-year-old yourself. Go in and wash your pretty face before you greet the world and show it you've been crying. You go on now, hear?'

"She did, and stepped into the cubicle beyond, some seconds later to emerge, composed far faster than myself."

* * *

"Physically gone, Lorelei left much of herself behind in my solitude. Her scent. Her beauty. Traces of it were printed on the air. And that embrace! What was I supposed to do? Had I been wrong to stand there and to let her hug me? Could she have read encouragement, compliance in my act? And yet, if I had stiffened or straight-armed her, would I have been rejecting to a supplicant? We would have to talk the darned thing over. First chance.

"Yes. I would want to think the business out, then trust to intuition. Timing. Dosage. Walk the razor's edge. Scylla and Charybdis! Maybe with enough experience you do that anyway. It called to mind a story."

"You're as bad as Hamlet," George complained, "plays within plays. But, please don't stop. I shouldn't have interrupted."

"I remember sitting back, swiveling around, my feet up on the desk. The sycamore was swaying. An evening breeze was bending down its topmost limbs. On the lawn, a dozen browning leaves—Damn! I had forgotten to irrigate it—and I remembered, oh, call it what you will, a kind of yardstick for the likes of Lorelei, except it tended toward apocryphal.

"My old clinical director and one of his buddies were still young residents working in an O.P.D. Both of them had as patients single women who came after hours, at night. The buddy's was a fading movie actress, fallen out from public favor. She had turned to drink and threatened suicide. One evening, seeking reassurance that she had a trace of some charisma left, she reached out with a plea that her doctor hold her, for just a minute, and bestow a tiny buss upon her wrinkling cheek.

"The fellow could not, would not violate his ethic. To comply was too seductive, which he told her in the kindest way he could. She didn't hear him, apparently. She went home and swallowed poison, killed herself—that night!

"The other patient who had voiced essentially the same sad wish expressed it to my teacher. He reasoned thus: 'a kiss! What's in a kiss? Were I to brush her forehead with my lips the way her father should have done—and say as much to her as I was doing so—what could that harm? Far better than reject her?' He followed out his hunch. Know where it led? His patient started screaming. Bolted from the room and down the stairs and out. Next day she hanged herself! A note she left said doctors, every one alike, were putty in her hands."

"I found no comfort in that flash, yet in my heart of hearts I did not feel much threat. I thought Mrs. Schultz was better 'put together' than that pair. Still, it would be mandatory at some propitious moment to expose her to herself—confront her with her histrionics, with her 'come-ons' and the way she chose to ply them.

"And there was another issue. Would therapy run counter to religious tenets? Not so much the superficial parts, more the possibility that getting her to accept forgiveness for her 'venal sin,' adultery, might compete with ancient catechism. Would I sprout horns and cloven hooves?

"Little Marie Renée. 'With shining upturned face.' On Lewiston's cobbled streets in patent leather shoes, immaculate, white, knee-high sox as she skipped home from church.

"And then the matter of the fee—speculations, idle all.
'One at a time,' I counseled me, just as I realized I had not yet
gone through the mail. It lay unopened on my desk, except for
that one article stating that income, on the average, increased by
19.3% after forty-seven hours of therapy! It sat there tauntingly!

"When Lorelei stepped through the door at the appointed
hour, whether by a trick of lighting and reflections, or through
my intense imagination, across the front of her gray, lifeless,
flattened halter, I could have sworn, emblazoned, stood the
Letter 'A.' Hester Prynne. *The Scarlet Letter!* Well, equally
they had the cause to wear it.

"For a while I listened, then, convinced of my position, I
made a summing up. She nodded her agreement with the gist of
my remarks, augmenting here and there to ask how often could
Jim plead his wife was ill. How long until he saw the awful
sham? What recourse, then what options did she have?

"Her eyes never left mine during my long disquisition.
When my head nodded up and down, hers did too; or if for
other cause I shook it left and right, she followed. Ultimately
she broke in politely, whispering.

"'You seem so kind. So friendly. And you've seen it all. So
clear. I need your help, I know ... but ... '

"'But what?' I interjected. She measured out her words:
'But the money for your services. We're so, so deep in debt. I
couldn't ask for favors or for special charity. Oh, we could pay
a little.'

"Then again a flood of tears—the old vicious circle! Ever
run into those George?"

"Yeh, but what did you do?"

"I'll tell you—only let me say a word about vicious circles
first. Did you ever stop to think they have their virtues? Ever
think of that? Or about the half-empty glass? Or about that
single straw that breaks the camel's back? Matter of philosophy,

George. The glass is half-full too. Or could you say that all you have to do to get the camel moving again is lift one lousy straw? That shouldn't be too hard. The nice part of a vicious circle is that it doesn't matter where you snap one. The whole thing falls apart. Funny, no one wrote that up before."

"Come on! What did you do?"

"I explained to Lorelei about vicious circles. Then she asked what my fee was. I told her. She went pale. I added that I hewed to local standards ... then, with a real inspiration I suddenly remembered that article, the one that I had been reading. I handed it to her, teasing just a trifle. She looked at it, puzzled by the graphs.

"'That paper,' I told her, 'was written for people with your financial problem. It's a study. It shows something that most of us have suspected right along but never measured out. About a year of psychotherapy usually puts things together well enough that incomes rise. Substantially. More than pays its way.'

"'But what about with wives?' asked Lorelei, eyes wide.

"'Them too!' And I told her why. 'I see it all the time. Do you think your Jim is concentrating well when you're at home depressed? Or if it gets to him when he finds you in bed?'

"'I'm sure no Doris Day,' she added. 'That poor guy! Sometimes I send him out for pizza or Colonel Sanders. He never kicks. Except I know he hates it ... mmm 19.3%!'

"'Well, yes! No! I mean you understand that that's an *average*. It wouldn't guarantee ...'

"'For just one year?'

"'That's what it says, but you have to consider that statistic ...'

"'A year would pass in no time. Think of it! I could hold my head erect, go out. Maybe we could get a hot tub, like the neighbors down the street!'

"The lilt in Lorelei's voice left me no doubt that she was

teasing, but before I could confront her with that fact she trilled out that Technocrat Computing had a Major Medical Insurance Policy that should further defray the cost. Did I mind if she brought the papers, and would I fill them out?

"Coquette! How long had she known that?"

* * *

"A sudden hot spell abruptly brought Valleyites to the realization that winter was waning. For Easter holidays the college kids went off to Catalina or to Baja where they camped out on the beach. Now the freeway folks could garden after work. Cut the grass. Water. Increments of daylight, bit by steady bit. Sprigs of apple, peach and plum trees blossomed overnight. Delicate as silk screens printed on the sky. I watched my lilacs bloom.

"Faithfully my dainty lady took her cue. Appeared. Each week. And like the season, gradually, albeit unrelated to the tilted axis of the earth or where in its trajectory around the sun, her smiles were also lengthened. Shed more light.

"I felt the vicious circle wearing thin.

"Her clothing colors brightened. There was laughter in the air. And recipes! She had started cooking, almost every night. But no solitary session passed without allusion to the 'countdown' and her query. Did I remember the article I had shown her? Did I realize, 'prorated,' she had earned fifteen per cent? 'Compute it, Doctor. It's my thirty-seventh session—only where's the extra cash?'

"To all of this, good-humoredly, I kept interpreting her taunting, teasing style. And its seduction. And its roots—content to watch the healing process work. Soon the camel, so it seemed, would walk again. And maybe run. One straw was coming off.

"We reassessed, perhaps the hundredth time, her mother's

gripes, her teachers and her sibs; we analyzed her mowing down
the boyfriends and her falling hard for Jim. And church. And
poverty. Few stones were left unturned. Always yielding her
more room in which she might maneuver, where restrictive ties
had been so tight before.

"It was a pleasure to behold:

"The twins had a birthday party, and she entertained some
friends. She took back her rotation in those endless carpool
chores and volunteered, mind you, to run double booths in
public at the school bazaar.

"The whole of that before our forty-seventh meeting. Still
two visits left to go, that is if she was counting days. She grinned,
and looking rather dreamily out through the open window at my
struggling sycamore, then past it, 'I'm a totally new woman,
thanks to you, and therapy. I've learned a lot this year. You
know, even if I've teased about it, it's been worth it, every cent!
No, no, I don't expect a miracle, as far as money goes. Not with
the austerity program and the cutbacks at Jim's work. You never
can tell though. He's got his dollar's worth, he knows.

"'I'm happy. I can hold my head up high. It's a glorious,
light feeling. Do you have any idea of the burden? Doctor, about
vacation, can't we plan it so that that will wrap things up? I'm
better than I've ever been—besides, by accident, it's forty-seven
hours! It did come out that way.'

"I could not contradict.

"Technocrat Computing, in its infinite arithmetic wisdom,
had calculated Jim's holiday precisely at that time. Why not
concur? Lorelei had fulfilled my every ambition for her. Any
more was frosting. We agreed.

"And when I took the silky fragile hand into my calloused
claw to shake it farewell, it was only a question who of the two
of us would speak aloud the joke on both our minds.

"Lorelei did so. 'A fabulous experience!' She would never

forget it; or me. 'Priceless' was the word, except that with his
antiquated slide rule Jim had figured out the cost. To them.
'Above two thousand bucks! So, if he got his raise ... 'Oh, I
don't know,' she giggled, 'Should I tell you *his* big joke? He
wanted me to ask you if some other patient in your practice got
our raise instead of us? That's Jim! He says that way you'd still
maintain the average 'cept it didn't apply to us!'
    "'Good-bye, good luck!'"

                              *   *   *

    George was first to spot the miniscule irregularity on the
far horizon. Broken relief after miles and miles of "lone and
level sands" that stretched so far away.
    "That it?" he asked.
    "You mean my story or that fly speck?"
    "Santa whazzis?"
    "It is. San Felipe. 'Crossroads of about two dozen private
lives!' Fifteen minutes more should do it. I'll take us in, okay?"
    "Fine! But what about your story. Is that it? Kind of a flat
ending, isn't it? I sort of expected an O. Henry finish. Something
that would pull it more together. That what you're working
on?"
    "'No, no, no' to answer your three questions. It's not the
end. But almost. Obviously. It has to be. Twelve miles or so,
we're there."
    "You running out of gas?"
    "Come on, you know me better. Oh, you mean the car.
Ha, ha! Okay. I'll wrap it up.
    "Lorelei was gone. Her life was livable again. She could
appear in public. Unashamed. Complete success—except in
dollars. No one wins them all, I guess. I know that the process

continued because precisely a month after our last session, there was a letter.

"'Private' was penned across the front. And when I opened it, perfume! From Lorelei. Nostalgically, I sniffed, then struggled through its script:

Dear Doctor,

I thought you'd get a kick! Just like you said. The other part worked out. Guess what! Me! Shy me. The gal who had to hide! On nationwide t.v. The twins right by my side. In color! Was I brave? Oh, how I hoped that you were watching. Bust the Bank! We did! We won five thousand bucks!"

Triptych

Books are keys to wisdom's treasure.
Books are gates to lands of pleasure.
Books are paths that upward lead.
Books are friends. Come, let us read!

—Emile Poulsson

*At the zenith of all philosophic esoterica, a Yin demands a
Yang. Goods adumbrate Evils. Love needs Hate and God wants
Devils.*

Ever a polarity.

Thus Libido and Aggression.

*Ought we then register surprise if at the nadir, as it were,
in an issue as pedestrian as playroom furnishings, the same
dichotomy exists?*

There are divergent schools:

*One of them inclines toward exploitation of whatever
happens to be there. It holds that children will utilize the paper,
pencils, clips, discarded envelopes, loose rubber bands, or string.
The miscellany of an office practice.*

133

The other, tending toward the sumptuous, more gaudy, and competitive (I feel), strives to keep abreast of all the latest gimcracks: Pachinko through to Pong.

I have worked both sides of that street. In clinics that bewildered kids with Disneylands of stuff, as well as where the budget kept things elemental.

In my consultation room are only basics such as chess and checkers—my opinion: simple things are best.

My room is hardly, if at all, distracting. Nonetheless, do not underestimate the mind. It towers far above our other instruments in its adaptability and its capacity to commandeer whatever it must have.

To document my belief that good psychotherapy is much a function of the craftsman's alertness and imagination almost irrespective of accessories, I have selected these three short stories, each of which centers on the diagnostic utility of the humblest piece of equipment, our stock in trade, the book.

Each offers proof that working with whatever is available remains the touchstone of our art.

10

Let There Be Light

Mrs. Finkel was a bird. A heron. Possibly a stork:

Beak, talons, claws, toothpick-slim extremities, a rounded disappearing mandible—even exophthalmic globes that looked to east and west instead of straight ahead—honestly!—each with its nictitating membrane.

Her hollow pigeon-chest, her stoop, her minijaw slung loose on her carina—well, had Mrs. Finkel but enjoyed the humor to do so, she might have bent a knee and tucked it underneath her skirts then masqueraded perfectly as a flamingo.

Except milady was depressed.

She lacked that needed levity ... and, face the fact, she had no taste for color either. No. Never would flamingos feather out themselves with plumes like Mrs. Finkel's.

To a viewing world she signaled her depression: sackcloth. Ashes. Grays on browns like shrouds, sans lipsticks, rouge, cosmetics, nor a piece of jewelry found anywhere upon her.

And she plunged so deep at one profundity of things, she tried to slay herself, which moved her husband, in despair as well, to clip her wings and nest her in a sanitarium.

That is where we met. Down in Sargasso's depths, so low in fact, myself, I very nearly was stove in just from the pressures of her grief. I sucked up her despondency without intending to and gloomily reflected, I expect, a pessimism back at her, and wondered silently within, if anything could buoy her vessel up, to surface it again.

Might I have been the wiser simply to withdraw with honor and assign her to another member of the staff who (with a rationale in which *he* full believed) would strap her down and send bolt-lightning through her cortex?

Convulsive therapy?

Was I too stubborn? And so proud in my indoctrination that perspective was distorted as to which deserved priority, my pride or her suffering?

Forgive my wandering. I shan't disclose her ichor's deadly source, nor rhapsodize upon my frailties. Muddy no more metaphors. Stick to phenomenology! Acknowledge Mrs. Finkel's basis for said melancholia whencever it derived, and me, my compulsivity.

We labored.

In a tiny, dirty, inconvenient, cluttered, noisy cubicle: the "Consultation Room," so dev'lishly conceived, it gathered up and concentrated and then amplified and funneled, as deposits, in between the pair of us, the clacking of the shuffleboard outside, the endless flatus of passing cars, the drone of circling aircraft, and the nightly tumult of those Big League baseball games.

We sat precisely at the focus of a parabolic cup that drew in every vitiation of the local atmosphere, which was enough to set up sound waves, and to such an incongruity, that even if poor Bent-wing chirped some little chirp, I scarce could more than see her lips move.

Well, complain to City Hall! Sure I belched out purple

words. In triplicate. With carbons. And waited for relief that never came, except in ultimata from a someone on "the top" who gave full leave to sign her out, "Against Advice."

To where conditons were "more optimal." To "Private Care."

Alright! I told her husband, and we told his wife. Also much of why.

Young maverick! Mr. Impetuous! Rushed in where angels feared to tread.

Into the silence of my suite.

Ungilded.

As I implied. My style has never favored regal furnishings. No throne. No subtly precious artifacts strewn casually there and here, nor splashy paintings to festoon the basic room. Indeed, I scarcely grace the walls with anything—no photographs, diplomas—better thus to draw a patient out. Know how I mean? Invite his fantasies of me and mine. Not hamper him with dates and titles.

I did have one accoutrement! Floor to ceiling books. Wall to wall. Shelves on shelves on shelves of books on books on books. Around me, behind me. Fat ones, thin ones, colored bright or buff, hardback, paperback, spiral spine or plain. No matter how she glanced. From left to right. Reversed. Below to up. No way at all to fix the therapist in view and not to see those books.

Now, back on course.

Mrs. Finkel, willowy, and with her waxen flexibility, the full-nigh ninety pounds, all gaunt and halting, had need to be escorted to my lair. Her husband, usually, his hand about her waist, across the threshold, frail, the owl upon its roost.

As I, with every artifice, attempted to enlighten: tinder, matches, candles, torches, laser beams; I gave it all I had.

I talked to her. I read to her. I prated like a magpie:

"Cheep cheep cheep!" Weather. Sports. T.V. I lectured about politics, philosophy and art. Was there no breaking through? No keystone loosed to snap her heavy arch?

Day after weary, wearing day. She sat. Her gaze upon the rug. Preoccupied and dumb.

Until, I do confess it, much to my surprise, that April, as the world outside responded to the hormones of the spring, an isomer of Mrs. Finkel flitted through the door.

Herself!

Fleet of foot! And rouge! Upon her cheeks its blush. A tint of color. On her lips the frailest floral wreath. A smile.

And perched, and actually looked upon me. With eye on eye. A virginal experience; then quavered in the hanging atmosphere:

"Oh my! You've changed your office, haven't you? How nice! And done it overnight! How ever did you manage? I see you've added all those shelves of books!"

11

Sometimes You Can Tell a Book by Its Cover

Parker Hill drops precipitously into Ruggles Circle. So steep is the decline, that standing on the promontory even up to twenty feet of the edge, one would assume that no ordinary city street could possibly connect the two together.

Behind it lies plateau.

Along the major thoroughfare which leads up to that brink are to be found a Catholic church, an elementary school, the Parker Tool and Die Works, and a splattering of shabby residences varying in age and states of disrepair. Woven in between these are assorted buildings of light industry, among which, awaiting slum improvement, stands the boarded up and padlocked Moxie Plant, soon to be razed.

It is a summer morning. Heavy, humid air wafting in from the harbor portends a sultry, sticky day.

Automobiles below the promontory are busy ferrying their passengers from rows-on-rows of new-built cell-like homes out in the suburbs, into downtown offices that honeycomb within the hives of an aged city's dirty, dusty high-rise monuments.

Some enter Ruggles Circle to run counterclockwise. Its centrifuge dispatches those in wide-flung arcs toward their vacations at the beach.

And contemplating the spinning pinwheel with its contradicting helices, dully aware of what its motions meant, from the vantage of those cliffs, are four galoots. The bonds that link them are the musketeer-like oath that dubbed them Cobras in the clubhouse two long years ago, their similarity in costume— leather jackets with a snake—and finally, a communality of rootlessness and dividends thereof.

Focus:

In pathetically familiar despair the boys enumerate their several options. What could fill a boring day? Hog says breaking into Bortman School and busting windows, or a variant, turning on the hydrant next to Spag's—then baiting Zinsky's guard dog. He'd "go bullshit" as he always did. And Specs suggests their stealing Chronicles. The ones deposited in wired-up rolls outside the pharmacy. Sail them down the hill.

Fats wants the laundromat: the coin machines are probably pretty full, but Aaron, who seldom dons the heavy mantle of group leader, keeps vetoing the other Cobras' schemes.

He's restless.

A dimly gnawing ache within anticipates that nothing of those kid stuff capers promises relief for what he craves.

He hungers.

Breathless cops and robber games, the risk, the racing— pranks repetitive and pointless, lacking in direction, purpose. Transitory pleasures. One-dimensional. Too fleeting. Lacking follow-through—and yet, abruptly he announces:

"Okay guys, I'll tell. ya what *I'm* gonna do. I'm gonna load my pockets an' my shirt with ammunition 'n' I'm gonna

bomb them tanks invadin' us down there." Translation: force an
entrance into the warehouse of the Moxie Bottling Plant, cart
off as many unpressed bottle caps as he can carry, and double
back to lob them into Ruggles Circle at the passing cars below.

"And the rockets' red glare, the bombs bursting in air ...
" Howitzers, grenades. A rerun of historic Bunker Hill. The
puzzled motorists unused to such guerrilla tactics, until (was it
purely accident?) Aaron loosed his most ambitious salvo at a
clearly marked police car which assuredly knew what and
whence.

"Run!" screamed Hog. Then Specs and Fats in unison:
"Yikes! Cheese it," as the knot undid itself, explosively, to north,
south, east, and west—except Aaron. Just as in his nightmares,
he stood transfixed, alone, and let himself get caught.

By the hairs of his chin, the youth qualified for the Adult
Authority. It remanded him to the State Hospital: thirty days of
observation. Parentless, and lacking legal guardians of record,
Aaron got swaddled in red tape. He might have spent a year or
more untangling it, but luckily he was put on voluntary status,
which afforded him some treatment by the staff with privileges
to come and go.

Those last details, I never wholly clarified or truly wished
to, finding more of moment that some quality that peered out
from his haunted eyes or from the lustre or the roughness of his
cut, whatever, induced a good samaritan in residency training to
care. Enough to pass with him an hour, periodically, and to
plant, however dimly in his mind, that in his whole "charade"
a classic flaw inhered.

Really, tossing bottle caps at passing squad cars! Then not
running! "Aaron, you were screaming out for help. You wanted
to get caught. No doubt of that at all, agreed?"

And then?

Reality. Stark and full and heavy-handed: residents are not

their patients' parents. At the end of the fiscal year the music has to stop. Then doctors jump about. To other sections of the country or the state. It's how the game is played. It says so in the rules—in black and white.

Thus Aaron and his "shrink" went separate ways.

The doctor? To wherever. And Aaron? With the former's help, enlisted in the Navy. Great Lakes Naval Training Station, then aboard the Haven as a Corpsman, ultimately ranked and rated and then discharged. Still young. Lonely, scarcely settled on a life direction, and festering with poisons from his youth.

May I introduce him?

Here he is.

In stocking feet a hulking six foot-eight. His frame: both spare and lithe. Without an extra gram of fat or flab. He's quick. He will jump or run, responding to the subtlest noises—always ready, watchful, taut.

Know him?

Prior to drifting to the coast with his mustering out pay, he thumbed to Indiana with a letter from a CPO. An audience had been arranged. A talent scout who did recruiting for the ABA. That meeting never happened. I mean the franchise was disbanded and dissolved, its players scurrying into the National or elsewhere—as you know.

Unlucky timing but for which his fantasied career in sports might well have come about. Thousands cheering hoarsely, Aaron dribbling down the courts or sinking free throws from the line.

Well, che serà....

You see those hands? Enormous aren't they? Large enough to cup a basketball in one. And strong. Was it an idle pipedream to picture how an angered Aaron well could crush a man of normal size? Hug him into limp surrender? Snap his spine? Twist and tear his head off (and then lob it in a basket even thirty feet away)?

But I seldom felt afraid within the giant's presence. You know why? Because I had a secret weapon of my own. A magic telescope. To humble Behomoth. Through the back end of it I reduced him to his baby days. And minified destrudo to a seed.

Planted by his parents who divorced when he was awfully small, then gave him to the State for foster care. He ran away. Summers sleeping in the streets. Scars deep through which his vital organs passed, and left a scarecrow filled with nothing more than straw. A void.

Were such the sources of the hungers that he felt? For acting like a naked "apetite"? All cavity? All mouth? A shell with long, lean legs and calipers above to catch what they could? They were. He had not the reserves to hear his life say "no" or urge on him to "wait." Can you imagine therapy with him? Will you believe we balanced on a pin?

Aaron, if I offered inches, almost by a reflex grabbed for yards. When I would offer feet, he whimpered for a mile. To him I responded with sincerity and effort; I tried to feed him, talking on the phone at night when he was in distress; I gave him extra hours and favors. Once I called the Auto Club to jump his battery—alert to risks of countertransference.

My hope? That slowly, deep within him, I was filling vacuua.

I recalled a demonstration of the indicator, phenolphthalein. Present in a beaker of strong acid. It was invisible as from above, in drops out of the burette containing caustic soda, the professor showed the class titration of that acid against base.

But nothing seemed to happen. Colorless, the liquid showed no change, except for transient little flurries. Stir them, they were gone. Until, with just one added micromillilitre everything became a splendid, flaming pink! Voilà! Like pressures on a trigger. Bang!

Freud had analogized the same phenomenon: full head of steam, and yet no motion, a tugboat straining at its ropes. Not until a deckhand slipped the last of them from the capstan did it churn off into waters of the deep.

Was I vainglorious to try? Hope springs....

I remember Aaron as he towered in the doorway. A Goliath. How he used to lumber in. And how he stretched himself one section at a time upon the creaking couch. Unhinging, slowly taking bearings, spreading out, and how repeatedly, despite his radar, he would brush the book shelves, going down. On one occasion how his shoulder caught on the *Psychiatric Handbooks* and knocked them loose. Another time he "hooked" himself on *Wayward Youth*. Was that a parapraxis? Had he seen it from the corner of his eye? I hear that "hoopsters" need unusual perception—that their fields of vision are angled out extremely wide.

I did not dwell on it, nor did he. Instead we probed the core of his distress, until, in mid-July, a month before my annual vacation, Aaron telephoned one morning, wondering if I had a cancellation and could see him Thursday. Then he telephoned again, same day, late afternoon.

I had to keep my answer pithy. "No." I was unable. I regretted, but we would meet on Friday as planned, the way it looked.

At the appointed hour, still one foot on the threshold, he began attacking, verbally, and kept it up, with fervor, as he settled into place: "I see that you don't really like me, do you, Doctor? Couldn't you tell how bad I needed something extra? Wednesday afternoon? You know, man, if I telephoned I wasn't shittin' you. I hurt!

"You're jus' the same as all them others, ain' cha? Promises and fancy words. Well, they're fer crap, I know. And so are you, besides.

"I shoulda' seen!

"Whatsamatter? Do I gotta have my Ph.D. to be important? Man, you stung me! You said, 'No!'

"Suppos'n I could pay your big fat fee. Would you have squeezed me in your 'busy schedule' then? You hate me, don't you? Jesus fuckin' Christ. You stink!

"Come on! So what's your answer? Why did you reject me? Couldn't you hear what I was askin'? I gotta be a 'white boy?' You hop then? Who filled up your hours anyway on Thursday? Lotsa white trash?

"Well, you go to Hell, you goddam turd! Your other patients too! I'm sick of comin' in an' you pretendin' that you wanna help. I've had it. Up to here."

He paused.

I mulled the wisdom of my interrupting—or defending. Aaron, in his state of mind, would never hear the fact that I had scheduled fourteen persons on that Thursday with needs no less than his. Twelve full hours of work.

I sunk instead down lower in my seat. On purpose. To assume, for him, the shape of Parker Hill. Of that fortuitous police car at which he had fired the bottle caps in order to get caught.

Oh yes, he let me have it!

Napalm. Hand grenades. Right on target—and believe me, but for being trained and well-apprized of Aaron's history, I might have taken flight. Think about it. He and I alone. Full six foot-eight. And fired by centuries of race discrimination. What kept me sitting there? The obvious:

Underneath the "violence" I heard him whimpering for love. That simple. I became the cop's car. Aaron wanted to be stopped, controlled, and taken in. A hint of which I gingerly suggested, adding that the timing of his outburst made me wonder if the issue lay in my vacation, which through no small accident concurred almost to the day with when the doctor of his youth had "upped and split."

My patient did what I should have expected: propping on one elbow, with a turn, he looked at me, and cried,

"That's hogshit, Hunkie! Your vacation! What about I ask you not to take it? Would you put yourself out one tiny bit? You give a big fat shit for punks like me? One little teeny favor for a black?"

Leaning forward, he held the top of his pinky tauntingly under my nose, and uncomfortably close to it, both to emphasize his words and to portray his estimated significance in my eyes.

"You're fucked!" Then eased on back. "So's all of it, your room, your couch, your books! Cause you don't care. You don't! Don't no one care for me. You're all of you a bunch of fuckin', slobbin', no-good, Hunkie, pig-faced, white-boy bastards. All of you, you stink!"

Then stopped.

I started, "Listen to the intensity of your feel...." But Aaron was not to be reached. He went on, ignoring what I had tried to interpose.

"They got divorced, they did. Yeah, they abandoned me. I begged them not to. Do you think they listen? So I wind up in a 'crazy farm.' That cool? I'm put in prison 'cept they call it 'hospital!' 'We're gonna help you.' Fuckers! Mother-fuckin' cunts!"

Look out!

He swung around—no, not in my direction. Just the opposite. Blindly, with his huge left hand, he grabbed the nearest book and hurled it straight across the room. It struck the door jamb fifteen feet away and lay, spread-eagled on the floor, its pages all bunched up.

What next?

Another hurricane of vicious, angry oaths. Need I record them? Street obscenities, sprinklings here and there of naval saltiness, blasphemies, indictments of our social system, invectives against prejudice, psychiatry, and me. I waited "clinically" within the lee of his ferocious blast.

"You faggot, bastard, kike! What would you do if I got up an' wrecked your goddamn fairy office? Huh? You couldn't stop me, know it? I think I'm gonna grab yer friggin' shelves 'n' tear 'em down. Yer books! Screw Books! So cool, so intellectual.

"They're shit. Yer shit! That's all! I'm gonna do it too. You watch. What would you do, call 'Help POLEECE?'

"Then kick me out? Huh, would you?

"You see the way I done with that one, over there?

"I know you always planned to. Go ahead, now. Call the cops! C'mon. You lock me up, g'wan, 'n' kick me out. G'wan! I give you your excuse!"

"You okay now?" I asked him.

Silence.

"Expecting me to do exactly as your parents did when they got their divorce?"

That's all I had to say. Goliath melted and the tears began to flow.

So I continued.

No new frontiers. No thrill of serendipity. I walked with him, hand in hand, across the bridge back into childhood, back up Parker Hill, into the Moxie Plant, through Ruggles Circle, into old familiar scenes and haunts and byways. Places I knew as if I had lived in them myself ...

Maximizing on the opportunity, assuring, reassuring, and interpreting—within the limits that had been defined by our parameter—nor do I wish to minimize ...

Violence within my office is rare—less than one percent. It

is tacit—written in the code—we "talk about" the action, not perform it. Only Aaron, he had shorter circuits than the rest. Even hints, however subtle, just the intimation of rejection impelled him to violence. It did behoove me, as the link between my patient and society, to urge controls on him. He could not live in comfort with most others primed that way.

Then he asked if I was frightened when he "ripped" me up and down, and about what I should do if he implemented his threat to tear the place apart or to attack me. Was I going to lock him up?

"I guess I would try to stop you. But the question still remains, why take it out on me? You're sure not mad at books, or shelves, or me! It's others in your life. We're scapegoats. I've tried repeatedly to help the child who's living there inside you to grow up. Remember how I used that phrase, 'delayed pardon,' and how I urged you to extend it to your folks?

"If you use your head, you will. When they broke up, it wasn't over you. You were an innocent bystander. I imagine you had your tantrums then, much as today.

"You sayin' this was a 'tantrum?'"

"Bet on it. Three or four years old, no more, throwing things, and threatening! We adults talk. Only toddlers act the way you did. Don't you see?"

"But you *did* reject me! And you didn't really answer if I scared you. Were you scared? I could have beat you up. Weren't you afraid?"

"Not half as much as you were. Listen, please."

Then I explained to Aaron, carefully, how unconscious dynamics had been working him over for years. In the laboratory of my office we had the opportunity, first-hand, to witness yet another example, so vivid and so fresh in its detail that neither of us could fail to grasp its import.

Was I "scared?" Yes. But that was precisely the point of it. He had succeeded in frightening me, or in configuring in me feelings that absolutely replicated those that he himself had harbored.

But for my experience, training, confidence, clinical acumen—not to mention other abiding built-in securities—I should have panicked under the emotional pressures, much as he habitually did, and had a tantrum too, or kicked him out, or called for help.

Did he see?

But, you know, here I am, once again guilty of this "uncontrollable behavior" of my own. My "m.o." I'm wandering wantonly. Wantonly. For all its nooks and crannies this was to have been a story about books. Concede me, therefore, that "in time the savage bull doth bear the yoke."

Aaron simmered down. His "psychitis" formed an abscess and we drained it. He was actually bigger, stronger, and quicker than I was; he might indeed have overpowered me. Sure, I had some qualms. But mainly I was being challenged over my empathy. I could pass his test and earn his trust.

It came together.

"Now then," I asked him, "what about that book?"

"How do you mean?"

"I mean you're leaving in five minutes, and you'll have to make a choice."

"Yeah. You wanna see if I'll be 'humble' and go stoop 'n' pick it up. Is that the deal?"

"Essentially. Or let it lie."

"You want me to apologize and get it?"

"All I want is that you understand," I said.

"But you would rather that I pick it up and put it where it was. What would you do if I just walked on past it?"

"I would retrieve it myself, but the point is we shall analyze whatever choice you make. Either way.

"Look, in my mind at least, there is absolutely no doubt that it's a Moxie bottle cap exactly like the one you tossed down Parker Hill to get yourself arrested and hospitalized. You blew your cool when the doctor 'abandoned' you at the end of residency training. In your view, I am doing the same thing by taking my vacation, don't you see?"

"But if I pick it up?"

"We shall analyze that too. Today it's time to quit."

"Stupid book," he grumbled.

Aaron slowly hinged himself together and stood up. He had been crying. The tissue under his short-cropped hair was sodden.

One huge stride from the couch and toward the doorway poised him by the book at which he sighed, then stared.

I watched.

Feinting toward the outside world, he showed he was tempted by his stubborness and his defiance, yet ever with that vital pivot foot in place, the would-be superstar bent down and took the book in hand, and passed it up to me. I thanked him. He shrugged, and started through the doorway. He would have driven off had I not shouted, "Hey, wait a minute! Come on back a second, will you? Something that you've gotta see. You know which one you picked to chuck across the room?"

"Uh, uh."

"You've no idea?"

"No. None."

"But you have occasionally noticed my books' titles. Remember those you flipped when you were lying down?"

"Did I toss one of them?"

"Uh, uh." I handed him the text.

Aaron slowly read its title. A friendly, easy, slightly guilty smile began to light his face. He muttered, "Jesus. Jesus Christ," and left.

I slipped the book back into place. The title? *The Mental Hospital.*

12

You Can't Tell a Book by Its Color

How come? I used to wonder. How come that flashing gold tooth when Silverman smiled? He seldom did so; nonetheless, it seemed incongruous, his being a dentist and all. And pretty much an American. And his name, *Silver*man.

During World War Two, I met a Philippino. He was proud of his display of gold. It typed him in a caste of affluence.

But Silverman?

Puzzling. The glitter simply did not fit. Not with his blandnesses, his washed-out look. Nor with his personality, his stoicism, his unchanging mien.

Nicely shaven, always. No blemishes. A dry and tight and pallid, faintly freckled skin with tiny threads of wrinkles at the jowls—first tell-tale marks of age.

His eyes: pale blue, dilute, the type you see invariably on men of light complexion. Whisper bristles, single-file along the upper lids—almost invisible. Broad, flat forehead, close-cropped hair, and sparse.

It was a Mongol facies to my mind, kin to Ghenghis Khan. That feature thickness. Almost like a man pressed up against a pane of glass, peering through. Foreshortened, spread.

And taciturn!

Sam Silverman, the Sphinx.

And motionless!

As still as any corpse.

He would ask me what to talk about, then wait, but here, come listen in and see:

"Good morning, Doctor," I ordinarily began, with cheer.

"–'d morning," he would respond, in pithy monotone.

"So, how are things?"

"About the same."

"Uh-huh. So ... what goes through your mind?"

"Not much."

"Well, just tell me what is surfacing."

"It's like I said: 'not much.' "

"Mmmmm. Whatever it is, allow yourself to say it."

"Nothing's there."

"That couldn't be."

"I understand that, technically. It's what you're always telling me."

"Because it's true."

"It's also true I don't get any thoughts at all. I'm thinking nothing. Nothing. Trivia that's all."

"How 'trivia'? What's that?"

"The commonest of things."

"Like what?"

" 'Like what?' Like objects in this room. The things I'm looking at."

"Which ones?"

"For Heaven's sake! Your desk, your chair, your books.

Yeh, I'm looking at your books. I sit across them every time I come. How not to see them?"

"Yes, sure. I should expect you would. You sound annoyed."

"I am a little. When I report that I'm not thinking anything, why can't you take my word?"

"Because your statement is not true. It can't be true as long as you're alive. The mind is always busy working over something. Constantly. It's a computer. It experiments. It attempts solutions for the problems we haven't solved. I have run through this for you before. Thinking is a form of trial action. Can you follow me?"

"I guess. Except that I don't get ... well ... pictures. Mostly blanks. I understand the point of what you've said. You *have* explained it all. Aren't there some people who are different? Isn't it possible the theory doesn't hold for me?"

"It's possible, but I don't see how you could be that different, basically. I would explain that your silence is what is left, that the fantasies and feelings are diving down, away, that you are repressing them. I don't know why. Do you?"

"Uh, uh. I really don't. I'd tell you if I knew. There's one thing that I feel. I feel depressed."

"I know."

"So now there's two of us. What next?"

"We try again. The only means we have is through following your associations. But that means you cannot neglect the faintest little clue. Even if you are thinking of what you ate for breakfast or the headlines. Call them out! Or what you dreamt of."

"I don't dream," said Silverman, then, "two poached eggs. On toast."

"How's that?"

"That's what I ate for breakfast. It's the same thing every day with me. A slice of bacon now and then."

"Go on."

"That's it. I've said it all."

"No, you haven't. Speak your mind. Don't worry if it sounds like nonsense—or if possibly you have told me it before. Don't worry about punctuation, grammar, paragraphs—you know."

Silverman flashed gold. He smiled his gilded smile.

"Make an Eisenhower speech?" he sniggered.

"Eisenhower?" I responded.

"Yeh, our President. He likes to murder grammar. His speeches always sound so good until you read them after. Ever notice? He forgets to put the verb in, or the subject."

Then he stopped.

I urged him to go on.

"That's it."

"Out of nowhere 'Eisenhower?' Are there other fantasies connected with the man?"

"There's nothing more ... except the feeling. Sadness."

"Try again."

"But nothing ever comes. Or will."

"Oh yes. There's something there. So, what about our President? You pulled his name out."

"No! There's nothing! I insist!"

"You sound annoyed," I countered once again.

"I am. Oh, not with you, With *me*. I really wish I could find the thing you're hunting. Others do, why not me?"

"Now there's a thought. Do you compare yourself with others?"

"I suppose. Naagh, not really. I don't want to fail. Besides, I'd like to drop a bomb on this dumb depression. You and treatment are the only hope I've got. I guess I'm scared you might give up on me."

"Give up?"

"Yeh, wash me out. Is that what happens when the patient is a failure? When the program never gets up off the ground?"

"Don't stop."

"You didn't answer."

"Right! But I did listen. 'Gets up off the ground?' Now how about *that* phrase?"

"I'm speaking figuratively—oh, you know what I mean. Boy, I couldn't do your job the live-long day. How do you stand it? I would hope for your sake other people talk."

"You've changed the subject," I cut in.

"I have?"

"I think you took 'evasive action.' I was asking you about that funny phrase you used."

"And so?"

"And so, I'd like to hear what next."

"That's all."

"Go on."

"I can't. I'm sitting here, my mind a total blank ... just looking at your books."

"Which ones?"

"The *same* ones. Those behind you. Occasionally I glance around. Your ashtray or the pen and pencil set. But mostly on the books."

"You seldom look at me."

"That's true."

"Do you avoid eye contact?"

"Sometimes. It's more comfortable to focus off in back."

"And think of nothing?"

"Right."

"No, wrong! To think of something, then repress it and

feel sad. This may appear to you to be nit-picking, but it's apt to
be important. What could you suppress, and why?''

"I'd tell you if I knew. I really would."

"What's your next thought?"

"Sad."

"Go on."

"I'm sad about my progress. My prognosis—that's a
different sad, discouraged. The other one is more, oh, general or
chronic. Yeh, 'chronic' says it better. Scratch the 'general.' ''

" 'General,' 'chronic.' What distinction are you making?''

" 'Chronic' says it better. I don't know why I spoke that
other word. I was trying to describe my feelings like I thought
you wanted. Does it matter?''

"Maybe."

"Books!"

"Go on."

"The books behind you."

"There are several books behind me. Which one now?''

"Jesus you're persistent! Okay, have it your way. Mostly at
that blue one. Right behind you. I can't read the title unless I
put on my glasses."

Dr. Silverman reached into his jacket front and flipped a
pair of "granny" glasses over his eyes. Standing and leaning
forward, then weaving his head in and out to maximize the
light, haltingly he said, "Stress ... under stress, *Men Under
Stress,* by Grinker, Grinker and Spiegel."

"You mean this one here?" I asked him, drawing it from
its niche.

"Yuh. That's it! So what?''

"Well, it does have a suggestive title."

"Uh uh! I never read it. It's coincidental. I don't wanna
rain on your parade, but I don't think I ever saw those words.
Not clearly. I look at it because I sort of like the color."

"What color would you call it?"

"Blue."

"Like you?"

"Oh, come on! No, powder blue. Gray blue. Light blue— so what color would you call it?"

I was about to answer, but when I looked across the desk I saw the gold tooth flash. This time not to smile. No. A grimace. More like pain. Then both his masseters and pterygoids clamped shut his lower jaw. Snapped it shut and held it as the dentist's nostrils flared. His face grew flushed, beet red. I heard the snuffle of a single, deep, spasmodic insufflation.

My patient turned his face away from mine and wept convulsively behind the shield of muscular, strong hands.

Blue. Powder blue. Blue as the Air Force blue. Blue as the gray blue of the General Eisenhower jackets worn by crewmen of the bombers flown in World War Two. Crewmen like his brother. His brother who had been a bombardier shot down and killed in southern France.

13
The Benzene Ring

Are you ready for a bit of whimsy, a slice of life, a plotless miracle, the kinds of things painters portray on canvas simply because they stir a human sentiment or tug upon some cord?

Remember Rockwell and his covers for the *Post?* Life's wistful moments? Charivaria?

Would I have justification, *sui generis,* to walk you through a poignancy, which may prove pointless after all? Or net you nothing more fulfilling than a taste of *déjà vu?*

I feel so, considering how very much of our mentation moils around like space dust in the vast, without precipitating out. Orts. Fragmented splinter thoughts or quark-sized puffs, cathected energies in search of unifying trends, common denominators, purpose.

Odd stuffs. Things which, they theorize, an artist collects with extra sensitivity. Later to record. If lucky, to remind us that we too had seen and felt a little. Underneath the threshold.

I conjure up the image of an elderly man. His leather face still wears the twist and droop of a slowly healing trigeminal palsy. Vainly he attempts to imbibe a simple mouthful. From the bubbler in the park. But dribbles. Is he seen?

His female counterpart. Transplanted from the Balkans. Ignorant of swank and glamour. Shuffling in her bedroom slippers, her babooshka, and her cotton stockings (tied by bagel knots an inch below her knees), past the chic display in the window of no less than Saks Fifth Avenue on Wilshire Boulevard.

Your sixth-grade sweetheart in those magic days of June. Pubescence and its flower. Her plaid skirt secured by that huge safety pin. Her brushing past your hand. By accident. A touch on private parts!

"A touch, a touch—I do declare a touch! A most palpable touch!"

What shall we do with these ... these nothings! Is there sense to stringing up such beads?

Another vagabond idea:

High school: Billy, my most trepid sidekick, was about as shy a version of the model as the series ever built. Spring zephyrs would intimidate the kid, and if an adult scarcely more than looked at him, he nearly swooned away—or blushed vermilion hues.

His father was a Civil Service physician. Good pay and "perks," among which those capacious quarters, furnished free, on the spreading acreage of the Brighton Marine–Naval–Merchant Seaman–Public Health Hospital. Rounding out that sesquipedalian address, to do it properly, one should have suffixed it with, "Officers' Quarters, Building L, Apartment F."

From the corner of a sympathetic eye I used to watch the kid, all flustered and apologetic, squirm and shuffle, start to write upon the Office Information Card—you know the type? The ones that leave two centimeters blank for "Name and

Address"? His anguish! Should he raise his hand and ask the teacher? Should he not?

Shy goose!

I wonder what became of Bill. Do you suppose he overcame his qualms, got married, became a lion tamer? Shot his wife?

Rare type. Kids are different now. They don't "sweat" things half as much. Bill crawled inside his skin, accepting that *he* was responsible. Whatever fault inhered was his. Our current crop would blurt out an attack upon the system, not themselves.

Hear them?

"Teach, this form is fucked! It's stupid! I can't stuff no address in this space."

O Tempora! O Mores!

Split to Korea. A commander in the Navy. "Scrambled eggs." Stripes of braided gold on six-inch épaulettes. Eagles on the collars of the blouse and shirt. Intimidators strung all over me. No way I could avoid them.

"I'm a doctor, son. I'm here to help you out. Please. Tell me all you can."

His answers: pure "cablese." Like rounds of ammo spewing from his gun: "Yessir. Nosir. I donno, sir. I'll try, sir." Trained that way:

Marine.

I was "sort of" a psychiatrist, mainly writing "surveys." Resumés that summarized the reasons for a sailor's being discharged, out. Bare facts. Fired in military jargon at a Board convened to hear the basics with no frills. Efficient. Crisp. I mean don't mention Oedipus or sibling rivalry. You want to "survey" him? Put in he "wets the bed," or "faints when under stress."

"Reject."

"Next!"

You know the type of report? No flowers. No adjectives.

No pronouns. Don't say "he"; say "subject named." And never "I" or "me"—"the writer," or the passive voice. Example: "It is felt," or the imperative: "recommend!" (Perhaps that is better than the way civilians murder "rather.")

I used to "interview" them (hardly "patients") in my so-called g.i. office. Not much on free association. Keep it simple. Get some words down on the form then fetch the sausage casing. Grind them out. Keep moving.

More than fleetingly, a bold, seditious thought that had the Pentagon seen fit to, it might profitably send—in uniform— a well-trained chimpanzee to act as my replacement and then "survey" me—and for but a handful of bananas!

Anyway, there he was, Pfc. Johnson or Hendrix or Adams or Schwartz, pimple-faced, ferociously youthful, faintly offensive from his underarms (through fear), callow, primed in half a hundred ways to kill me with his knuckles, fists, or knees, or stab or shoot or blast, yet white-faced at the prospect of our talk.

"Son, what's your name? Okay. Where were you born? Okay. How long is your constructive service time? Okay. Father, mother both alive and well? Okay. And brothers, sisters? How many and what age?"

He choked.

But why?

What's happening Pfc. Outlandish? Born in Dayton. Cedar Rapids. Ames, Seattle or Dubuque?

What spawns that purple blush? My query about siblings? I'd impaled him on that question? Now he stands there dully staring. Soundless. Foolish-looking.

Narcolepsy?

Petit mal?

Would I squeeze into that allotted centimeter space, "Mentally retarded?"

"Out!"

Here comes the space dust; let's digress. Flashback. Ever heard of Wöhler? He was the patron saint of organic chemistry. First among men to synthesize urea. In leaps and bounds the progress after, but it had to halt. Got stuck. C_6H_6. Another genius would discover how six hydrogens and carbons and their valences could stabilize into *benzene*.

A ring!

Remember? August Kekulé (von Stradonitz). From a burst of insight in a restless dream. Dreamed his famous dream about the serpent bent upon itself, full circle, tail within its mouth. The famous *benzene ring,* contenting all the atoms and their double-bond demands.

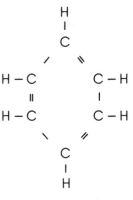

That celebrated lozenge that became the keystone of the arch. The steroids, DNA. Cholesterol—the lot!

A most impressive brand. But why think of that?

Because I had asked Outlandish if he had been graced with siblings. That was it. His answer, when we finished would repeat the benzene ring.

How so?

Try to follow:

"It's routine," I urged him. "You supply the facts, then I'll fill in this form. In ninety days you'll be back home. Dubuque. You'll see. Released. Okay?

"Pick it up on 'Brothers, Sisters.' Have you any? Tell me names and ages. That's not asking you too much. So. Let's hear it, huh!'

"It's hard to tell," he choked.

Know why?

Outlandish framed it as it actually was: his mother and his father married. Quickly, one, two, three, they sired four kids. Outlandish was the last. But strife and storm, in volume, supervened. His parents, rived, then went their separate ways.

Uxorious, those two, not made for single life. Hence each unto himself was quick to take a spouse—but spouses both with progeny of former wedlocks and from whom more offspring yet came forth. Flying halves, and steps, once and twice removed, by mother, father, present-day and "ex."

Bewildering!

And more so when those newly welded unions broke apart. His full-blooded parents left their recent mates, and after drifting aimlessly about, were caught another time within the primal magnet's field. They married one another again—and had more kids, all siblings, as it were.

Outlandish and his parents came together, split, moved down, came back at last and reunited, thus reclosed the ring.

Is that too gossamer? Etheral? Symbolic?

If you were sitting on the panel that awarded or denied those military "surveys," wouldn't you understand the reason for my penning in that centimeter space—you know, where it asks for the "complainant's family relations," a picture only, of a *benzene ring?*

14

And Nothing But, So Help Me

"You advocate being truthful?"

"Yes, I do."

"Always?"

"It's hard for me to conjure up a time when lying would be better."

"What if you were guilty of some tactical mistake? How would you handle that?"

"I would probably admit it."

"You say 'probably?'"

"I do. The first obligation would be analyzing the structure of the situation. Beyond that, if it was appropriate, I would probably admit it. Listen, an analyst acquaintance of mine didn't; he was wrong. I'll tell you what happened. It was spring. As usual his nose was either stuffed or running from an allergy that had dogged him all his life. He had been medicated with a new and potent antihistaminic. During one of his sessions, unexpectedly, it caused him to doze. Behind the couch.

"He must have snorted once or twice. His patient, as I heard the story from her later, accused him of 'dropping off.'

"The analyst lied. He denied it. Worse still, he took recourse to the rather shameful tactic of turning her accusation around and onto her in the guise of an interpretation:

"She was too 'suspicious, critical, projecting her own boredom and resistance."'

"What happened?"

"The patient knew he wasn't being truthful. He destroyed her trust irretrievably. He would have been wiser to analyze those qualities if they were present in her, but also to admit his lapse, without necessarily elaborating."

"I see. Yet, being totally truthful must get you into some, well, uncomfortable situations."

"No, not really. Look, there's a difference between telling the truth and telling the *whole* truth. In analysis the orientation is principally toward detective work—finding out why, but if one makes declarative statements instead of the more frequent interrogative, they must reflect integrity. Build trust, trust which must be generated if one is to be believed and helpful ultimately."

"I do see. Still.... Okay, let's say that a mother phones to ask if her teenage son is taking drugs."

"What is your question?"

"Well, suppose he is, and that the youngster's transportation to your office and his subsidy depended on parental cooperation and good will. You would be obliged to respect her concern, but wouldn't you shy away from telling the mother the truth to protect your patient's confidence?"

"Let me help you. You are mixing several issues. In working with kids, it is very often necessary to enlist a lot of support from their parents. I often ask right at the start if I may be allowed to depend upon my judgment about what questions and whose I should or should not answer. In the main, I would say that has proved to be the best technique.

"But you are also muddying the issue of who is the principal patient. While I don't lie to anyone if I can avoid it, I do try to focus clearly on my chief therapeutic target. In your example, that should be the child. I do not have the same commitment to his family as I have to him."

"So how would you respond?"

"Chances are I would say, as politely as I could, that a question such as that ought not to be asked. Then I would repeat what I have just told to you by way of explanation."

"Yet, aren't there times when such a handling of the issue might be misleading? To seem to give an answer you didn't intend at all?"

"For sure! Many of the less sophisticated parents hearing anything except a staunch denial would read an equivocation into my response, and fear the worst. But I could point that out as well ..."

"What if you were treating a little boy or girl who was fatally ill? Suppose *he* asked you—say he had leukemia—suppose he asked you if he was going to get better?"

"I would have to say I do not know."

"Would that be true?"

"It would."

"But suppose he pressed you then to learn his chances?"

"Still, I would try to plumb the basics. What is the real question? Is it fear of pain, disfigurement, or death? But going along with your hypothesis, if he pressed me for statistics, I would most likely confess I was not all that current on them."

"Yes, but suppose he came right out and asked you, 'Am I apt to die of this disease? To *die*!' What would you say to that?"

"Actually, I would have to be there in the real situation to know, but I can imagine myself formulating something honest yet hopeful."

"Such as?"

"Like cases of remission—ones that have fooled the biggest doctors. Or the fact that that particular disease is getting closer every day to 'cure.'"

"Is that the fact?"

"It is."

"In other words, the truth and nothing but."

"Right. But, as I have said, that is not identical with blurting out or volunteering unsolicited black gloom—or wielding the truth as a club. You use it when you must. Let me give you a couple of instructive examples:

"A young psychiatrist opened his office immediately upon completion of his residency training. When people telephoned for an appointment, he wished to appear to be very very busy and much much in demand; he would hesitate as if he had to search to find a spot to fit the caller in: 'Um ... How about say Thursday ... no ... no ... um. Let me see, a week from Friday? Wait ... no ... gee, the only time would have to be today. This afternoon.'

"Do you know the impression he gave? Universally? One of a young practitioner who tried to give an impression of being busier and more sought after than he was. He might just as well have skipped the phony act."

"I see."

"The second example is more subtle: My wife and I were invited to dinner by a psychologist. Several other mental health workers were also guests. It was a pleasant evening. During the meal, conversation was animated.

"Unexpectedly, one of the host's children, probably kept awake by the unusual commotion, pajamaed in one of those space-suit buntings, drowsed into the room. Proudly, and with exaggerated indulgence, his daddy introduced the boy around, then turned him over to the distaff side for trundling up again.

"'Darndest four-year-old I ever saw,' paternal pride said,

boasting. 'Do you know what that kid asked me at the dinner table Thursday night? If God was real and I believed in him. A bit precocious. don't you think?'

"The group acknowledged him. He was advanced alright, only someone chirped, 'What did you answer, Maury?' Everybody laughed except the speaker who kept pushing for a reply.

"Flushed, our host spluttered defensively, then finally fudged, 'I don't recollect. I do remember that he'd rattled me a bit. I didn't want to bother his young head with theosophic crud.

"'Come to think of it I sort of beat around the bush, then told him that I did—which isn't true you know—but made a mental note that some day I would hold forth in greater depth.'"

"The group swooped down on him. Good-naturedly. One of the analysts suggested that the issue, at its root, had more to do with Oedipus than God. Another spoke of basic trust. Another quite upheld the host, professing that he, too, would do the very same. Would have finessed it. What sense to make mountains out of molehills? At which point the spotlight turned on me.

"'What would you tell your son?' I then heard Maury asking.

"I replied, as usual, 'The truth.' Again confronting Maury I asked him, 'Bud, what are the facts? Where do you stand with God?'

"Unflustered, he replied, 'At his age I believed with all my heart. As I grew older, I became unsure. It's actually an issue I hardly ever think of. At this stage of life it isn't much important.'

"I could not resist a chuckle. You see why?"

"I don't."

"Because when Maury was off guard he gave the wholly truthful answer to the group. What he told us he could have told his son. I'll say his words again. Just listen, 'When I was your age I believed with all my heart, etc.'

"Wouldn't those have been near perfect as response?"

"You've got a point. It's a good story; even so, you must get into heavy waters now and then. How about white lies? Is there a place for them?"

"I should imagine. Let me follow up on your 'heavy waters.' I am thinking of a situation in which, irrespective of my devotion to the truth, I could find no bright side whatsoever nor any consolation. Think about treating a person who literally had no prospect for improvement.

"I was interviewing a middle-aged woman whose suicide attempt had induced a local social welfare agency to send her in. Weeks earlier she had taken a fistful of barbiturates, but somehow had survived. Hers was about the bleakest landscape I had ever looked upon.

"The attempt was her solution to a rare form of chronic heart disease—heredofamilial. Do you know the term?"

"It was passed on through the genes."

"Close enough, and being rare was much unknown, so incurable. Some sort of progressive, degenerative process involving those nerve and muscle fibers that are needed to conduct the impulse from the s-a node. Ever hear about Purkinje fibers?"

"No."

"Well, now you have. She was fifty-five years old, destitute, unable to work or even move with comfort, facing increasing suffering. You know what made it worse? She had four children—all boys."

"Why was that so bad?"

"The condition was 'sex-linked.' Of the sons, the oldest two had already died of that same illness. Her faulty genes. Heart attacks at ages eighteen and nineteen!

"She held herself accountable. Fully, however irrationally.

Of the two survivors, one already had had attacks and was considered to be living even then on borrowed time; the other suffered angina at age thirteen!

"Her husband? Divorced her and took off! He couldn't stand the gaff.

"She tried to kill herself a short time later. Penthothal. I don't know where she got it. Took enough to choke a good-sized horse. Care to guess what saved her? I asked too.

"She raised the midriff of her blouse and pointed to a scar. 'This!' She spat out, with contempt. 'This did!'

"'This' was a pacemaker implanted near her solar plexus. Apparently it had kept on ticking, pumping blood despite the load of medicine she consumed.

"I found myself casting about for solaces. For hopes. She had no prospect for a cure, a heart transplant, or anything mechanical. Certainly no husband would come peeking over her horizon. Broke besides, on welfare, facing increasing infirmity and death.

"Not to mention guilt for 'murder' of her sons.

"Well, she didn't let me do much rummaging. She told me, 'Save your breath.' She had a plan to kill herself and would. You know her scheme? One vestige of her erstwhile pride remained. She'd trump them yet, she would. She said, 'You ever write about your weirdo patients, here's one for your book! You put *me* in it. See this button in my gut? Inside it's got a battery. A battery that's going all the time. And running down. Except it's underneath the skin. They're gonna have to ask me for permission. 'Cause it's surgery when they replace it. There's my ticket out; I'll never sign.'"

"That's a horrible story."

"I agree."

"So, were you wholly truthful with her?"

"Yes, I was."

"Well, I mean, did she back you to the wall with your philosophy of sticking to the facts, or were you able to gentle them at all?"

"I really can't be sure."

"How so?"

"I never saw the lady after that one visit. I invited her. She accepted the appointment but never did return."

"Those were 'heavy waters,' I agree. If she should happen to come back to talk with you again some day, do you still feel that simple honesty would be the best approach?"

"To tell the truth, I do."

15
Whodonit?

Martha

"Martha! See the lighthouse! Hey Martha!" Shrill. Imperative. "Lookie here! Hey Martha, see the lighthouse?"

Martha overplayed her part. She made as if to glance their way, turning her head slowly, then of a sudden jerked it fully about. The boys screamed and disappeared beneath the splashing waters.

In mock disgust, she clucked her tongue.

Again, further off, but from the other side, "Hey, Martha! Over here! See the lighthouse?"

"Lighthouse, pshaw!" she muttered. "Them's water spouts. Ain't good fer nothing 'cept to piss in bed. Come back when yer growed up. Come back in eight, nine years."

Eban floated by. Silently, expectantly, the others from a distance watched their emissary do his act. He arched his back and urged his erect genital skyward. Martha saw it from the corner of her eye. She spun around.

Anticipating her move, Eban folded in the middle, commending his flashing brown-white torso to the depths. All the boys laughed. In unison they sang out, "Martha loves the lighthouse! Martha loves the lighthouse!"

Then it stopped.

Whispers. Giggles. Crickets. Water lapping at the smooth and slippery stones. Sluicing. There would be few more swimming days that year. School already open. Leaves were yellow-orange. Soon the State of Maine would be one shocking color burst despite this last reprieve—Indian summer.

And nine months gone, breathless, uncomfortable, impatient with the sultry, sticky heat, cranky, Martha dully reflected on the weeks to come.

Eban. Him and all them others.

The town's tom fools.

They didn't really bother her. Theirs was a game. No game for her, this pregnancy, her future. Could she cope with Sam? And had she made the right decision about Joel? When somethin' is fit it doesn't natter at your brain, she told herself, and then she shifted her position slightly where she sat.

Sweet Jesus and goddam if it wasn't there again! The urgency! Relentless! Lord gawdamighty! She'd have to rouse herself to pee. Another thimbleful. Every fifteen minutes. And them hemorrhoids.

And that stinkin' outhouse!

Sam had promised her on his mother's grave that the lake would be on sewers. Five years ago. Fat chance! Him and his inside tips! All them stories picked up from his passengers. Hogwash! Everyone the same. 'Ceptin' the bad news. Sewers, sure! Like blacktop for their road. Oh sure. Sure bet!

Well, one thing sure. She couldn't wait for them much longer. That was mighty clear.

"Can't see the whole damn baby thing is worth the troubles that it brings," she mused. "'specially the way I'm gonna hafta do with Joel, him stayin' with his Grandma. He'll have conniptions. Well, I certainly can't manage no three kids 'n' no one here to help. Uh, uh. No way. Anyhow, the boy will make out better down in town. Not fit to live in, this here lobster trap. Stupid ice-box!

"Sam won't miss him none. That's flat. I never see a father take a little boy as bad as Sam. Which ain't to say he favors Mary better, 'ceptin' Joel's right smart. Ah me ..."

"Hey Martha, Lookie, Nubble light!" from starboard. They all laughed. Someone screamed. The lighthouse sank from sight.

Martha often wondered why she had stuck with Sam. There had been other guys. All fools, the lot of them. Only Sam turned out to be the biggest. Him and his cab.

She hated everything about him nowadays: his never changing clothes, his musty odor, his smoking, and the messy trail it left: matches, butts, the spit-rimed pipes. But most she couldn't stand his "act." His "high-falutin' it." His kissy-assy shinin' up to cadge a fatter tip from summer folks. His puttin' on his "down Maine" accent and that stupid trick of drivin' tourists in a half-circle from the depot to the lake. Or gettin' them to ask to see them "fossil tracks."

As if they didn't know. Gawd! Could Sam have thought that he was smarter than all them big lawyers and professors and them doctors down from Boston and Connecticut? "He don't fool nobody. He never will. No way!"

Oh Christ she had to pee!

Six feet away from Martha, little Joel was sitting in the sand. Rounded still with baby fat, his pudgy hand and clumsy fingers were attempting something with a fallen needle from a spreading pine tree overhead. A game of Don Quixote, or its infantile equivalent, thrusting, jabbing at a pillbug, watching it curl into a ball, then jousting with it once again when it surmised that it was safe enough both to unfurl and crawl away.

Over and over. Parry, thrust. Recoil. A tireless and endless game. With deep absorption.

Three years old. Could Joel be toying with philosophies? Extrapolating universal wisdoms from those moves? It's doubtful that he understood. His mother surely didn't, nor did the splashing, sporting "lighthouse keepers" in the lake. Yet it is imperative for us to mark his words and mark them well. There will be need to resurrect them later on.

"Mommy see?" said Joel. "Bug go 'bye-bye?' No go 'bye-bye.' Mommy see? Bug no 'bye-bye.' Bug no go. See?"

* * *

The swimming ended. Suddenly.

Something magnetized the leader of the gang. He hollered, "Follow me!" Then, kicking up his heels, he ran off through the brush. Like mercury.

The others chased behind, down the winding path hidden to the main road in waist-high grass. A cloud of dust rose with boyish shouting back and forth, gradually fading, dying out, and gone. Then all was quiet once again. Pastoral. The sky, the lake, the trees.

"Lighthouse indeed," Martha smirked. She shouted to the wind, "Ya little pissant! Where ya runnin' off to now? Ya gonna' stick that 'lighthouse' up some poor gal's ass 'n' knock her up? Like all the other rabbits in this town? Good riddance! Don't come back."

She sighed.

Then sighed again, then shifted her center of gravity a "smidgin" forward. It responded, pushing her back again. With a lurch, she managed to stand. Authoritatively, to Joel, "Now you stay put!" Then, balancing a second to get steady, she debated whether on the spot to lift her skirts and relieve herself or.... "Oh Goddam it!" She decided to attempt the longer trip.

Slowly, grudgingly, an oath with each step, she started up the wooden stairway from the water's edge to the outhouse.

Every progress of that climb was dearly gained. Galumph, pause, shuffle—all the way to the landing. Turn. Galumph, galumph. At last, the weathered door.

Winters in those parts were invariably severe. Frosts and heavy snows had mangled that crude stairway many times before. Both would again this year, or next. And Sam, as sure as clam broth, would "Christ" and "Fuck it!" through some hapless patchwork reconstruction.

Actually, it didn't matter how sturdily he did so. Wind and water, relentlessness of heat and wet, age, termites, or the combinations—something always pulled it down. Like everything around wore out, got wrinkled, and had to be replaced—even the Natives—Old Man Mayben, Fosdick, Purdee, Martha's mother, showing signs.

She reached the mildewed, warping door. Then held her breath and in. Pine boards, blue-green, soggy-damp, mouldering. Ugh! Just to put a woman's private parts on them. Fech! Yes. Joel would have to stay with Grandma. Mary and the new one would take everything she had. Yes, that was that.

*　*　*

Indian summer.

Cobalt waters. Forest like a crazy quilt. Unusual resurgences.

The weeds that had perished on the first frost were

regenerated. They grew thick along the riverbanks. So thick in places that they fouled the outboard motors. No one ventured in the shallows. Not this late of season.

Instead the city folk were busy putting up their gear. Scraping hulls, washing down, locking up. And one by one even the stubbornest of hangers-on fell victim to the calendar. Each day another packed his things and left. Thinner herd. Trickling south.

Folding canvas chairs. Ragged hammocks. Old tents, bright rubber rafts, khaki jackets pinned with fish flies, good-luck yachtsman caps, tricycles, bicycles, barbeque pieces, stowed beneath the tarps of U-Hauls or part visible through station-wagon windows as the exodus began.

A Coxey's army wending homeward. Off to Lowell, Hartford, Providence, Pawtuket, New York City, Boston—who knows where? Wagon masters in Bermuda shorts and jersey shirts and sneakers. Princes in disguise, the lot of them, who would resume their winter roles as lawyers, teachers, doctors, architects, tycoons.

Another summer done.

Why chronicle their march? Because Joel did. He watched them wend away. He had no other choice. Snared by his age.

He saw. He registered. He stored in some compartment of his mind the knowledge that a festive, peopled, teeming summer spa could be abandoned. Ghosted overnight. Epitomizing something for his future use. A raw material he could charge with sentiment should ever need arise to resurrect aloneness in a lonely place—as rest assured it would.

In late September, two weeks earlier than planned, though well into her third trimester, Martha had a baby girl. She called her Grace. She labored and she suffered perilously long. Sam? Forsook her to the mercies of a midwife, then got drunk. And Dr. Fred? Till close to daybreak had been unavailable. And Joel?

Frightened, hiding, crying, standing vigil outside Martha's door, then shooed away, repeatedly, at last to fall asleep, curled up, exhausted in his bed, his fingers in his mouth.

Within two days transported off to Grandma's in the city, dropped by Sam, who set the boy on her doorstep, knocked her knocker twice and drove off in his cab.

*   *   *

That scene, so vivid in its portrayal, was put together piece by piece over several years of psychoanalytic therapy. It formed a cornerstone on which later frameworks would be built. To Joel, grown up, and to myself, the architects of healthy, newer structures, it became increasingly significant as we progressed.

Within its narrative, much like a regular "Whodonit," there are seeded several clues. Others will be furnished as his story moves along, but for several cogent reasons I now take a literary license and play hop-scotch with the sequence of events.

Come, I should like to have you meet my patient face-to-face:

Picture a tall, slender man. Imagine him with sallow complexion, such as you have seen on people whose time is spent indoors. Thread lines along his face, deep at the jowls and redundant underneath his puffy eyes.

He is forty-five years old.

His look? Like a beagle's, sorrowful. His hair? Calvites and canites: balding and gray.

Corduroy jacket that had seen far better days, brown, "spiffy" once with its heraldic emblem at the breast, and leather buttons, but slightly threadbare now, if you look carefully. You see the cuff rims? There! Okay?

His trousers? Oxford gray. Beltless. Loose-fitting. Cinched

by a broad, flat hook-and-eye affair, off center of his middle,
and tucking in a broadcloth shirt—dark blue with piping, open
neck, wide collar.

"I'm Dr. Benedict," he says, and offers you his hand, then
strides the three short steps to stand before the chair. He seats
himself as you do.

A handshake diagnostic? Bet on it!

I pumped at cotton wadding. The doctor's was too tenta-
tive, too ineffectual, too delicate—so much so that I was not
surprised to hear his next remarks:

"I've come for my depression—besides which I suck cocks.
But, I don't want the latter fixed, just the former.

"I have tried to take my life. I know the way you work, so
here's the nub of it: I'm active in A.A. I used to be on drugs.
On both those counts I'm clean. What else? I married once,
divorced, no kids. I'm trained to do psychiatry, but don't. I'm
living on the dole. I'm homosexual, not latent, but overt."

Grandma

Print of Currier and Ives.

A criss-cross picket fence. A broken gate latch. Weeds
everywhere. Carrot tops arched over, lying on the ground.
Exuberant tomato vines, but brown and withered. Two loose
wooden treads that led up to the door, and flagstones out of
kilter in the path. A hundred year old house, neglected, raggedy.

In it lived a feature actress in the plot: Joel's Grandma.

That elderly woman, widowed long ago, maintained it by
herself. And every evidence bore out that she had long ago
grown rusty in the knack of looking after things—her house,
her person, and most certainly young kids. In fact, solitude
as it so unobtrusively but incrementally is apt to do, distorted,
then destroyed whatever had been penchant to adjust or

compromise—with anything—and finally entrenched her in a bunch of border-eccentricities as much attached to her as bits of her anatomy, like talking to her pets or spending days in bed.

So much that it was unkind of Martha to impose on her the burden of a three-year old. "The terrible threes"—or twos—whichever.

"Them's the little Dickens that gets inter everything 'n' climbs, Martha. Now I can't promise nothin'!" were her words—aware that she had long since reached and slid beyond the point where life's trajectory accelerates its downward slope— aware that she preferred to coast, to take as comfort that her few possessions might lie undisturbed. In their "fittin'" places. And her habits, good or bad, "just left alone"—the lot of which made Joel a foreign element, intrusive in her scheme.

But she "owed" Martha.

Twilight or no.

Something about Sam. I never learned. Besides, she heard it on her radio that there might be "foster money" takin' in a waif, and God knew she had use for that. Dr. Fred could help. Real smart at legal ins and outs. And paperwork.

Again, why linger on these orts? Because they too must furnish necessary clues: a youngster, hungering for food who would pick upon such crumbs.

*   *   *

"Joel, yer gonna fall asleep in that bowl. Yer Ma is gonna think yer Gran'ma didn't feed ya none. 'T'sa' matter? Ya moonin' over stayin' here with me? Ya miss yer Ma?

"Not much on talking are ya? Yer Ma did at yer age. Like all my kids. Real bags o' wind. How old you now, gone three? Yeh, that's yer father's nature in ya, Sonny. Mopin' in that window like ya do. Hmp!

"Lookin' fer yer Daddy are ya? He ain't there. Ain't gonna be there neither. Oh yeh, I know. He's drivin' through the town. That man! Ya think he drop around 'n' visit with his kin? I mean, besides ya bein' his son? Would ya? Er come 'n' nail my fence?

"Here, see my hands? I uster sew. Look here! Balled up like this? Ya think 'at I c'n holt a hamma or a nail? That's rich. It's everythin' I got ter buttin this here dress. Look here!

"Uster keep chickens. All run off an died. Behin' that shed. Couldn' manage by m'self. No, not since Gran'pa went ta heavin.

"Joel!

"Come back here! You set down 'n' eat this oatmeal. God's witness how I fuss to fix it. Gran'ma knows what little codfish needs fer growin'. Oatmeal. C'mon. Here! Brown sugar! Mmmmmm! Yum. I'll eat some too.

"Ya got teeth. I ain't. I hafter. See! Watch yer Gran'ma taste it. My gawd, yer skin 'n' bones. Lookit them holler eyes!

"Joel, if ya was any older I say ya got wim-wams. Ya down 'a dumps? A little midge like you? Ya miss yer Ma? Sonny, ya don't know nothin' about nothin' yet, 'n' believe me 'at's a damn good thing, 'n' I ain't gonna scare ya none neither with no stories how yer baby sister almos' kill yer Ma, comin' like she did, her tail bone first. Squeezin' out that way.

"She'll be a 'backward' one, you'll see. I hear about a lady once't who died deliverin' like that. Was down Webhannet way. Calls it 'breecher's birth' ... anyhow ya wouldn't understan'.

"Dr. Sam says all his years 'n' babies that he brung inter this world, that only five or six like that 'n' half them dead besides. 'At's why that Martha calls her 'Grace.' Grace o' God it is. His grace that *she's* alive. I mean yer mother. Course yer sister too.

"Yump! Wouldn' that fix everything right smart if Martha hadda died?

"Ya think yer Gran'ma gonna hop acrosta broom 'n' fly up to the Lake 'n' tend to you three kids? Uh uh! I done my baby work. I raised my brood, not sayin' I'm not proud to show off what I got 'ceptin' Martha. That's yer Ma. Martha's growed a little ragged on the edges here of late. I mean she shoulda held Grace up another year or two.

"She's still too good fer Sam. Yer Daddy, Joel. Like all us Hollisters. We marry shoddy, seems.

"Joel! Ya ain't eatin' nothin', son. Ya miss yer Ma? C'mon. She's much too busy to be fussin' about you. She's got that backward baby ta be lookin' at. Yer third claw onna lobster, son. 'At's why she sent ya here.

"Hup! Eat this now 'n' Gran'ma gonna take a nap, okay?"

*   *   *

Hop scotch!

"That's right. Principally the sadness. Like a brooding, dark cloud. I want to say 'miasma.' Sometimes I actually sob, especially at night. About my future—and my past, and my present. Not a pretty picture, is it?

"My homosexuality? Well, I'm assuming that I don't shock you with that. I expect that I've been referred to someone sophisticated and experienced enough to handle it for what it is—and keep my confidence, of course.

"I mean, it's no secret that I'm in A.A. Part of their program as you must realize is open confessional. Exposure and self-flagellation. *Mea culpa!* I shouldn't knock it, really. It's kept me alive for years where nothing else would, even therapy. Oh, forgive me, I'm rambling.

"I think they go a little overboard with the contrition part, but as I say, I'm in no spot to criticize.

"Then there were drugs. I thought that I was taking dexedrine to diet, and that I could control it. Great at rationalization, aren't we doctors? As if the rules apply to someone else, not us.

'Always self-prescribed. Well, I abused them. I started needing 'whites' to perk myself up in the morning after I had drunk too much at night.

"Do you know the pattern? Alcohol or barbiturates 'h.s.' to fall asleep with, and then benzedrine to jolt me back into harness again next day, then both together to release me from the 'high' that I'd been riding in the hope that I could sleep the whole mess off.

"Vicious, ugly circle! Well, as far as all of that, I'm 'clean.'

"But, what I don't want circulated is my 'gay' habit. Perhaps that's an addiction too except it spares my liver and my brain, I think ... though God knows I'm actually so lonely most of the time that I might as well be 'straight.' It's been so ... long ... which goes with this depression. No real friends. I can't keep them. Jealousy! I get so desperately possessive, almost paranoid. Beyond bearing it.

"Oh, do forgive me. I sound as if I'm whining. I'll be fine in just a minute. Do forgive me, please."

Dr. Benedict turned his long, pale face toward the window. A light beam caught a sparkle in his eye. One welling, salty tear. He sniffed. From the pocket underneath his jacket flap, he drew a clean white hankie, and into it, at last, he blew his nose.

Twice.

Then twice the other nostril ... with an unused section daubing at his eyes. He mumbled, "This is what happens. Sudden uncontrollable emotional outbursts," as he reached behind the crested monogram of his blazer to procure his cigarettes. Fresh pack. Unopened.

Picture the man. Watch his movements. Every one of them has purpose. Meaning. Each inscribes itself upon our record. Each has future use. Dr. Benedict the thaumaturgist. He's about to do a trick. A sleight-of-hand.

Smoothly, evenly, gently, he pulls at the red cellophane leader, winding it deftly around the top of the packet. The piece thus freed, he dangles delicately over the clean, ceramic ash tray, then allows it to drop. It lies there. Disposed of.

Across my mind (for reasons I would understand three years later) there flitted the single word, "placenta." I didn't know why—the paper's shape, the way he chose to let it drop, perhaps its color. Dark. Blood red.

Meticulously as any surgeon would, with his long, slender, bony fingers, he dissects loose, then folds back, one tin foil corner, then the other, then the flap remaining, so that just a third of the top has been opened, and the duty stamp affixed across it yet remains untorn.

Now, behold!

Out of its wrapper skin, he extrudes the package by pushing along its bottom with his thumb. The cellophane, plaited thus into a miniature accordion, is used to play a tiny crinkly tune, several times. Back-forth, in-out, the package sliding up and down and up again, until he sheds the "instrument" at last, rolling it into a ball, which he deposits in the tray beside the ribbon already lying there.

. My thoughts?

He voiced them for me.

"You're noticing my habit, I imagine. Yes, it's 'Freudian.' I really hadn't meant to do that, yet I often do. And even I see the sexy implications. I openly confess them. Masturbation. Right? You needn't comment. I'll go on."

The doctor cleared his throat. He eyed me surreptitiously as if he felt discomfort at my scrutiny.

"I'll admit that I'm self-conscious too, and rather out of practice with sitting on this side of the desk," he stated, then continued, "From what I've come to learn about the subject, I suspect that I should have come into analysis years earlier. When I was younger."

He grasped the denuded package and knocked loose a single cigarette. Its tip came within the pincers of his thumb and index finger—pinkie-high—strangely reminding me a little of a lobster's claw. And I watched him draw it out along its extraordinary length and tamp it on the crystal of his watch, then turn it over and repeat that gesture several times allowing the cigarette to slide between his fingers as he did so.

"Forty-five is too brittle. Don't you agree?

"Only there was no way I could have afforded it then, and there certainly isn't now. God knows, the money that has slipped through my hands would have been more than adequate. Worse yet, I never will have sufficient. Rest assured. I can't practice anymore. I can't even work at anything."

He put the cigarette down on the table at his side instead of smoking it.

Why such niggling detail?

Because his every movement had significance. Much as a puppeteer's. Much as a pantomimist's. I sensed that without knowing how I knew it. Nor did I realize what he was trying to tell me.

Like semaphore, waggling flags across the room—another ciphered message. Ready?

In order to lay his cigarette down, he was obliged to move the box of tissues slightly to the right. He did so. That I took as evidence he had seen the tissues. Yet, he chose to lurch across the room to take one from a dispenser set beside the couch. Out came a "man-sized" napkin, meant as cover for the cushion underneath the heads of analytic patients. Benedict knew that to be its function, yet he did a "double-take," opening his mouth and widening his eyes, remarking, "My, this is enormous! Is it this big to correlate with people's troubles? Oh, of course! How silly of me. These are for analysands aren't they? Like a head rest?"

I smiled, "Yes."

'I guess I'm acting out, except I didn't see the smaller box beside the ashtray. Would you interpret that as reaching out for analytic help, or is it something deeper?"

"I guess it could be both of those and then some, but go on," I replied.

"Well, as I was saying, money. It eliminates me from that consideration. At least from private work. I get a paltry check from disability and it, plus a five-dollar birthday gift from my mother, pretty much constitute my yearly income."

He reddened.

Automatically his fingers tapped a second cigarette from the package. It, too, he held lightly just a moment. Then "I'm smoking shamefully." He pushed the cigarette back into its berth. "I've got to curb it. I must do that little trick a hundred times a day—ambivalence. I take one out and put it back again.

"May I be totally frank? You need not answer. I went to your institute to ask about the Analytic Clinic. I imagine you know Dr. Goldstein there. One of my classmates is a friend of his. He was very kind. I told him the whole story ... er ... well, most if it, that is, about the depressions. Oh, he more than likely read between the lines about the rest, although I try not to be 'swishy.' Well, Dr. Goldstein told me I ought to talk with you to see if you had time to take me on in treatment.

"I could pay something, but it wouldn't be a lot."

Hat-in-hand. For an instant Dr. Benedict transmuted to a

hungry five-year-old. He was embarrassed. Naturally long and slender, his face was even further lengthened by a pursed, puckered, expectant pouting of his lips and a sideways-downward look which set his bony chin upon his shoulder.

Then he sent another message. (It's important too!)

He reached into his jacket pocket. Out came a matchbook. How colorful! On its cover, unmistakably, a Mondrian design. Dr. Benedict had bought those matches! Odd, speaking as he had a breath before of poverty, its pinch.

"I suppose, it's one of those 'many called but few chosen' affairs. Am I right? A lot of people who could conceivably benefit from analysis either have to wait their turns or ultimately do without. That wouldn't surprise me, but I must get on with it."

At last he seemed prepared to smoke. From the table, he retrieved the cigarette he had left lying. He swung its distal end into his mouth. Slightly garbled, then his next remarks:

"My 'Chief Complaint': Depression. Present Illness: The patient is a forty-five-year old, white, divorced physician whose loneliness and despondency have driven him to still another suicidal posture."

Benedict the surgeon, as if selecting a scalpel from a case, teased loose the corner match amidst its fellows and worked it back and forth. At last he tore it free. Across the roughened surface of the booklet, he honed its tip, stroking smoothly and away from his body.

Fire!

Tip to tip.

He sucked in deeply with profound satisfaction.

Then, counterclockwise windshield-wiper motions, high in the air, in front of him, fanned out the flame, finally dropping the match into the ashtray, mincingly, disdainfully, I thought. As if it were a dirty object, or one loathed.

Those gestures were effeminate, stereotyped, and I absorbed them totally. Why? Why make such infinite prolixity of lighting up to smoke? Why comment also that there was a rather lovely something in the blue and grayish swirling smoke rings as they rose and curled around, and patterned through the sun?

We watched them silently, the two of us, until he spoke anew: "I had to leave my work. I couldn't concentrate at all. Resigned. So desperate in my loneliness—but mustn't drink again. No! It would kill me sure."

Another tear welled up.

"Where do I live? A little guest house in back of an elderly widow's home. Over on Arminta. She's a hideous bore, but just about my only living contact now for weeks. Oh, I've reached out, only nothing, no one is fulfilling.

"This I find awkward to say: I go cruising. You look puzzled. Hunting pick-ups. I see them standing, thumbing at the freeway entrances, young men, like lollipops—so sweet and fresh! I give them lifts. Only what could they want with an aging, wrinkled boy like me?

"Sometimes, even if I'm going in the opposite direction, I try to turn around. It's always too late. Someone snaps them up before I'm able to get back, wouldn't you know? Could the vice-squad set a person up that way? God, that's all I'd need."

He sucked hard on his cigarette, bringing the tip to an intense glow which gradually turned dull, then gray with ash as he exhaled.

"Shall I continue with my anamnesis? I'm trying to compartmentalize to keep it clear for you."

"You needn't," I observed.

"Well, I imagine it would help."

"Whatever way you can," I said, reflecting inwardly that the doctor was more than likely unaware, despite his expertise and sophistication, that I was very busy observing the unfolding of several other themes besides the verbal—even to the extent of comparing him to prestidigitators who engage attention *here*, in order to sneak past you something *there*.

To wit? To wit those matches.

How come? Alright. Consider this as I did.

In an affluent country where every bar and bank and restaurant and bowling alley hand out free, as advertisements, fistfuls, gratis, all you want in matches, this needy man, by his own confession on his uppers, for some reason, had laid in a private stock of great artist match books.

Artis gratia.

Because their beauty had appealed to him? Because he touched the tragic lives of fellow sufferers and similarly starving artists to support their work this way? Because the pleasure of his smoking was enhanced along this visual dimension? Far more than lighting up to logos of "Joe's Eats"! I could at best but guess. A relic of an erstwhile elegance. A trace. Or more? We'll see.

I wondered too if he was drawing my attention to a "dangling-carrot" type of confessional to camouflage bigger, darker kinds of crimes he wished to smuggle through. No harm to wonder. Only patience, patience, patience.

"Do you know Maine? My birthplace? Aroostook County? Where they grow potatoes? Born in 1922. We moved, they tell me, down the coast when I was six months old."

He crossed one knobby knee astride the other, hitching up his trouser leg along his slender thigh. "I have two sisters. Younger. Both of them. Mary was born in 1923, and Grace in '25. My earliest memories go back to around then. Her birth. Because I had to live with my grandmother in the city at that time. I was sent off."

Again the cigarette was sucked at hard and long. His gaze grew gentle and remote.

"My father is alive. I shouldn't call him well. He's in his seventies, and Martha, Mother, she's alright, I guess. I couldn't swear to what her true age is. She's seventy, I think. Both girls are married and have children. We swap Christmas cards each year. I'm not close to either one of them. What else? Where can I go from there?"

"Just say it as you think it. I'll keep up."

"I know. It's just ... I sort of drew a blank. Okay. Past History—My education."

He took another puff then settled in the chair.

Miss Bleek

Joel was Whistler's Mother, in miniature and spatially transposed. Hour on hour he did *his* sitting in the window, at his Grandmother's house. There were two. At the larger one downstairs he could tuck his legs up underneath (being careful lest his muddy shoes touch the cushions of the seat). His forehead pressed the pane; his elbow rode the sill. Upstairs at the smaller one, miraculously circular—it didn't open—well, that was "special," if he was special good or special bad.

Bad if he had been restricted or confined as punishment. Good when coal men came and other things like that. Then, climbing on the hassock and sliding far out into the dormer, he was snuggled in the crow's nest of his ship.

His pinnacle. Its altitude to match the heights of Loomis's dump truck rising up. Fifteen feet? Not more. But high enough to scrape the vaults of heaven. High as giant's bean stalks in his ken.

"Ya gonna watch fer Loomis, Joel? Grandma's puttin' in her coal. G'wan, get up there, matey. Lively lad! Ya peel yer eye 'n' get yer telescopes. I'm gonna do one chore then I'm fer upstairs too. Yer Grandma's gonna nap. I'll keep ya company."

Loomis was Ralph Loomis. Son of Loomis Coal and Coke.
A tall, good-looking somewhat simple youth who had, through
nepotism, steady if not inspirational employ. He did not drive.
In fact, it is doubtful that he ever passed the test or took his
license.

No! His task was climbing up the elevated rig and, once
the chutes were set, to shovel so the flow of coal would keep on
moving through the hatch. If lumps should plug it, Loomis
would sing out, "weigh up," then, as the lifting engine idled,
with his shovel handle or its blade, dislodge impediments and
make ready for the next.

Sometimes loads delivered were so small he wasn't needed.
The truck bed could be split in thirds by using boards, though
usually, because the winters on the shore were long and bitter
and because there was a drayage fee, the customers laid in a full
load every time, as Joel's Grandma did.

So Loomis rode along.

"Yer too little ter read Joel, but I see in *Farmer's Almanac*
we're in fer one good mighty heavy winter. Seem strange don't
it? Here it is 'most Labuh Day 'n' Grandma buyin' coal? Well,
I know things. Ya see them geese fly by last night? Well, they
know somethin' too. Ya recollect the frost nip yestidday? Okay.
Mark my words. A good one this time. But we'll ride'r out, we
will."

Together then they heard the straining vehicle as it turned
and climbed the hill. "She's comin', Joel. Don't wait on me!
G'wan. Hop in yer winder. I'll be up."

Joel flew the stairs and dove into the dormer. Sure enough!
It was! Loomis's sooty face and lumberjacket shirt. Rolled
sleeves. Oh his would be a job for Joel, full-grown. "Tap, tap,
tap" upon the panel with his knuckles. Futile. Too much noise.
Perhaps he'd look that way. So wave, Joel, wave. No luck. The
truck was slowing. Wow, just look!

Loomis eased his frame gracefully over the side. With well-practiced motions he loosed the pair of chains that had been securing the chutes beneath the dump bed, and with a dextrous, clever maneuver used the vehicle's slow but continuing forward momentum to slide them along its length until they both lay free. From the cab, he swung a blackened barrel, which he positioned at a point equidistant between the basement window and the delivery hatch, and then upon it he rested first one then the other chute to form a path along which the stream of coals would flow.

Ready?

The driver emerged with a clipboard full of papers. He approached the downstairs door, then rang the bell. "I gotta get your signature on this here invoice," Joel could hear him saying. "Snappy weather ain't it? Thank you, Mum. That otta do 'er. Thanks again," as with a wave he sent the signal to his cohort who, waiting on it, yanked the lever to release the coal.

How black! How shiny! And beautiful! Dissolving mountains. Surely that will stand. Its base erodes. So topple crests. Bit by bit. A giant's ebon hourglass. Dusty lumpy grains, in turn, all find the hole. Some tumble off the chute. "Thud-clunk" upon the pavement. Smashed to powdered smithereens below. They flow and flow.

If only every day might bring to starving eyes such spectacles, such keen adventures! Loomis! Shovel, sir! Don't stumble! Strong man. Hero. *He* could be a small boy's father.

Could he? Push! Push! Push!

And then a strange thing happened. Loomis saw the youngster watching, and he grinned. He winked at Joel, he did. Then he saluted. Then he kicked the last survivors through the gate and laughed. Enough that something of the echoes could be heard above the racket, even through the sealed-up window. And what then? Why then the part of which a lad would dream of repeatedly—into adulthood, into middle years—for reasons fathomless to him, but not at last to us (you'll see).

Loomis lay full-length upon the empty truck bed, slid himself out through the aperture, and down.

The clown! Joel clapped his little hands with glee. Through the aperture and down! His lissome body, feet first, out the hatch into the waiting world. Bravo!

*   *   *

Infinite the span in Grandma's windows. Five years old. Surveyor of the city traffic. School yard inspector. Joel could see a piece of Bailey's park way off.

Beaulieu's rotting Cracker Box and Norton's Cape Cod, both were visible with ease, then, if he angled down the street and scrunched a little, the corner of the fire station, leaving thus, in center stage, the school.

Marshall Elementary: kindergarten and the first three grades. It had as well two "temporary portables" to service fourth- and fifth-grade students, but their structures lay beyond his line of sight.

As intimately as the operations of his body parts, Joel came to know the details of that red brick building. At the top of each tall window perched a horizontal vent that different students opened every morning, with a pole. He smiled to see them seek, then find, then pull. Behind another window, stood a yellow balance, exactly like the one at "Uncle" Doctor Fred's.

How wistfully, how fruitlessly, Joel waited for repeat performances of a drama witnessed once—how many moons before? The day when one by one, bare-topped, there stood upon that platform balance, in parade, each student getting weighed—first boys, then girls—a show that lasted, class by class, a whole week long at least, filling boring mornings of those boundless days wih ultimates of entertainment.

And the fire escape. The metal grillwork running round the second story. And the stagings where the kids stood when the special bell rang. "Fire drill," croaked out his Grandma. "Darn good thing! It's case their heater blows," then showed him burn scars on her withered, skinny arm. "Ya see that piece tucked up, looks like a spindly stork? Well, it comes down. They got it balanced. See that block?"

One Sunday or what may have been a holiday, when school was out, Joel saw two kids who scaled the iron fence. They had a broom. The big boy gave the little one a piggy-back and handed him their "tool" to pull that "stork leg" down. He got it. Climbed right up and peeked into the windows. Pried a latch and entered, and emerged, and wrote some letters on the panes with soap. Joel asked. But Grandma clucked, "It's somethin' 'dirty' 'atcha wouldn' understan'."

And then another day a paint truck parked outside the school. "Mr. Benson," Grandma told him. "Gonna paint the fence, I reck'. That keep the two of ya from gettin' inter mischiefs."

Coveralls. Brand clean. And going to paint the fence! Wow! Cans, a million of them. Pouring, stirring with a stick. And brushes! Orange, garish, lovely. Will he leave it that way? Better than the ugly, dusty black. So, bar by bar. Top down, behind, the right, the left, the front. Another shocking brilliant rod. How slick! Six pickets, teeth of an enormous comb, tines of a giant's fork. And with each unit done the paint can moved along. Then Benson stopped to eat his lunch.

Joel eyed the sandwich, the wrapper, the thermos, the apple. He eyed the pipe and matches and the funny sweeping windshield-wiper motions of the painter's weary fingers as he fanned the flame to put it out with his wrist, his arm. And then the shocking contrast when the fresh black shiny tint lay coated on the orange. Halloween! Black magic.

"Lookit Grandma! Has Mr. Benson any little chidren of his own? Is there a little Benson sister?" If a youngster had a painter for a father ... and to look at lovely colors all one's life. Could Grandma please find the other crayons she once spoke of? In the attic? Please.

*   *   *

"I'll set a bourne," the poet said, "how far in to be loved." Bind up the boundless. Define the infinite. All those on the morning that his Grandma took him into school.

It was a hazy time around his birthday. Pencils. A handkerchief. Dressed up in fancy knicker-bocker pants. Walked down the path beyond the ragged weed patch, holding Grandma's hand. Lookit there that fence! Paint bubbles! And right through the gate of it. Chain. Lock. In the "Office." Transoms. Lookit, in the corner, see that pole!

"His name is Joel. No. I'm his Grandma. Martha's livin' at the Lake. He's her first. They's two sisters. His daddy's name is 'Sam.' He stays with me."

Then writing. A hatched-faced old woman with a pug. She smelled of something musty. A machine was blowing air into the room. "Say 'bye' to Grandma Joel 'n' you behave. An' when they ring 'at bell, ya skitter, hear? I'll watch ya through the winder. Now behave!"

And standing with his thighs together, pressing tight, frightened, wanting urgently to pee and to cry, Joel looked at the ceiling and the floor and put his index finger in his twitching mouth.

"Oh for shame!"

Miss Hatchet speaking. Miss Pug-hair.

"We don't suck our thumbs or fingers in this school. Don't let me catch you either. Six years old! Act big! Come on, I'll take you to Miss Bleek; she's waiting. Come on, boy. Let's go."

Yes, clues!

More clues.

How luckless that that hungry little mouth should find a Mistress Bleek to suck on. Kinder Fate had named Miss Bleek "Miss Full." Starved again! Write in Joel's record what it took him years and years to recognize, to ferret out; this twist:

Miss Bleek. Single, fortyish. Her jet black hair wrapped tightly on her skull. Pierced by a comb. Her plain, white face made deathlike by still whiter powder, and unsmiling. Wearing practical square shoes with solid "Cuban" heels. Sensible. And flat, flat, flat her upper dress front. And those foolish doilies on her shoulders. Épaulettes? This dried-up witch his first-grade fountain and his lifeline?

Do you know what more?

That only days before the little lad's enrollment, this spinster teacher's roommate sister, Julie, had committed suicide by hanging—in the shadow of which deed "Miss Full" went off to feed her class.

*   *   *

" 'Martha, see the lighthouse?' I remember that. It's my earliest recollection. Oh, we've kidded enough about it that maybe I don't remember *it* actually, rather the later talking about it. Except I think I see the lake, and Eban. I would have been about three years old. Do you believe that memory goes back that far?"

"We recall selectively," I explained. "Isolated scenes or vocal utterances we retain are usually representatives of broader situations. They epitomize. A whole class of experiences could be

subsumed under that one vivid image. Do you have some idea
what 'Martha, see the lighthouse?' might have meant for you?''

"Of course! In the main it's depression, but I know there's
plenty more. Rather shapeless, as I've told you. Seasons. A whole
way of life.

"The change of seasons that I miss so. Color, swimming,
pregnancy. 'Lighthouse' was Eban's penis. My mother's disgust
with my father, and the pregnancy. I know the story. It's all
completely inventoried in me somewhere—not that I can pull it
out that simply—but I feel that something there wants definition
and expulsion."

"So do I."

"Did I ever mention Martha's 'black clams?' No, I couldn't
have. Ha, ha! The time I saw her nursing Grace? I saw her
nipples. I was consternated at their color and their shape—I
mean how black and long.

" 'What's Grace eating?' I expect I asked her.

" 'Them's 'black clams,' " she told me. I still hear the
mockery. She wasn't happy to be stuck with Grace. I mean the
whole experience. It was a bad one for her. Sam, the living
conditions, money—I don't imagine that she relished sending
me away. My sister, Grace that is, she's paying the penalty
today. Badly 'screwed up.' Not a very apt psychiatric diagnosis,
is it? But it conveys the picture.

" 'Black clams.' In her own way she was intimating
something poisonous, it sounds. Funny, I never thought of that
before. It impressed me how the nipple stretches out to get so
long. Inches long, literally.

"You know, come to think of it, a nipple gets to be rather
like a baby's thumb. I can see why the baby sucks it for a
substitute. Almost identical.

"I didn't suck my thumb. Mostly I was a finger-sucker. Do
you know what I'm associating? Ha, ha! I'm embarrassed. It's a

joke, an old joke, about how you can tell the size of a man's cock from the length of his index finger—not that I think it's true.''

I interrupted, "Do you hear that?"

"Hear what?"

"Your chain of associations?"

"Well, I ... wasn't ... listening closely, just 'freely' as you want. What part of it?"

"I'll repeat it: your mind pretty much linked up *sad* with Martha's *nursing*, nursing with *breasts*, breasts with *nipples*, nipples with *thumbs*, thumbs with *fingers*, then *finger-sucking*, then *fingers* with *cocks*. Do you want to supply the missing bit?"

"I sort of see what you're driving at."

"Do you know what I extrapolate?"

"Of course, that my cock-sucking derives from the wish to nurse more. That's theoretical, isn't it, I mean the classical interpretation?"

"It sounds more than just theoretical. But I am also calling your attention to the 'sad' part. Somehow it feels to me that our biggest work is there. It does suggest that at the root of your 'homosexuality' is a deprivation or a hunger, and that you have been starving almost all your life."

"Good God!"

"I'm only using your 'material.' "

"I know, but ... "

"But what?"

"You're intimating that my depression goes that far back?"

"Could be. If I recall correctly, in the very first words you spoke to me on the day we met, you made virtually the same linkage. Do you remember? You asked me to fix the *depression* but not the *cock-sucking*.'

"You know by now, I hope, that when I listen to you I don't respect negatives, subjunctives, imperatives in the usual linguistic way. I go for content. Those two items were associated together, so I made a mental note. Forget that you tried to disguise the connection with a negative command. Am I clear?"

"Perfectly."

"Even so, I want to belabor the point. Because it's time that you heard your own thoughts better. If a man says to me, 'I'm thinking of an elephant,' I hear 'elephant.' *Elephant* is in his mind, okay? And if he says to me in the most ridiculous roundabout, 'If for a second you think I would give consideration to the possibility of reflecting upon pachyderms or their relatives, elephants ... ' do you know what I hear? Still *Elephant*, but as a corollary, an attempt to deny his so doing.

"Simple, isn't it?

"When you tell me 'depressed' and 'cock-sucking,' I have a right to tie those two together despite your denials and all the in between. Do I make my point?"

"You do."

"You even asked me *'to leave that last alone.'* To me that meant the area was tender, wouldn't stand much probing right away, but maybe later."

"I follow, at least intellectually. I suppose ... it's as if ... whatever the verb form, past, future, whatever voice or mood, if the subjects come together, then they are 'associated.' How simple!"

"Yes, elegantly simple, really. Can you use it?"

"I can try."

Dr. Benedict did try. Wobbly legs. A new-born colt. He reminded me of a corps of Army Engineers who also try to build a bridge across a wild, forbidding stream. Somehow one brave soldier swims with a rope and gains the other side. Having done so, the rest is detail; once that first firm foothold is attained, what follows will be easier. His buddies tie stouter ropes to his for him to pull across, then stouter still, then more men follow, then thicker cables till at length huge tanks.

We had made one vital contact. Now to strengthen it, to try.

Sam

Grade nine. Geometry. Instead of becoming a priest, Mr. Robbins taught junior high. He liked to make curious, apocryphal remarks, among them: "Things equal to the same thing are equal to each other." Fair enough, that much. And fair enough its fellow, "The whole comprises the sum of all of its parts." Later, in their travels and their studies, the boys would hear about the inviolable laws of thermodynamics, he promised. Never would men construct machines to run on perpetual motion. Nor could one ever hope that out of nothing any substance might emerge. He preached that too.

But puzzling in the extreme his philosophic addendum: that those axioms were invariably true in blackboard games but *not in life.*

But not in life? Heavy words! Contradicted in the "actuality of living," Mr. Robbins said. "Just wait and see."

Nice man. Florid face. Clean-shaven. Jolly. Joel sought him out to ask him after class. How could that be? And Robbins put his girlish hand upon Joel's shoulder and exposed him to the famous syllogism about cats. And dogs. For openers.

"Is a dog an animal? It is? And what about a cat? That too? Why so it follows algebraically then that dogs *are* cats, pursuant to your logic. Simple a, b, c, *n'est-ce pas?*" he asked with a smile. And walked away.

Joel laughed too with admiration and perplexity. Absorbent. Impressionable boy. Yet, would need to chew upon it more and more until at last, within the confines of my office, I would show him how he had been living with a prime example of such contradiction in the person of his father, Sam.

So many trees screened him from the forest! Joel was fragile and vulnerable. Nature had wrought him a passive, timorous, cowerant, unobtrusive lad who rather chose to skulk in shadows, fearful of the sun. He quailed at confrontations. He hung back, and to help him with the insecurities inherent in that state, like others similarly frail, he looked out for heroes from whom to draw. When he did not find them in abundance, he imputed heroism to key figures in his infantile surround: to Mr. Robbins, Loomis, Mr. Benson. Can you plumb the reason? Pathetic, really, that in such imputation, he could make them reverend and strong, then *borrow back* from them the very strengths he had needed from the start.

Won't compute? A house of cards? Sam's "father image" crumbled. Hard to lionize that man in the face of all his contradictions. Yet Joel tried. Repeatedly. He had the need.

*   *   *

Grandma didn't come down to breakfast one morning. That wasn't too irregular. But when Joel returned from school mid-afternoon, she still had not stirred. And when Lester Priddy rang the doorbell to collect for the paper, and together he and Joel tip-toed up the stairs and found her dead in bed—good grief! Passed on in sleep. Near eighty. Skimpy funeral. Joel went, then packed up and returned to the lake.

He was thirteen, a time of life when baby fat supposedly has given way to muscle mass and fibre—you know, when soft-ish guys become self-conscious and lift weights and jog, work out with barbells, footballs, baseballs, and a secret manual they sent for from Chicago on the promise that ten minutes' daily exercise would make them men. A time when fathers supervise in Little League and take their budding replications fishing, hunting, doing "macho" things, even elbowing their ribs with jokes of girls and blushing double entendres.

How Joel? Look first on him, and later on his father.

Joel grew up. Skinny, meatless, hollow-chested owl, spider-legged with flailing willow stems that hinged upon his torso corners, up and down. Pale and phthisic. Like a youthful Karloff, hovering near death.

Worse yet, he was hopelessly gauche. A disaster. Dyskinesic. Uncoordinated. That was hard because survival in that frozen quadrant of our country demanded combat with the winds, the weather, and Her Majesty, the Sea. A natural selection bred the inhabitants burly, physical, and quick.

Truly! When the junior high clanged out "dismissal," herds of buffalo would thunder down the stairs. Leap them twos and threes. Or hurdle ramparts, swinging, vaulting with their lithe bodies. Liquid, flowing movements—so much reflex. Riding bikes. Like Lester who could pedal with his feet and fold and toss a paper, never breaking stride.

Not Joel. He faltered. Paused. Deliberated. Took steps one by one. On bikes? He shoved off sitting down. Like girls. Do you wonder he was never chosen up for teams? Left there standing. Odd man out.

"I don't care," he lied.

Not much! That is why he used to trail off to the woods and weep. At length he sought solace in his books. In art. In music. Then in poetry, one day.

His hero: Dr. Fred, the only other "intellect" in town, graduate of Yale. Poor little lamb who had lost his way. Started helping out summers, then presumably divorced and moved up "permanent." Some gossip. Big diploma on the wall.

Shelve him for the moment. He comes later. Simply note

Joel loved him, tentatively at first, and would have had him as
his father, if he could.

See Sam, *Pater noster*. Crude. So basic. Crass. Taxicab and
fish. And cuss. So much disdain. So patent his defenses against
deep inferiorities. Sam's was a wasted, useless life. Ask Joel.
Watch him shrug his slender, sloping shoulders. Lobsters, clams,
slaying precious time, a pole between your legs—fie! There were
far better things to do.

Sam used to bait him. "Like what? Like them sissy books
ya always got yer nose stuck inter? You 'n' Dr. Fred, some pair!
Why doncher go to doctor school yerself? So's all them wimmen
lets ya feel their tits up—or stick yer finger in their bottoms.
That wha' cher want? Keep readin' all that sissy junk!"

Sam's principal earnings were generated from his hack.
Summer, give or take a little, ran between the Fourth and Labor
Day. Winters were real slow. As did most of the other indigents,
he set a string of lobster traps up and down the bay then peddled
his catch to markets in the city or to a couple of favorite
customers with whom he had clandestine deals.

Like the Hospital at Fergus. That was a story unto itself.
Account of Jethro, Sam's drinking buddy. Jethro, "clean-up" for
the lab. Original Mr. Step-'n'-fetch-it. Shrewd enough to filch a
dram or two of pure grain alcohol from the huge ten-gallon
bottle, then top the carbuoy back up with distilled water. Nifty
trick. And nip around to the kitchen for a can of fruit juice, then
light out to the copse among the birch, sheltered from the winds.
Hot sun. Balm of Gilead. And the black man sang.

Sam cussed. Funny about spiritus frumenti—brings to the
surface whatever lies lurking underneath. Old Jethro's bitter-
sweet. Sam's mad.

Sam would fume and rant about the tourists and the taxi
business, about how much everything was costing, and Martha.
Growin' old and fat and dumpy. About the ice, the snow. His

having once again to fix that "friggin' stairway," about lobsters runnin' bad, inspectors, taxes. His bread-and-butter issue: Joel, his son, his "one and only." "Only part o' him that's Benedict is like that Arnold guy they tell about. He's turncoat, Jethro, mark my words. That boy's a 'sister.' He's a 'fruitcake.' Got too much Hollister in him is how I figure ... ," and then he would do his coda about the "Jew-man" down in Harpswell "movin' in a fleet of cabs next spring," to cut Sam's "livin'" out.

Mostly Sam handled the "lobsterin'" alone. Help occasionally was available in the person of Mooney, the "idiot boy" who didn't ask many questions, and was "built like a ox."

Ordinarily he would seed eighty or ninety of the open-slat boxes up and down the coast, but when "they were runnin'," Sam paid out a hundred, even more. Then he had to have a second pair of hands.

There was additonal reason: The other fishermen started the "natural way," like Sam, but gradually gave in and mounted winches on their boats; not Joel's daddy. Money, myopia, stubborness, stupidity, whatever, he hung by the tried-and-true technic. Yanked them manually. Up and over, into the starboard quarter abaft the beam. "Don't bother ya 'lessen ya ain't uster it,'" to advertise he was.

And then, one dull, wet, Saturday afternoon, looming in Joel's doorway, speaking at him—no preamble, knock, or pleasantry—"Young Mooney's taken off. I set a hundred twenty traps. How's about ya give yer Dad a help? Go to Harpswell, Ellsworth, Pemaquid. C'n you get outta bed fer four a.m.? I know ya ain't much on that line o' things except it do ya good. Give ya a appetite. Gawd knows ya lookin' peakèd late."

Joel winced. He had been reading the *Ancient Mariner* by odd coincidence. Was it a sign? "An ancient mariner ... but wherefore stopst thou me?" How apt! "Water everywhere." To help Sam out?

He wished. A chord was struck. Was there yet hope of congruence? Could synods still be met? And was it true that he could hang some muscle on his frame, smooth out his motions? Besides there was a beauty to be found at sea. Jack London found it. So too Coleridge, and Conrad, Melville: water, mist, Sam's antediluvian Chrysler engine slipping past the dock. "Putt, putt, putt, putt," then echoless against the morning fog. His father's smoking mixture hanging on the droplets in the air. Wrapping frozen fingers round a warming coffee mug. Sea gulls' cry and beams that creaked. A poetry lay there.

Yes, but Bluebeard! Captain Hook!

Remember Joel, "you're *not* the same as other kids in town." Remember how you got "them hemorrhoids" from straining. Isometrics—for your troubles just one single baleful bulge, down in your groin. A "hernia" was what Fred named it. Besides you know that you can't even start the doggone boat.

"Gawdamighty! Any one-armed half-blind jackass got the wits to give up grindin' it before the juice conks. Ya run my friggin' battery dry, stupid. All ya gotta do is push the stahtah."

There was seaweed everywhere, and slime. The fusel made him bilious. Something in his ears used to go all queasy if he ate—or didn't. Yet it was possible that all Joel's recollections fit the past. Outgrown. Perhaps with effort he could pull the fenders smoothly out and do the necessary to shove off and hop aboard the craft.

Mixed feelings.

Stay home? Another empty day?

To sit alone, perchance to sleep, be bored and restless, reading of the sea *in vitro*—how "the very boards did shrink"— or go to the source "in vivo"? Perhaps acquire a breath of that resurgent inspiration that suffused a Masefield, Homer, or Ulysses ... possibly to register experience. Yes, even from a day of lobstering, accumulate stuff from which to weave a novel or a play.

"What say, Joel? Four a.m.?" Joel hung his head and muttered, "Yes, that's fine."

* * *

Sam left him to his books, heavily trudging off to bed after rummaging about, presumably arranging this and that for their early departure. Joel tried to read but couldn't anymore. Nor did he literally catch one wink of sleep all night.

A hoot owl called. Incessantly. His tinny Mickey Mouse alarm ticked out its merciless tattoo. No slumber came. It might have. Circa two-fifteen, except that Sam came thumping in, his pillow and his blanket trailing after, muttering, "Yer Mother kick me out fer snoring. I'll jus' bunk in here with you."

In seconds he was out, interspersing tortured utterly irregular snorts between the hoot-owl calls until, responding to some inner stimulus, he sat upright and went below to perk the coffee. Four a.m.

Joel smelled the brew and heard it bumping in the pot when he dragged in. And sourdough sliced into man-sized chunks, stacked up, beside the maple syrup in its unmarked can, and butter on the table.

"Syrup. Fuller energy. Ya'll need an aig er two. I'm gonna make us some. Aboard ships cooks is men. This otta do it."

The three eggs spluttered in the fry pan. Once they had congealed slightly, Sam slid them onto the sourdough slices, sunny side, added syrup, salt, and pepper, then evenly divided the concoction into halves with a clam knife from his belt.

"Ya know how I like aigs? Tabasco. That's yer Mexican: Ain't got none. Hot! Here, this here's yers. C'mon."

"I'm really not too hungry," Joel protested, but Sam heard

little of his words. "Won't hit Blue Hill till noon, with luck. Be four o'clock er five before we finish up." With his mackinaw sleeve he wiped a spot of egg yolk off his lip. "Gwan'n eat. We gotta move."

Joel tried. He knew from past experience that food could substitute for sleep. At least a little. He wished he had a heavy sweater underneath his jacket and a pair of worn-in boots. He wished Sam had cared enough to get him some for Christmas, or that once, just once, he might have said, with feeling, "Here, you wear this mackinaw. Don't worry about me."

Instead, "Boy, ya sure got dressed up stupid, Joel. They ain't not time ter change. We gotta run. Let's go."

*   *   *

Gray-black cosmos out of doors. A damp, mysterious, and tender fog enshrouded landmarks. Gentled every contour. Even twelve-fifteen feet ahead lay hazy and obscure. Soft, the raggedy dilapidation of the weather—rough garage. Cheeseclothed, the paint-peelings of its bivalve door.

Joel approached it. Sliding the bent nail out of the latch loop, he folded back the leaflet, loosening the clasp. Then he tugged trying to swing open the resistive boards whose top half made response, but the bottom edge was stuck.

He yanked again.

The door became a fan. It floppered forth and back. "Ya gotta lift it. Christ! Like this!" Impatience spoke.

The door swung clear.

Sealed up in the tinny car, still hopeful, Joel slammed his door with resolution. Luckless kid! It refused to click. He tried again. Sam reached across, annoyed, "Sweet Jesus Joel, ya gotta *mean* it." Slam! The tongue struck into place. Clicked shut for Sam.

Their day was well begun.

At the quai, silent at her moorings, the pudgy little boat kept bobbing up and down. Waves lapped. A fender squeaked. Far off in the mist a muffled buoy-bell. Cotton padding in the air, all cushioned yet by fog.

Sam clomped his lucky bag upon the wharf. Two gas cans thudded down beside it. Then the lunch pail. "Joel, ya gimme these, then yank them fenders 'n' shove off. Ya lemme do the engine." One smooth movement swung him to the deck. He primed the motor, pulled the choke, inveighed against some salty demi-sea-god, then put curses on the weather, wind, and age.

"Rum-ga rum-ga rum," for all his troubles, then commands to Joel to come on board; he needed help. "Friggin' choke head's busted. Get me them pair o' pliers. Inna lazaret. C'mon! Can ya do it, or I gotta leggo here 'n' do it f'r myse'f?"

Joel tried to leap with dexterity. Tried to time his grand jeté to tiny undulations of the craft. Poor clown! His sneaker ticked the beam rail. Damn near fell! Which pliers? Did he mean the monkey wrench or some other oily instrument whose name he interchanged so freely? Do it right Joel, just this once! Don't smell the fusel.

The engine coughed and ran. Joel's father laughed. He praised his trusty, faithful land-built superannuated Chrysler rebored, rebuilt motor. Pulled it from his cab himself. One hundred twenty thousand earth miles. God knows how many hundred leagues at sea. "Sunk'er in the hold single-handed." Took "a 'hol' dang winter," but he did it.

"Putt, putt, putt, putt," slipping past the jetty out into the dappled, thinning haze.

*　　*　　*

From below decks, to a height of sixteen inches above the cabin canopy, unlagged, a rusted old exhaust pipe carried off the hot, unburned gases. Damnably in the way of every movement around the starboard side of the cabin, and terribly tempting to the uninitiate as a pole to cling to in a sea-swell, it demanded conscious energies of Joel, continuously, lest he grab it.

More than once he had got bitten. And knew he would again. No matter how he tried.

Sam?

Reflexly curved around its presence. Even used it. Touched his wooden matchtip to rusty pock marks, bursting them to flame to light his pipe. Or scratch it. Cavalier. At one with its hot dangers. All his movements nonchalant, graceful, strong but apt—the product of some maritime tradition. Generations. Father. Grandfather. Poseidon.

Yet not Joel. How come?

And another question. Was Sam worth the effort? If Joel could conform and dovetail, was it worth the struggle? Even if he got his muscles, did he want them? Did he want to be a merman to do battle with the fish? Did Martha have the answers? Did Grandma? Mooney? Lester Priddy? Loomis? Mayben? Was there anyone or anything in town to justify a fight? Battling up against the currents? What the dividend? Reward?

When Sam lay mouldering and dead. Did Joel want this boat? Sam's cab? His boots? More questions. Dizzying. Annoying. Irresolvable. Assailing him that long long day between the shoals of Ellsworth and Webhannet Bay.

*   *   *

Twelve hours. Gray to crystal clear. Along the ragged coastline. In and out. Blue Hill. Pejepscot. Spot the buoy. Idle

up. Hook the rope, then pull, pull, pull. Strings of sea slime.
There's the box! What's in it? Tug!

Up and over. In.

Water's running out.

A bunch of crabs!

Okay!

Again.

A lobster! Better yet! Another in the net.

Forty, fifty, sixty traps by noon.

They ate (Sam did).

Hot coffee from his thermos. That felt good! Fish taste.
Fish smell.

Start the engines! Wells, Ogunquit Yarmouth. "Toss,
them babies back. No, that one's long enough. Here! Measure!
Use my gauge. No, Joel! Get the rhythm. Slap the fucker in yer
apron. Get the motion of it. Grab a peg 'n' shove it in 'er claw.
Don't trust 'er. Watch it! Nipped ya, ha, ha, ha! No, Joel. Ya
gotta slap that fucker in between yer legs like this. Sweet Jesus
Christ! Yer standin' like yer pissin' up a rope. Like this! Like
me."

Forty, fifty, sixty pinioned lobster claws at last. Their
exoskeletons. A growing pile of spindly shellfish parts: antennae,
eyes, and claws. Until back sore, bone weary, drooping lids, up
the back door stairs at last and in. Scant energies enough to fall
upon the mattress, yet enough to forge one ironbound resolve:

His life and Sam's would evermore diverge.

That inchoate awareness cut him from his obligations and
enveloped him in dreams.

*   *   *

"That was the last time that I tried to make it with my
father. It was hopeless. We're of different worlds. I watched

him welding once—two metal pieces, but the solder didn't take. It looked good momentarily, then broke apart. Both pieces were unaffected by all the heat and effort. There was no lasting result.

"Oh sure, I know about ambivalence. How do I mean? Well, last year he got sick. I expected him to die. I called. I wrote. Yes, you could say I 'cared,' but only within certain well defined limits. I cared about his condition in the way I cared about the razing of my old grade school. No, that's a poor example. More like the twinge of nostalgia I got reading about the Ellsworth dump, with sort of an acknowledgement that I was familiar with it, even if it's rather loathsome."

"You didn't spend more time with him?"

"Hardly. Not when I could avoid him. I dove into my books. Read everything that I could get my hands on. Poetry, drama. I haunted the library. Once I had started down the divergent path there was simply no return. Then I began to recognize how almost everything in his style of living was alien and repugnant. All of it disenchanted me even further."

"Go on."

"I made my own life ... pretty much."

"I see."

"It was lonely, but I managed."

"Yuh."

"I didn't thrive. I survived."

"Go on."

"Well, that says it."

"Okay. And what more?"

"Are you suggesting that I'm holding something back?"

"Are you?"

"I feel tight."

"What are your thoughts?"

"Something utterly ridiculous. That maybe I had more affection for my father than I realized."

"Did you?"

"Blank."

"Blank?"

"It's as if something dropped out of the script."

"Say what you can."

"What I'm thinking is ridiculous."

"Say it."

"It has no relevance at all."

"We'll see."

"Okay. When I drove up I noticed that you'd fredilized—oops!—I mean fertilized your lawn."

"And?"

"Well, alright, I was talking about missing my father with the same nostalgia as I'd feel about the local dump. He 'crapped' all over me. Is that it?"

"I doubt it. I mean your association is undeniably valid. There's no such thing as a 'nonassociation,' but I thought I heard something else too."

"My slip?"

"Your slip."

"I tried to say 'fertilizer.' It didn't come out that way."

"No, it didn't."

"What did it sound like to you?"

"You tell me first."

"Fretilizer."

"What could that mean?"

" 'Fret.' A 'fret' is a worry, a rub, a stop on an instrument, isn't it? On a guitar? Oh I don't know! What is it? Fret, don't fret; it's a rub.

" 'Ay. There's the rub.' "

"Hamlet—'to sleep. Perchance to dream. Perchance to dream. Ay, there's the rub.' Alright, Hamlet. So what am I saying?"

"I don't know, but whatever it is, it's full of resistance."

"As you've told me. I'm 'treading water.' "

"Yes."

"Why?"

"Let's find out. You made a slip. You said 'fredilized.' When I called you on it you took an 'evasive action' and called it 'fretilizer,' then you started to throw red herrings across our path. Mind, they're all significant enough, I suspect, but I'm after a 'bigger fish.' "

" '*Fred*ilized.' You know, to be perfectly honest I thought that I said that too."

"It sounded pretty clear."

"Well, there is something I'm resisting."

"Are you?"

"Yes, I am."

"What stops you?"

"Feelings. If I weren't lying here so helplessly, at this point I'd light up a cigarette."

"Just speak your thoughts."

"I want to smoke. I crave one. It's dreadful, really strong. I imagine that if you wanted to, you could let me. I mean mechanically. All I'd have to do is twist a little. I could hold the ashtray on my chest. What is the reason you forbid it on the couch?"

"I never forbade you."

"That's true. Actually. But you told me it might be better to forbear. To acknowledge the craving and analyze it rather than to 'act it out.' "

"Right."

"Well it's here! Smoke, suck. In, pull, cocks. 'Martha, see the lighthouse?' Pricks. Lollipops. Beautiful young lollipops. Standing at the freeway ramps. I saw the most gorgeous young man yesterday standing at the Vanalden entrance. Rugged. Curly

hair. Blond. Clean. Tight jeans. I stared at his 'basket.' My
God, I wanted him ... this hurts...."

"Go on!"

"I wanted to take him home. I find this awkward. I wanted
to take him home with me and bathe him, touch him, kiss his
body. I wanted to hug his head.... My God. I'm hurting. Oh,
this sounds dreadful, out of context."

"What happened?"

"I was headed East. By the time I turned around he was
gone. Someone else had picked him up. They don't wait long. It
felt like this when I would need a drink. If I weren't here right
now, I'd probably call A.A."

"And?"

" ... and it's been so ... so long between 'loves.' Too long.
Funny, that boy reminded me of someone. He looked sheepish,
forlorn, like a little lost lamb. Sheepskin. Diploma. Oh, Jesus!
No! I can't ... I know I have to. He reminded me of *Fred*, Dr.
Fred, our town physician. Have I ever mentioned him? Of course
I have. A poor little sheep who had 'gone astray.' I think he
came to stay in Maine once he got divorced. Funny that I never
learned. More bones in the graveyard. I don't even know if he's
alive."

"Fred?"

"Fred, Dr. Fred."

" 'Fred' and 'lying there.' 'Fredilizer?' "

"Oh my Gawd!"

Fred

By the time arrangements had been made for Joel to
register in school at Arlington, the emotional distances between
him and the major dramatis personae in his life had grown
beyond all bridging. Sam had almost killed the boy in a violent

dispute over the meagre legacy his Grandma had left him, ear-marked for education. "Out of town."

Pundit Dr. Fred, doubling as a kind of legal counsel (after stitching up Joel's eye), sounded reason's voice—which maneuver wrecked forever any vestige of rapport he ever held with Sam, but deepened his with Joel.

Seesaw. Marjorie Daw. Up here. Down there.

So Arlington for aye. Boola boola boo.

Arlington Prep. Shuffle the deck. Change his luck.

Sometimes, surely, it is possible that a lesser remedy succeeds. A new hat. A vacation. A change of scene. Depression's physic might be found therein. Might blunt its bite, its constant low-keyed gnaw.

If only he could plumb the object of its search. Joel tried. He read. Surcease was brief in books. He studied. Some small distractions came. He prayed for genies in glass bottles to come washing up on shore, to lift him in gigantic skyward arcs beyond the mire below.

He wrote. Notes in his journal. Depicted his wrenching agonies as "mordant," "hungry," "angry," "lonely and relentless," struggling ever to define the contour of his hell, unaware those days that having failed to drown it, drug it, numb it, reason it away, he would slash both wrists with misdirected stabs to slay it—and would fail at even that.

Eternal hope.

Matriculation.

Arlington.

Application papers. Fee: Ten simoleons, drawn from his trustee bank account. A one-page character reference. A history and physical examination. His willing local medical doctor, accessible. No fuss.

Does it seem strange that phoning for an appointment would have been excessive? Fred was in or out—that simple. His was a very casual, basic practice. There or gone. His cardboard clock left dangling from the doorknob let any caller know when he would return. No beeper, phonemate, secretary.

Oh yes, he had a nurse on the ready, Mrs. Priddy, Lester's mother. She was "part-time." Now and then. Living with her teenage son next door, in widowhood, she welcomed any opportunity to service the practitioner—on demand. She had use for money. The flexibility much suited. Even days when she assisted "heavy" she could still nip over back to monitor her cooking and her home. She kept Fred's books besides.

She knew as much about his past and present as did anyone around. Which wasn't a great deal. Sparse and pithy his allusions to his former life. One sensed a bitterness, suspicioned a remorse.

Fred was not going to kill himself with toil. He painted, read, walked through the woods, wrote papers now and then and delivered them to his colleagues at conventions "up in Boston" and New York. He made trips to libraries in Portland if he wished. Good physician—educated, kind, attentive, known by every soul for miles around, and comfortable under the mantle of responsibility imposed on those who modulate the throes of life and death.

His negatives? Folks ragged him for his knowledge of the arts. Slightly suspect as was anyone who quoted Wilde or Whitman, while suturing.

*   *   *

Joel rang the pull-out doorbell. "Hello!"

"Hello. I'm home," the echo answered.

"Are you busy?"

"Not for you. Come in—not too, really. How're you doin' Joel? What's up?"

Fred laid the green-covered periodical on the desk. He had

been sipping something colorless and clear and unmistakably identifiable as alcohol. "What are *you* reading these days?"

"Branch Cabell."

"You finished with Molière?"

"I guess."

Le Médecin malgré Lui, Fred mumbled, somewhat distantly.

"Pardon?"

"Oh, nothing, just a twit of self-indulgence and showing off."

"Would you pronounce it one more time?"

Médecin malgré Lui. Doctor in spite of himself, the victim practitioner."

"I read it, but I didn't know its original title. I also read *Tartuffe.*"

"Don't mind my mood. Say Joel, you're as hung up on the classics as I am. Are you sure you're just starting high school? You'll kill 'em."

Joel flushed. How sweet to be so flattered. Understood. Encouraged.

"Stick with them. They endure. The classics I mean."

"I know."

"Yessir, you're quite a youngster, Joel.

"Know what? I'd bet, excepting you and me, there's no one in a forty-mile radius who's ever heard the names the two of us just mentioned. Even having an enlightened conversation. Morons! Aagh—forgive me. I'm just pitying myself I guess ... and *à propos* morons, if you will indulge me one more solecism— your father, Joel. That man! You know I had to twist his arm to free you up for school. Boy, he's something!"

"Not a 'Bourgeois Gentilhomme,'" Joel smirked.

"Touché! No, although he's half-way one, *bourgeois.*"

Joel beamed.

"What brings you skulking through my premises on Saturday 'on little catlike feet?'"

"Carl Sandburg. 'Fog.'"

"Right! Good boy! "'The fog comes creeping in,' eh? Is there anything you haven't read?"

Joel literally swelled with youthful pride. "I've brought these papers." Producing the bulky envelope from the book satchel he so often carried, he unsheathed the blank sheets labeled, "History and Physical Exam."

"What's that?" Fred asked.

"For school. I'm leaving in two weeks."

"So soon?"

"Yessir!"

"Well, that's bully for you. I'll miss you. The town's collective I.Q. is going to suffer. Count on it!"

"I'll miss you too," Joel managed, choking slightly, suspecting that his visage must have turned beet-red. And there it hung momentarily, until resolving the awkwardness, within the bounds of full propriety, Fred clasped the youngster's hand and pumped it, then found Joel's slender shoulder muscle, which he kneaded gently, searching, seeking words.

And was it strange that Fred then circled Joel's small superstructure in a hug? A fatherly, aseptic momentary clutch? It gave only confirmation that he cared—intellectually, clinically, of course. But what was that he quoted in a whisper, and from where?

" ... speranza ... che entrate?" ... blankly peering into space.

"Did you say something?" Joel started.

But instead of verbalizing, the older man reached around behind him to procure a bottle standing on his instrument tray. His movement faltered slightly. Strange tools of the trade. A bottle standing amidst napkins, scalpels, gauze.

He double-checked its contents, then from it, calculatedly, into an empty glass cylinder, graduated with equidistant little horizontal lines its full extent, he poured precisely sixty milliliters, finishing off the gesture with hauteur, raising high in the air the slender liquid string. It ended in a drop.

"I keep a very accurate account of how much I use this way. Grog ration. Like any good God-fearin', sea-farin' man. My quotidian allowance. It cuts the salt, it does."

"Dissolves the barnacles," Joel offered sportingly, quoting Sam.

"You see these lines? One cubic milliliter each. Read the meniscus. See it? Sixty cubic centimeters. Metric."

Joel asked, "Is that a double shot?"

"Bull's eye!" Fred responded, " 'Double, double, toil and trouble.' 'Twining, twinscrew turbines!' to mix a metaphor. At Yale they claimed that if you could say that without a square knot in your tongue you could go on drinking.

"Yup. It's a double shot. Ever tippled, Joel? I mean just between the two of us?"

"Once," the youngster whispered. "Sam's scotch. Tasted like turpentine. Burned. I can't see much in it really. Besides, it's hard for me to be objective. I mean the way he gets so stupid and abusive—but I didn't mean to moralize with you."

"No offense. I know my limits. Alcohol. Arabic word, Joel. It used to signify a kind of make-up that the women painted on their eyes. Collyrium. It's a medicine. It's a drug. Almost a universal one: it's antiseptic, analgesic, an hypnotic, I mean it puts you to sleep—nutritious—name it! Oh, you can't get fat on alcohol. Not itself, but it spares the other calories you eat. Turns *them* to fat.

"Funny stuff though. You drink it and it gives you license to let out whatever's lurking. Me? I get maudlin, sentimental. Feel it now.

"I start delving into the past. Oh shit! You need a history and physical exam, you say?"

"I do, but what you said is true. Sam gets cruel. As if that's always lying underneath his surface. I tried one last time to be a kind of son to him. He needed help with pulling traps. He got blind drunk by the time that we got home. That ended it. I'll never offer again. Of course, there was much more."

"There always is. You want to whet your whistle?"

"To join you in a drink? I guess I should learn. Oh, I don't know ... "

"One libation for the road as it were? To Arlington. There's a can of fruit juice in the frig. That cuts it down."

"Okay, but just a drop."

"Use this beaker. You don't even have to rinse it out. Like I told you: antiseptic. Don't bother you, does it, Mr. Norton's urine was in it?"

Joel grinned. He really loved to banter with this man, he did.

Fred took a little sip, kissing the rim of the cylinder with tiny pursed-up lips. "You had better learn to hold your liquor. Prep school, eh? Well, you'll knock 'em on their round and rosy asses, Joel. By Christ, I hope you do. You need some little victories, I guess. Arlington, eh? Didn't I read something in the *Chronicle* about two 'townies' got arrested for fermenting garbage into schnapps?"

Joel laughed aloud. Had he the right to flirt with happiness? How delicious when it came.

"Well, well, this history's a cinch." Fred glanced at the printed captions, then turned the paper over. "I delivered you. I know everything you ever had. Roseola, rubella. Did you know you had 'exanthem subitum,' my boy? Well, it's not as awful as its name. Mostly spots 'n' fever."

Fred was rambling in a mildly euphoric way.

"I could even make this out against your future, know that Joel? Statistics. 'We don't know who, but we do know how many are going to die, and of what.' Big insurance tables. Actuarial. Damn! It looks as if I've gotta do some lab work. Yessiree! And examine you. Jesus Christ they're getting fussy 'up in Boston.'

"Cephalin flocculation! VDRL! I can't fluff those. I'm gonna have to draw some blood. Better take your shirt off. Ever had V.D? Yikes! Better take it all off, son. You see that johnny? Go behind the screen and put it on, okay?"

Moving smoothly, Fred stepped over to the autoclave. Depressing its outer lever arm, he opened its lid and raised up its sieve-like tray. A wisp of steam emerged. From the assortment made thus accessible, he selected a large-bore needle and syringe parts. Careful to keep everything sterile, he locked the needle hub in place with a twist, then slid the ground glass plunger home into the outer half of the glass cylinder.

"There, this ought to do it, free and easy are you?" As he worked the surfaces against each other several times, "Sometimes they get frozen stuck." In and out, back and forth.

Joel watched.

He watched from behind his curtain. Curiosity? Fear of needles?

Was some simple silly question on his mind—about the johnny? Or yet more?

He watched the plunger slide itself back out, and in.

"Gotta keep it sterile while you test it. Ready Joel?"

He picked a cotton pledget from a jar, squeezed it semi-dry, and lay the hypodermic on it. He then took a test tube from a rack and shook it up and down. The crystals in its bottom jiggled loose. Fred scrutinized the label on it, holding it a full arm's length away.

"See how your arms get shorter Joel, with age? I guess I'm ready for bifocals any day."

"Doesn't that happen to us all?" asked Joel as he stepped sheepishly beyond the screen.

"It varies," Fred pontificated, drawing once again from the double shot left standing on the tray. "I sort of hoped I'd fight the monster off a while," upon which words he tipped the tubular receptacle again, still faced away from Joel. "Don't I remember that you were starting on a hernia back when? Oh sure, you were. See here? They ask that. Well, we'll check it."

"I'm all ready," Joel replied, still hanging back slightly.

Fred turned.

He roared.

"Oh Jesus Joel, you're precious! Forgive me. You might as well have come out 'bollicky.' You've put that johnny on totally backwards, and besides, you could have kept your shorts. Oh my! Oh my, my, my. You have grown up, haven't you? When did all that happen, overnight?"

Joel choked.

"Oh, forget me. Don't be bashful. I do this all the livelong day. It's just ... I didn't realize so long had passed since your last exam. You're quite a man, er, youngster, aren't you? Yessiree!"

"I guess." This time Joel sipped from his beaker. "Shall I put my shorts back on?"

"No, never mind. C'mere. C'mere. Here, face the window. Look at this flashlight. Now follow my fingers. Good. Here! See them wiggle? Okay, up and down and in and out! Good! Say 'aaagh!' No, open wide, wide, wide."

Did Joel hear the doctor falter? Slur a word? Somewhere on the wires of his internal abacus were beads of alcohol sliding over, adding, multiplying? Dame Nature never drops a single stitch nor loses the perfection of her count.

A universal drug. Elixir. Bathing now the central nervous cells and lulling them, beguiling them, about to lift the veil.

A routine physical. How many hundred had he logged in his career? They could be done and well with half a waking mind. Need proof? Had he not managed to, exhausted on the wards? O.B? Emergency? Or in the service where they marched them past in droves? World War Two?

"I'm gonna check your eye grounds, son. A funduscopic. Pick a spot and fix it. Over there. Got it? No, don't move. Again."

And then did Joel imagine what transpired, or was it possible that eye-to-eye and cheek-to-cheek, Fred lingered? That his stubble rubbed the youngster's peach fuzz with a message? A caress? Was brushing back and forth this way "routine?"

Cologne?

Or was it alcohol?

How could he hope to know? So few in all his life the men who had come so close. What if—but only in conjecture—if the two of them had been conjoined on some other purpose? In a friendship? Seeking warmth. In an embrace. It felt so good, so good.

Oh God!

Forget that Joel! Forget it now! Control, control it, Joel. Don't think of that. Think something else! Please God! Oh no! Not here! Not now. Fred's going to see it standing up.

And that it was. Full-turgid. Totally beyond the point of no return. His member. At attention. On the ready. Firm, erect, like an animal whose leash would never hold it—straining to be longer, fuller. Huge. Pulsating. Ripe.

"Hey, what's with you, son?" Fred started. "Did I press a button that I shouldn' a'? Jesus, Joel, your heart is racing. You alright? You chug-a-lug that drink? Is that what pulled your trigger? Don't go off."

And mortally embarrassed, struggling for composure, groping for a word, a toe-hold, anything at all, Joel nearly swooned. He could not suppress the realization that within seconds Fred's clean, cool hands, the ones he wanted now so badly on him, would reach below and touch his penis. For hernias. To retract his full-retracted foreskin as before. Syringe! The in and out. The back, the forth.

Would touch and linger on his private parts the way a doctor must, but more. Some stronger feeling. A feeling he had dreamt of. By himself. At night. So strong. Compelling—utter tidal wave. High-cresting. Surging, bursting out. Directing him through channels, over cliffs, down an abyss.

To touch, to rub, to fricate to a heat, to fondle, hug, embrace, insert, to mouth, to kiss, to suck, to eat!

This man!

When it did unfold he saw it just as if it happened to another. Someone else apart who took the elder's unresistive hand and wrapped it, willingly, around his member. Gently, gently, pushing back and forth, then, guided by some knowing unknown force reaching out for its counterpart in Fred.

Yes, there, and hard!

Enormous behind the zipper.

Let it flower.

Unfold petals.

Peel it out.

Proud pistil, stamen.

Joy!

Exquisite!

What salt tears!

Dizzy. Stop! Don't stop!

Oh Glory be! How long!

Oh kiss it! Hug it! Stroke it on your tongue. Embrace it. Bite it. Devour it!

Together they were done. Joel left for Arlington next day.

*   *   *

"That started me on my career, or should I say 'infection?'
As guilty as I was, I loved every second of that contact. I loved
Fred. It wasn't really sexual. He was accessible, responsive. I
don't know how to describe it. Both of us were ready for
something that ... precipitated out at that point.

"I have thought of that incident a thousand times. I doubt
that Fred was 'gay.' Maybe I reminded him of a son he never
had, or of himself.

"He was the only person I had ever got close to in fifteen
years, except my Grandmother—sort of. She had some warmth,
remotely.

"But here I am talking about homosexuality. I didn't really
intend to. I'm committed pretty much to my style of life. I don't
propose to change that. Just this damned depression!"

"What if both are two sides of the same coin?" I queried.

"I was afraid you'd ask that sooner or later."

"Well?"

"I don't know. But I don't understand. I mean the love
affairs I've had have been so positive. Not depressing. Excuse my
banality, but 'You're the doctor.' Do what you must. Okay, you
want to know my thoughts, I know. Love. I skip around. Love.
Homosexual love is more 'pure.' Ugh women! The purest form
of love is homosexual."

"I don't understand you," I responded in earnest.

"I mean ... it means ... well, I can't explain it accurately
except I've heard it said, argued. Are you suggesting that I'm
rationalizing or intellectualizing?"

"Are you?"

"Oh, Jesus! I suppose so. You are relentless! Intellectualizing what? Don't you grant anything at all? Must you analyze everything? I've told you rock-bottom truths about myself. What could be left?"

"We'll see, but first, please, you use the term 'homosexual' quite often. Actually what *do* you mean by it?"

"Queer, gay. Oh you're looking for a deeper psychoanalytic bit, are you? Not just the cock-sucking part, eh?"

"You seem to use the expression rather globally, loosely."

"Well, would you want to define it for me?"

"Yes. To your surprise I shall. Because I suspect that it's imperative for us to comprehend, and to concur. If you follow my definition it could lead to a fuller understanding of yourself. I'll be overly simple; do realize that, and that things can get very abstruse too.

"I consider homosexuality a form of developmental arrest. Are you familiar with that term?"

"I think," Dr. Benedict replied.

"Or as a 'regression.' *That* I'm sure you've heard. I'll begin at the beginning. I picture the newborn mind as 'asexual.' Fleetingly, like an unstable sub-atomic particle. Almost immediately thereafter, and then for a sustained period, it directs its 'loving' energies upon itself. Narcisstically, it focuses on the self. The asexual evolutes to autosexual. Follow?

"The baby mind doesn't even know or conceptualize the existence of anything out there beyond itself. It can't delineate where *it* ends and the environment begins. It's all 'me.' 'Me hunger.' 'Me be fed.' 'Me wet.' 'Me be changed.' 'Me tired.' 'Me sleep.' Babies don't realize (we imagine) that nipples or the bottles aren't as much a part of themselves as their own thumbs—and about as much under their control.

"It's a narcisstic world, totally.

"But, for some reason a growth force impels us toward

altruism—altruism at the polar extreme—awareness of 'otherness,' the 'nonme.' Have you read Buber? *I—Thou?*

"Anyhow, the distance to altruism is enormous. It has to be accomplished in stages. One of the first is a transitional phase in which we discover self-like objects in creatures other than ourselves. As I love myself, I can love the reflection of myself in someone outside who is not myself. That's important.

"And there's a bonus—a convenience. Two people struggling that way, identically, can be mutually helpful. They can reciprocate and assist each other."

"Do you mean physically?"

"I could. Yes. If we restrict our consideration to the physical aspects only."

"Does that explain why—Gawd, I blush to tell you this—but, well, I used to try awfully hard to get my own penis into my mouth. I couldn't. Once when I was doing 'sixty-nine,' I flashed back to that memory and it occurred to me that my partner may have had the same frustrated ambition.

"We were sort of helping each other out."

"Exactly! But do you see the narcisstic root? And the transitional? You were making love, and so was he, to yourself—and him."

"I see, sort of."

"What you have told me with so much embarrassment is not unique. Actually about three percent of males can accomplish autofellatio. It's a terribly lonely game. Pathetically self-contained. Risks a person's struggling toward friendships and psychic growth."

"You mean it's less than 'sixty-nine.'"

"More like 'zero,' if you want to pun."

"Well, I see what you mean, theoretically, now that you point it out."

"Yes, but I want to carry it further. I would like you to recognize how altruism or its counterpart, heterosexuality, would not necessarily be a permanent attainment. Varied pressures imposed from above, or pulls from below, can make a person regress."

"Lose ground, so to speak, or tumble?" Benedict asked.

"Well said! In fact, I often conceptualize the process as a four- or five-story building with a penthouse. That's maturity on top. Genital heterosexuality, selfless, altruistic love—but to have got there gives no guarantee that you'll stay."

"I have never heard it presented quite that way before. I follow you. Parts of what you've explained I've been exposed to—I mean about regression. And it's true. When I'm too much alone I get hypochondriacal. That's narcissistic. And I masturbate."

"Down to the basement, eh?"

Dr. Benedict laughed. It was a pleasant response, mixed with the satisfaction of having understood, and relief over his masturbation confession—but he continued in a manner that appeared to reverse that positive trend.

"Should I feel any less depressed for understanding? I don't. I'll think over what you have explained. But don't expect me to change. Women are still ... disgusting. I could never touch one again. I was married as you know. Ha! My real loves were 'on the side'—men."

"You have told me."

"I could never think of warming to a girl. Uh, uh. Narcissistic, eh? I'll have to think that over."

Hawker

* Arlington. Another world. One hundred-fifty miles from home and yet so strange. Stepped through the looking glass.

Teeming with people, traffic. Metal monster street cars.

People. Buses. People. Ever bent on getting somewhere in a hurry. Always carrying. In trucks, on bicycles, in shopping bags, in packages.

The climate? Well, the seasons were the same, yet summer's heat was different—sultry, humid. Utterly unwelcome. Soaring temperatures made sticky liquids trickle underarm and shirts that clung. Clung in damp ellipses on the backs of walkers, sitters, standers. And stifling. Lifeless breezes that brought no relief. Nor any from the sudden showers falling from a sky shimmeringly clear and blue scant minutes earlier.

And fall? Different too. Its winds were smoky, dusty, pollenaceous.

Winters? Not like home at all. No, not at all. The snow drifts were a menace. Dirty, gray. Impediments. A nuisance to be cleared as quickly as the ploughs could push them off.

And spring? Restricted to a scattered dozen linden trees in leaf along Joel's dreary route to school—and in his yard, a single lilac and a rose bush. Humph, some spring!

But studies came with ease. Alas, not friendships.

With the unexpected swiftness and the devastation of a thunderbolt, a fulminant and rare leukemia, monocytic, cut Joel's roommate down. Joel visited Bruce once only. In the hospital. He saw him, bag-of-bones, struggling for breaths, his last, inside a plastic tent of oxygen. Dead in three short weeks! That was a shock.

And yet, there were advantages to living all alone: his things could lie there, undisturbed, somewhat like the stopping of a motion picture on a single frame. Frozen his researches into Robert Graves. No need to clear the table of the index cards or references from the library. Turned to page eighteen, his half-completed honors theme for Dr. Hawker, by the breakfast dishes. Casual this way, and he could start the film again precisely where he had left it. When he wished.

Close on Hawker: Try to see him. Conjure up a bachelor. Tweedy. Fortyish. Leather elbow patches on his jacket and a flap, slits on either side. Spare build, scant shoulder padding, long, narrow shoes with buckles. Don't forget the pipe.

Hear him? High-pitched nasal tones? Hyperarticulate. His every *mot* precise. Well schooled to turn a phrase. He literally peppered Joel's papers with them: *Bravissimo* or *multa bene!* Now and then, *Excelsior!* to urge the youngster on, and finally, for Joel's last effort, "Please contact me for a conference at your convenience."

Hawker smoked a private blend concocted by the tobacconist near school. He liked a meerschaum. His tastes in music ran to classical (of course) and favored Telemann and Bach. Athletics? Tennis with Doug Sanders from Biology—and good.

Need yet a little more?

In winter he wore scarves. No overcoat. Enormous brightly colored wools. Hand-knit.

That ought to say it. Let us get back to Joel. His thesis? E.E. Cummings. A critique.

* * *

It was Saturday around eleven in the morning. He had slept until ten, then wandered to the square. Somewhere in the back of his mind was the notion that by now the themes would be corrected and available at Simpson House, each in its numbered box.

He could eat as he perused his paper, also Hawker's comments on it, if any.

It was there: In red, an "A" across its top. "You have fine sensitivity for Cummings. Please contact me for a conference at your convenience."

Another victory, wahoo!

Small pickings all those other snobbish dumb rejections! Hawker liked him. He wanted then and there to call. Why not? At least to set up an appointment. He'd die a thousand deaths by Tuesday and the class. Hawker, Hawker, Hawker! Splendid sort of man.

* * *

At the corner of North and Linden streets, next door to Agate Books, beside the twenty-four-hour laundromat, Haggerty's Bar! Run-down, bordering on insolvency, its policy increasingly grew liberal insofar as challenging the ages of its clientele. The boss served all alike: halt, hale, young, old. There, in a dark and high-backed booth, his monograph before him, page by precious page, Joel read and sipped a beer.

Nay, line by line and word by word. How hard he had toiled. Every phrase was good. Each fitted, truly well. Hawker was responsive. Super! Maybe he would do a spot of writing, or become a critic, or a poet—time would tell.

"Bites this universe in two!" There was an image. "Dawn of a doom of a dream." Could he write as crazily as Cummings who lived nearby in Cambridge? Was it possible that Hawker knew him? Glory, glory, glory! Beer, beer, beer. "Peels forever out of its grave and sprinkles nowhere with me and you."

Transcendent, resplendent, magic!

The youngster credited himself with adequate sensitivity. He had experienced pain. All poets must have suffered ... yes, he was qualified. Yet what if he had been born to other folks? Suppose that Einstein had emerged amidst the Maori? Or in the Bush? Or Tanganyika? Would *his* genius have shone forth? Was Joel then lucky to have moved to Arlington from Maine? Could Sam and Martha—could all the shackles of his childhood dungeon, those days in Hell, be turned to his advantage?

Lobsters, hernias, the morons of his youth? Hope springs. And
Fred?

He gasped a guilty gasp. Ah well ... he would not return to
Maine. Ever. *"You can't go home again,"* he mused. No,
nevermore. No, "croaked the raven, nevermore!"

He resurrected Bruce. Leukemia. Struck down. *Vita brevis.*
Yes, it was. Why Bruce? Would Bruce have been a friend, a
lover? Thoughts again of Maine and Dr. Fred, and then a call to
Haggerty to bring "another round."

Yes, Joel would toast the audience—except, he was alone.
As usual. The beer was painless, pure Nepenthe, in the cool and
dark.

Regrets? Had Wilde not said it? That the only things in all
his life he would repeat were his regrets? Repeat. Repeat. So,
what regrets?

Had Bruce regrets? Or Grandma? Or Miss Bleek's hanged
sister? Jesus! Maybe Fred was right. A thimbleful of beer and
here he was, all muddled and sentimental. Twining, twinning,
turbans, turbines. Maybe he would be wise to leave the bar and
go lie down. No, he'd be fine. Focus, focus hard on the report.
"All nothing's only our hugest home ... the more we die ... "
"We die," said Joel. "We die."

He would be better off to eat a bite, and soon.

He quaffed the beer. "Mudlucious." "Puddle-wonderful."
"Eddieandbill." Crazy Cummings. Well, Sam was crazy too.
Who wasn't if he drank enough? Or ... crazy ... yes, it would be
crazy to ... and yet ... *why not?* Regrets? How tempting. Phone
Hawker now! Ring him up in the pay booth. He could be in.
Well, well, well, well, now look at that. His address. Right on
Linden Street. About two blocks. At Elm, most likely. Why not?
Why not? Why not?

Joel watched a depersonalized self rise up and chug-a-lug
his beer. How fine! His synchrony was smooth. Slide. Glide.

Don't drink if driving. Drunk don't drive. Jive drunk. This dive.
Ha ha! Cummings!

Hawker! Two short blocks, 440 Linden. On the left.

Sunlight, bright and harsh, assaulted the youth. It hurt his
eyes, forcing definitions on him and repeating its demands. Two
beers for breakfast in the damp dank pit of Haggerty's had
utterly unhinged him for an outdoor stint. Just maintain.
Maintain. Elm Street. Linden. Odds *were* on the left. Go on.

Graceful linden trees actually lined the sidewalk. The day
was growing warm. Mottled patches of relief where clustered
leaves were filtering the sun. Patterns in concrete. Patterns on
the tar. A "Little lame balloonman, far and wheeeeee."

Walk straighter, Joel. Maintain.

Sam's voice: "Shit-faced drunk!" Fred's voice: "Antiseptic,
analgesic. If you ever drink too much, breathe oxygen, that
burns it." Deep, deep breaths—but they brought dizziness and
nausea. Just maintain.

Wisdom would have called the lad a taxi. Sent him home
to bed. To sleep. Detoxify. Return refreshed. But youth is
known more for its impatience than its wisdom. Joel gathered up
his forces and moved on.

"R. Hawker" was printed in artistic scroll—like longhand
across a tinted name-tag, slid behind a celluloid cutout. Beside it
was a bakelite bell button, black, centered in a round brass cuff.

Even to his fuzzy, shifting perception, it was clear that
buttons set in cuffs like that were breasts. Nipples. Black clams.
Did Joel dare to touch? To push it in? He watched his finger
moving through the air.

"Buzz."

"Buzz." The moving finger moved then rang again.

A garbled squawking voice came from the brass meshwork
of the speaking tube above: "Who's there?"

Joel fumbled. "Dr. Hawker?"

"Yes?"

"It's Joel, Dr., Joel Benedict. One of your students. A conference. You said to ... conference with you."

"Who?"

Neither made further reply for an instant. Joel had drained the utmost of his concentration to achieve those scant remarks. Hawker? Probably beguiled or puzzled in his rooms upstairs.

Then the striker plate began to "click! click! click," indicative that whosoe'er the caller was, he now must push the huge glass door to pass on through. Joel lurched. He shoved. The door swung in.

Ah, dark again. His senses returned to him, aligned his wishes and his acts. Back in control. Breathe deeply. A smell like creosote. Some oily cleaning agent? Enough of that would turn his stomach, sure ... ai! What was Hawker's number. Was he certain? 2-B? 2-A? Joel grasped the newel as a door above came open. A mellow voice called, "Hullo, up here!"

The voice continued. "Benedict! How unexpected. And how nice. Come up."

*   *   *

Hawker's "digs" were rather unusual. Books stood everywhere. They lined the walls, lay on tables, some in piles or clusters, open, markers sticking out of pages. Papers. Signs of busy writing, reading, work. Yet not untidy. Not at all. The hugest volumes anchored down the lowest shelves: Art books. "Plates," according to their titled spines, of much reknowned impressionists. Medium-sized volumes at the level of the shoulder. Easy reach. Every color, binding, size. On top, both perpendicular and wedged in niches, horizontal, brightly jacketed, the paperbacks. So Hawker was a reader, a literary man!

And yet, as much as books predominated, centered, precisely where it best might catch the glance, hung an oriental tapestry on black velvet, depicting in its white relief a dancing unicorn—horn-proud and darting eye. How smart!

And plants! Hanging from the ceiling. See, Hawker had obtained an alchemist's retort. Sphere-bellied, with its neck a tapered arch, suspended on a ring of cork, as if it hung on air and in it, hydroponic stuffs, not dirt, and sprigs of philodendron, trailing out and winding up and down. Resplendent work of art!

And statues. David there, by Michaelangelo. Oh lovely boyish nude! And lighted by a spot. From where?

"How nice of you to visit! Do come in. Aha, you brought your thesis."

"You wrote that I should contact you," Joel managed, gaining slightly in his struggle to be poised. "Is it alright? I found it hard to have to wait till Tuesday."

"Oh, yes, of course," said Hawker. "Only do forgive me. The place looks dreadful. Saturday, you know. I wasn't expecting anyone until much later on. It's fine. I often do tutorials up here. Here, have a seat. Be comfy. I'll be back in just a minute ... er ... could I offer you something while you're waiting?"

Joel sat.

His senses were returning. Dare he ask for coffee or a bun? "Tutorials?" He had not been that far out of line then. Maybe not.

Hawker hung there, anticipating Joel's response. "Might I fix you one of these? Or is it early? 'These' apparently referring to a shallow bird-bath-shaped glass in which floated an onion on a toothpick.

"It's a dry Martini. I'm being naughty I suppose, but, devil-take-it, it's Saturday and it's my time to unwind. Here, here. Please just take this one. I haven't touched it. I'll prepare myself another. Do excuse me. Sip it. It's possible you'll find it slightly strong."

For the first time Joel noticed Hawker's attire. A black silk robe, "Chinesey," monogrammed "R.H." It reached his mid-thigh only. A loose sash tied it round the waist. Open-necked, its top was spread apart to show the doctor's hairless smooth white chest. Sandals shod his slender, sinewed feet.

"Ah, you're taken by my raiments? I've been exercising. Oriental ballet. Keeps me limber. If you like I'll show you ... no? Here, just glance once through your theme and we'll discuss it. I'll be back."

Hawker wove the slightest bit unsteadily across the room. Exercising, Posh! He had been toping. Even in his haze Joel sensed enough to sniff that out. But then again, why not? Who made the rules? It was even possible that Hawker hadn't been to sleep yet, that his Friday night had been extended through this morning. Bachelors could work what schedules they preferred.

His head was getting clearer. Clearer still. Perhaps if he moved slowly he could stand. Best not. His theme? Oh look! A monograph by Branch Cabell—*Jurgen*. On the table and in easy reach.

Joel skimmed, "Poictesme—Petronius Arbiter ... Caverns of Phigalia...." The poem struck him. He rubbed his eyes, then read it through aloud.

Cabell. He had talked to Fred about him. Daring writer. His books caused quite a stir. When Hawker came back he could ask about Cabell. Joel's eye fell on the cover. "By now the fretful babblings of the prurient over the amatory excursions of Jurgen...."Good lines. Great words. Could he one day write that way? Could Hawker help him? The Caverns of Phigalia. Aloud he read again:

> I enter.
> Proud and erect.
> I take my fill of delight. Imperiously, Irrationally,

And none punishes. Not yet.
But in three months
And in three months
And in three more months,
The avenger comes forth
And mocks me, by being as I am visibly,
And by being foredoomed to do or I have done,
Inevitably."

"Bravo!" Hawker exploded. "Nicely read. You understood it?"

"Mostly," Joel answered, noting as he lay the book back on the table that the doctor had slipped out of the robe and into a black net shirt which billowed about his hips. A Buccaneer! It's peek-a-boo, it's décolletage, the older man's smooth pasty flesh, were working something on the youngster.

"From up Maine, aren't you?"

"We say 'down,'" Joel twitted.

"What part?"

"Near Ellsworth. Squantum Lake. You know it?"

"Is it near Bar Harbor?"

"No, much further south."

"I used to go there on our summer holidays. It's lovely."

"Ellsworth?"

"No, Bar Harbor, Dr. Sanders from Biology—have you met him? His parents kept a cabin by Dorr Mountain. His father worked at Roscoe Jackson Labs before the fire."

"That's interesting," Joel said, dutifully.

"Oh it isn't at all, and you know it," Hawker twitted him back. "Both of us would prefer to get on to your paper wouldn't we, rather than dwell on middle-aged bachelor reminiscences?" He took a sip from his bird bath. "You haven't touched yours. Is it too strong?"

"I'm not much of a drinker, but I'll try it," he suggested,

slowly, cautiously raising the glass to his lips. Tart, but interesting. No, not strong. No. He could handle it with ease. In fact, he rather liked the blending of the alcoholic flavors. And the onion. Nice concoction.

"A martini?" Joel asked.

"Is it too 'arid?' " Hawker smirked.

They laughed and opened up Joel's theme.

"For a young man you show considerable maturity," Hawker started. "I liked this bit about Cummings's 'dreaming wide awake.' How did that notion strike you?"

Quickened pulses. Pounding sounds. A man who cared. Joel sipped again.

"And this paragraph comparing Cummings's 'A leaf falls in the loneliness' to Herbert's 'Atlar.' Rather nice. You have the feel for poetry, Benedict—or may I call you 'Joel?' "

Could he?

Should he?

Should Hawker have crowded Joel ever so slightly, leaning over, or have placed the theme, its arching papers, its hard cover, in Joel's lap? And deftly, ambiguously, dubiously, inadvertently have pressed upon it now and then to make his point? Or hovered by so close?

"You must have had a wealth of intimate and personal experiences Joel, to be as geared to nuance as you seem."

And so Joel talked. Someone who cared. Or seemed to. He talked of Martha and the lighthouse, Grandma, Grace, his father, Loomis, Miss Bleek, and he talked of all his dearest dreams. Too much. Yea, much too much. He even knew it was "martini talk" and that he would regret it; even so. Cascades. The currents of it flowed. Tumbling, rushing out. "The whole 'shittin' kaboodle,' " as he would once to me characterize it, everything, the lot of it.

Dr. Hawker was most kind. And tender.

"You moved from the Lake when you were just that young? Because they couldn't cope with both the girls and you?"

"It's the first thing I remember."

"How awfully sad!"

"Yes, I supppose it is. I've been sad all my life."

"Well, I'd say your suffering has molded you some character," Hawker offered, lighting his pipe. "I'm proud to have you as a student. Don't let this go to your head, but you're one of the brightest I've ever ever worked with."

"And you're one of the ... no, *the* best teacher I've ever had," Joel got out, thickly, "but if you don't mind I think I'd better go. I'll finish up my drink and run."

"You'll nothing of the kind," said Hawker. "I'm going to fix a snack. I'm certain that you've taken next to nothing all day long."

"Please don't bother."

"It's no trouble. Here. You can help ... although you do look a little green around the gills. Are you alright?"

"I think. I'm ... just ... not used to drinking two martinis. Yes, they are strong."

"One gains a tolerance, which I confess I have. Here Joel, here, let me help you to the divan. I'll brew up some coffee. You'll be fine."

On rising, even with Hawker's supporting arm to help him, Joel discovered that his equilibrium was far more compromised than he had realized. The room swayed. Objects swam. The unicorn was playing Don Quixote with its horn. Black spots. They really happened.

Hawker took him firmly about his slender shoulders. Joel's hands reached out to find his friend's support. His head fell limp upon the teacher's bosom, then he totally surrendered to his weight—a sack of grain beside the divan, on the floor.

Whirlpools, flimsy fragmentary visions. Statements. An-

swers in his voice, from outer space. From inner space. And
Hawker's cooing, pleading, gentling reassuring sounds. "Only if
you're sure you want it." "I could help you if you'd let me.
Harvard. Yale. I have contacts. Joel, I love you. May I, now?"

His shoes slipped from his feet. "Poor darling. How you're
sweating. How you've suffered. Sent you packing, did they?
Well, no matter. I'll protect you. Here. I'm going to kiss you.
Now. Like that? Again. I love you, Joel, and you love me."

Joel did. At least he thought he did. He felt he felt he did.
Although only semi-conscious, he was totally alive reflexively;
he was done to and he did, or thought he did, whatever Hawker
wished, what he himself had wished. All tenderness. How
smooth. Fingers delicate as light beams on his skin. And stroked
his hair. Lips like butterfly's. Brush and touch. And urgings.

Branch Cabell.

Proud. Erect. The thrill! The sigh. In love.

Beyond restraint.

Hawker, in due course, entrenched Joel, secretly to be sure,
in alcohol, fellatio, sodomy, and drugs. On Saturdays and
Sundays. And most holidays besides.

Until.

*　*　*

"Until something happened. Actually I never knew how or
what. It was different. I'll say it as I think it. Did you ever read
The Last Hurrah, Edwin O'Connor's book? Oh, believe me, by
now I know that you won't answer. I'll go on. *I* read it. Anyone
who ever lived around Boston would realize how thinly it was
disguised. It was really about the life of James Michael Curley.
Big crook! Plenty old-time charisma though. Anyhow—I'm
rambling—he was the last of the baby-kissing, hand-shaking
politicians. In the book it tells how in the 'smoke-filled room' on

election eve, while all the party henchmen were watching the returns and slapping each other's back because of obvious victory, the 'Old Man' saw one untoward sign! Just a fleeting microscopic contradiction on the tally board, but small as it was, from it he could read the handwriting on the wall. Defeat! His long incumbency was over. The upstart would displace him.

"It was like that with Dr. Hawker.

"I had utterly surrendered to him, soul and body, even to the point of doing those stupid oriental ballet exercises, but I don't regret it, not a jot. In fact, I imagine he loved me too. Except that his dependency was less intense, less desperate than mine. I hung upon him, drew from him. Was that oral? I suppose. Something I had missed from way back when. I sucked his breast. Figuratively ... er ... aah ... anyhow I sort of realized that however much that man could supply, it wouldn't be enough. I mean it didn't touch the core."

"Which was?"

"Which must have been the earliest deprivations. My mother. Grace. The rotten timing of her having Grace and Mary so damned soon, and sending me away. I'm sad just resurrecting it."

"And Hawker couldn't undo that, eh?"

"I felt he could. In retrospect, I saw that he had problems of his own."

"Perhaps. From your descriptions it sounds as if the two of you were performing, each his own charade, to some potential audience. Pantomiming what you needed most. *You* missed your 'suck.' "

"Oh, here we go again."

"I'll stop if you can hear it. I mean, 'hear it!' "

"I understand you. Academically. But I'm still yearning. How come with all my enlightenment I haven't changed my 'style'?"

"Well, let's find out ... but listen, I want to be certain that you do follow. It is as if your behavior, ever since your childhood deprivation, has been trying to set the balance right, to make up lost supplies. Unfortunately you have been busy trying to paint out shadows. There was a futility in every symptomatic thing you did."

Benedict replied, "I see it. I'm aware that Hawker was old enough to be my father, and that he was also entitled 'Dr.' just as Dr. Fred. And I know that his loving me was how I wished a father or a mother would have done. Still, there is this awful sadness. That's what I was getting at. Like O'Connor's book.

"I saw a subtle sign, a hint that the situation was changing. I asked him; he denied it. Then I actually caught them together. Blond. Blue-eyed. An Adonis. Today I couldn't blame him. An athlete and a freshman!

"I reacted totally. I tried to commit suicide. That's when I saw my first psychiatrist."

"I know."

"He helped a little, but I wasn't honest with him—not fully. I never spoke of Hawker or the homosexuality. I couldn't have. I was afraid that Hawker would be fired. But he did get me out of my depression. That was good.

"He was supportive. Kind. Incidentally, that was around the time I started that weird 'compulsion.' It did start about then. Have I ever mentioned it? I'll say it anyhow. I know.

"I used to go into Boston to the analytic clinic to consult with Dr. Freedman. You probably knew him. No answer. Well, I'd guess he's dead by now. It was a low fee set-up, come to think of it, like this.

"Hmmm. That's funny isn't it? 'History repeats.' Anyhow, it started with a movie I had gone to, an anthropological thing about New Guinea, as I recall, *The Sky Above the Earth Below*. I had seen the preview. Natives running naked. They showed them on the screen. They wore some bizarre pyramid-shaped cones over their privates, as if to burlesque their penises, then they sewed an enormous snakeskin together and all of them crawled through it. Symbolized pregnancy. A ritualistic 'abreactive' business I suppose."

"How do you mean?"

"You know perfectly well how I mean."

"I want you to hear yourself say something," I insisted.

"I mean that the primitive peoples probably saw pregnancy or delivery as traumatic, and so they devised a ritualistic 'safety valve' to work their feelings off."

"People do that?" I asked, leadingly.

"You know perfectly well they do."

"Okay, so long as we have established it. It is possible that later on I may remind you of that."

"I saw the movie. It didn't do much for me, but from that date I started my 'game,' my 'compulsion.' I never related them to each other before."

"What's the 'game'?"

"Frottage."

"What's that?"

"French for 'rubbing.' "

"I know, but what was the 'game?' "

"This is embarrassing."

"Go on."

"I played it on the subways. They were always very crowded around the rush hour. Once you had squeezed into a car you would be pressed up tight against the other riders.

"And?"

" ... and ... this is awkward. Damn! I would spot someone beside whom I might wish to stand. I liked to get his buttocks up against my groin. Sardines. I didn't know if everybody realized how it worked and winked at it or if some were really unconscious."

"I have heard others speak of 'frottage,' only most men play it with the girls—their breasts," I offered.

"I have heard that too. So what?" Doctor Benedict asked, showing mild annoyance.

"Was that your 'compulsion?'"

"Oh no! No, no. I liked that part though, especially if I got slightly hard—I think that the bouncing of the cars was stimulating—no, the other thing was different. I would ride very close to the door. Maybe I feared some disclosure of my fantasies and wanted to escape. I would ride near the door as often as I could, but once the door would start to close, at least half the time, I'd feel an urgent need to squeeze out, and then did."

"How so?"

"I would squeeze out onto the platform, catch another car. Was that a 'claustrophobia'?"

"Was it?"

"Well, if I did it once, I would have to do it *twice*. Then I could forget it for a while. Never more than twice squeezing out on any single trip."

"You noticed that?"

"I did."

"What could it mean?"

"I have no idea at all. It started after that movie. Then it went away."

"The movie that supposedly was 'cathartic,' culturally speaking, for the 'pregnancy trauma'?"

"I remember that you marked those words Exhibit A," he said.

"Know why?"

"I don't."

"Well, speak your thoughts."

"A poem."

"A poem?"

" 'Backwards, turn backwards oh Time in thy flight.'...''

" 'Make me a child again just for tonight,' " I added.

"I really feel horrible right now. Incredibly heavy. Right now. This is when I want a smoke, or drink."

"Okay, notice that too. Exhibit B. Go on."

Mrs. Buffum

"How do you take your coffee?"

"Black, thank you."

"Sugar?"

"No, thanks."

"It's very nice of you to stop in."

"It's very kind of you to have me."

"I don't entertain much anymore, not since Horace died, and Melvin gone to do his doctorin' in West Virginia."

"Melvin?"

"My son."

"He's a doctor?"

"Mostly; he's a 'cheiropractic.' Oh, they give him an awful time. My Melvin wasn't much on studyin'. Not first. You know how boys are! Settled down tho', he did. May helped him. You can't say too much for her. Or Millie. Study? Every night. Did his garagin' and came home 'n' sat up in his room. Readin'. Three whole years. She helped him. She's a dear."

"May?"

"No, Millie. May was Cyril's by his first marriage. Millie's the baby sister."

"I don't see ... "

"Big family. Came here from Alabama or Georgia. Marry young down there."

"I'm afraid I ... "

"Cyril was married once before. Yup. He's a 'cheiropractic' now. Very successful too."

"Cyril?"

"No, Melvin, our only son. Wonderful practice! Of course he has to stay down there. Something about licenses. Can't get one here. I don't know why."

"Are you certain?"

"It's what he wrote me. I miss him so. No, you sit still. I'll get it."

Mrs. Buffum placed the sugar bowl on the table equidistant between them. She laid napkins beside the coffee cups. Irish linens. Very nice. They matched each other, though the creamer and sugar bowl did not. The silverware was monogrammed with "W."

Joel wondered what was its relevance, but opted to forbear. Atrocious bore, this woman. Besides her other dreary aspects, she had the dreadful habit of assuming that even total strangers whom she trapped into conversation could be miraculously, immediately familiar with all the characters in her life. Joel had encountered that vexing quality elsewhere (furthermore, albeit unawares, he tended on occasion to be guilty of that very breach himself).

I felt that with it Mrs. Buffum simultaneously expressed both hostility and its polar opposite, friendship. On the one hand, no one could possibly follow such a story line: that was hostile. On the other hand, implied at least, were openness, intimacy—instant invitations into the dramas of her private life.

From the cupboard drawer, she procured twin napkin rings. Into their embrace, she tucked two tissues rolled up into cylinders. From the stove across the room came the aroma of freshly perking coffee. It smelled good—familiar, promising.

It set limits, reassuringly, to the purpose and duration of this meeting, for the occurrence of which Joel was self-remonstrating. Yes, loneliness was bad, but this was worse. He heard himself speak out: "Are you much of a coffee drinker?"

"Only sociable. At my age it keeps you up all night. I uster drink the Sankers, but it didn't taste right. Would you have wanted tea instead?"

"Oh no, no, no, indeed! No, coffee's fine."

"Of course, for something special like having company, I love it. I take one cup regular at breakfast then just half a cup at night. Keeps me awake. I'm so glad you stopped by. That calls for coffee.

"Too much acid for my system," she went on, as Joel realized his head was bobbing up and down mechanically. He had phased her out. Better tune back in. "My, she's prating! I'd be happier asleep back in my place."

"Never usta be, too acid for my system, that is. Age, age does it. How old would you say I am?"

Joel's head continued up and down. After an awkward instant he caught himself and clung almost desperately at the echo of her "acid." He repeated that aloud as if the word had plunged him into thought.

"Well, I'm seventy, I am! No one believes it. But you're right about the acid. Mrs. Topham—she's the one who has to wear the bag?—she sips coffee and it runs right through her. Burns her insides, she says. She can tell. It comes straight out her side. Had to give it up.

"You bein' a doctor that don't bother you I take it."

"Not at all, Joel fibbed. "No, not at all."

"She's not long for this world, I figure, pity! Dear sweet thing she is."

Mrs. Buffum stepped to the stove. With a twist she shut off the gas, then rubbed her hand across her apron. It had been freshly washed and ironed. "Be just a minute now. I always let it settle good. You comfy in your rooms?"

"Delightfully, really. And now that you mention it, I had wanted to get your permission to plant a few things outside my door. Would there be any objection? Roses are my hobby. Do you like them?"

"You go ahead. Plant anything you like. That would be nice. You keep a garden where you lived before?"

"I've gardened now and then," was his tangential answer. "I love the colors and the subtle shades."

"Roses are just grand, so cheerful. Molly Wattle, she had the greenest thumb! Sugar?"

"No, no thanks!"

"Cream?"

"No, thanks. I take it black. Smells rich!"

"I call it 'cream,' except it isn't. Milk, actually. I don't take milk either. Melvin says too much cholesterols. 'Mother,' he says, 'you keep away from milk and butter.' Cheese is poison. Do you believe in them cholesterols?"

"Well, I have read a bit about the subject, but I understand it's controv ... "

'I know! Seems you can't eat next to anything except it kills you. Everything tastes good is bad it seems."

"That's true," Joel shifted. He wanted urgently to leave.

"Puts weight on you or plugs your vessels. I don't know what this world's coming to, I swear! I should think *you* wouldn't have to worry."

"How do you mean?"

"Bein' so nice and slim!"

"Oh, thanks," Joel smiled.

"'No dairy products, Mother,' that's the lastest thing.

What next? I could understand the sugar. That ran in my family."

"It what?"

"Diabetes. Mother Buffum had it too. I worry that my Melvin's going to catch it. Both sides! She died skin and bones. Wouldn't see a doctor though, not her. Christian Science. Horace used to scream at her, not that it helped."

"Horace?"

"Mr. Buffum. He didn't hold with Christian Science. Not that all the doctors helped him none when his time came. A stroke. Just fell right on this floor. Rolled under the table! Gone fifteen years this April."

Joel cleared his throat. He sipped. In replacing the cup on the saucer, he tried in vain to sneak a glance at his watch. Across his mind, distressingly, flashed the notion that this tiresome woman was, perhaps, the product of too long a life of solitude. Beware! Was he himself a bore? Had he, unbeknownst, offensive characteristics to which others would react?

"Your coffee strong enough?" she asked.

"It's fine. It's really splendid."

"Next thing you know they'll find it gives you something too."

"That's possible," Joel smiled wearily.

"Like migraines. Mother Buffum had them too. Held her belief. She knew she was dying. Didn't swerve, no sir! Melvin missed her. Six years old! She used to tell him stories. Oh, he was bright. That's when he said he wanted doctorin'. Help his Grandma. Course he didn't know she was a Christian Science. That some joke? Grand work. I think it's grand. How come you studied medicine?"

Joel fielded that too a little from the side, "Well, I'm not practicing just now."

"I know. You said."

Mrs. Buffum took a sip of her drink. "I always eat alone. I set my table though. You think that's funny? I put cream out, and sugar, and napkins even if I never use them. For myself. Know why? I put them out then put them back away. Every time. You think that's funny? Well, I've got my reason. I'd lose my mind if not. When Horace died 'n' Melvin moved away, for the longest time I'd set two places at the table. Just like he was here. Oh, I didn't talk to him or nothing'. I just kept up. Like now. I miss him still, ya know?"

"Melvin?"

"And Horace. Both. All the company I got now's my dog. I dream of them."

"That's natural," said Joel shifting again. He knew. He knew that irrespective of the enormous radii of her conversational circles, there was a central point. Sooner or later she would spiral in upon it. Some favor? Some damned hypochondriacal question? Some piece of plumbing or of carpentry? Fat chance! No, more than likely some symptom nagging at her, keeping her awake with worry. How he would like to leave!

"I fresh that up for you? How about a muffin? Got one warming in the oven. Smell it?"

"Thank you, no. I mustn't. I really have an awful lot to do. Besides, it's rude to wear out my welcome."

"Pish, tush! You're more than welcome. Any time."

Joel cringed.

"Do you believe in dreams?" she continued.

"Oh God help us. Here it comes," Joel thought. Is that her pitch? "I have studied them a little," he began before she cut him off.

"I still dream of Horace."

"You most likely miss him."

"Lord, I do. And Melvin. Can you imagine? Things need fixin'. Leaky water faucets, stopped up tub ... "

"I'm utterly useless when it comes to those," Joel parried. "Simply ten thumbs. Always have been. Could you get a handyman or plumber? Surely someone hereabouts could help."

"They cost!" She interrupted him. "You know, it ain't that pipe though, come to think of it. I'm more worried about somethin' here"—she pointed to her middle—"that's actin' stopped up too. Got me worried."

Joel squirmed.

"All swollen 'round my tailbone in the morning and my stomach's twice the size of what it oughta be."

For an instant she fell silent. Then she slid the paper napkin from its ring and, with a corner of it, daubed at the angle of her eye. The room seemed awfully quiet. How to break the pause? With what to fill the void? He tried. "You were saying about dreams?"

"Are you sure you won't have another sip of coffee?"

"No, I mustn't. Thank you."

"Could I ask you just one simple question, you being medical and all? My digestion. Not the same. I'm twice the size I oughta be through here. Oh well, I know that you got better things than listen to my worries. You mustn't mind an old lady talks too much. I hope I didn't bore you."

"Not a bit," said Joel. "I've enjoyed our chat."

"Will you come again? Whenever you feel like coffee or tea or muffins? Just knock. I'm always home."

Joel rose to leave. Strangely, as he did so, an enormously oppressive weight settled upon him. Like a tachistoscope flashing, his mind presented millisecond images of criss-crossed picket fences, carrot patches, dormer windows, stairs in need of fixing, and of Eban in the Lake, his brown-white torso floating by. Sickly feelings. Sox too tight and pants, and shirt, "Martha, see the lighthouse?" He could almost hear that clarion outcry. He broke into a sweat.

"I've got to go now Mrs. Buffum. Thank you."
In his room he phoned his sponsor in A.A.

* * *

"I had a dream," Dr. Benedict started. "It was very short
but very puzzling: I was in a hall, yet I was watching myself in
that hall. The feeling was familiar. Maybe school. I had to go
into another room where I had an appointment. I can still see
the door. It was huge. On it was printed just the single letter 'F.'
In red.

"Usually I don't dream in colors. Doesn't that mean intense
emotionality? Anyway, I got it open with great difficulty, by
pushing and finally by backing into it.

"Ha, ha! I used my rump like a battering ram. There was
water on the floor. Someone shouted. I felt great danger. I
wanted to get out.

"Now, here's the upsetting part: There was a kitten in the
water, a baby kitten with its hair all mattered down and its eyes
stuck tightly shut. I woke up in a sweat."

"What do you make of it?" I asked.

"Not much. Something terrifying. I tried to analyze it, only
I can't never do much with my dreams. The red 'F' was very
vivid. The passageway reminds me a little of my Grandmother's
house. Did I ever tell you that she had a kitten?

"I used to play with it. And the door, it was so huge ... "

"Just tell me what occurs to you."

"Nothing much."

"Whatever," I persisted.

Dr. Benedict lay motionless before me. On his behalf *I* had
a dozen quick ideas related to his dream and what it might have
meant. I chose to let them lie sequestered for the moment,
hoping that the flow of his would bring us confirmation.

"We were inseparable companions for a while, the kitty and me," he started. "It was a lonely life even then. Strange, that particular feeling hasn't really changed. Oh dear!"

"What else?"

"Not much."

"Would you mind running through the dream once more?"

He did. As usual, I listened carefully and followed every word, intent on spotting any variance from its first rendition. There was one.

"You left out the part about the battering ram. How you used your rump to back in through the door."

"I did?"

"You did."

"Well, what of it?"

"As I have told you, that's apt to be a sign that extra camouflage is being added at that point. Your mind has sensed some need to beef up its repression at that spot."

"So I'd be wise to analyze it there," he started.

"Yes, you would, but the only way you can is by associating freely, and out loud!"

"I'll try. I guess that means my telling you that I can't concentrate on the dream at all. I'm too upset about other things: my landlady. She caught me once again. With symptoms. And a request.

" 'I've got to ask you for a tiny favor, Dr. Benedict, if I may. It's my stomach. Like I was saying, I'm so irregular. I guess my bowel's just wore out. That happen? I'd be so pleased if I could get them regular again. Once each day. I don't feel right if I don't. And I'm so swollen. My doctor wants me in the hospital. For tests.'

"When she told me that she swept her hand across her lower abdomen, then she tried to take mine to palpate her. Down below. I drew back of course. Really! I couldn't offer an opinion anyway. I'm no clinician. Ugh! Well, I managed some platitude about hoping that she would soon get back to normal, but she persisted, and reminded me that there was 'this tiny favor.' Know what it was? That if anything should happen to her I might have to move.''

"To move?''

"If anything should happen to her, if she died.''

"So what was the 'tiny favor?' ''

"Oh, yes! Well that remark shook me right between the eyes. Thor's hammer! To move? Again? I actually reeled. So much that *I* almost didn't hear the favor either—simply to look after things a bit while she was gone—to feed her dog and to leave a light on above the fireplace, to scare the burglers off. I shouldn't have minded, but I did. That damned old fool ... especially asking me to touch her stomach, or her remarking that she hadn't been that swollen up 'for thirty years, since Melvin.' I was beside myself all day.''

"Your comment?''

"Oh, I can see in retrospect that I over-reacted. Why? I don't know. Somehow, though, the entrapment, her having no one else to ask, her going to the hospital, the possibility that I might have to move—the whole package turned me queasy. I wanted to throw up. I should have vomited all over her. That's hostile, isn't it?''

Dr. Benedict paused, sighed, then continued:

"Well, she did, wouldn't you know! I mean she did go to the hospital. Large bowel carcinoma—obstruction. So there I was. She called to tell me, and reminded me to leave a light burning above the mantel and to be sure that all·her faucets were turned off.''

"What happened then?'' I prodded him.

"What happened? Why I went as she had asked. The light was off. Of course the door was locked and she hadn't left me the key. I managed to get in, but after complying with her wishes I spent one of the most miserable nights in my entire life.

"I had an old-fashioned anxiety attack. I very nearly phoned you."

"Don't stop. What more?"

"That's it!"

"Uh, uh, there's more!"

"That's when I had the dream."

"Please. Speak your thoughts."

"I'm seeing that huge door. Say, here's an idea: Maybe the door wasn't huge. Maybe *I* was little!"

"Go on."

"Maybe it was a dream of childhood."

"Okay."

"Red 'F'."

"Go on!"

"Red 'F.' Red 'F.' That's it."

"What are you thinking?"

"That red 'F.' That's all."

"And something more," I pressed him.

"No, just that letter on the door."

"Say it then."

"Red 'F.'"

"Say it just as you were saying it before!"

"I did."

"You didn't."

"Yes, I did. Red 'F.'"

"You said it several times before."

"Red 'F,' red 'F,' red 'F!'"

"You hear it?"

"Hear what?"

"Let me say it my way: 'F red. F red F red.'"

"Oh! Jesus. Oh Jesus Christ!"

Joel was transfixed. "Do you suppose that I was dreaming about Dr. Fred? It figures. Trying to doctor that old fool! Hmm. Yes it could be, I suppose. It could. Her asking me the way she did to diagnose her stomach. Ha! That's a laugh."

"It would be typical of dreams to twist the picture that way," I encouraged him. "Can you say more?"

"I could," Joel started, then laughed unexpectedly. "Oh, this is funny. Do forgive me. It's a riot. Ha, ha, ha! Do you know what?"

"I do not."

"I'll tell you, except that it has nothing to do with the dream. I just recalled something. How stupid I am! When my landlady went into the hospital she forgot to leave me the key. When I tried to put her night light on I had a problem."

"What?"

"How to get in. I tried the front and rear doors, then the glass slider in the patio. Locked. Even the windows. I was about to give up when I saw the doggie door. I thought, 'Why not?' I mean, it was better than going the whole way over to her. So I got down on all fours and pushed my feet through. Hee, hee, hee! It was a squeeze. I got my rump in. Hey! Is that the dream? Well, I'll be damned! I wriggled and I squirmed and finally got in.

"Oh my! Know what? There *was* water on the floor. Yuh—that's in the dream too, isn't it?

"But here's the funny part ... "

Joel struggled for composure. It was nice to see him mirthful for once, even if the reason for his mood was puzzling and I felt a trifle uneasy lest his joy should prove short-lived.

"Yes, here's the funny part. The back door was just like yours. It had a knob lock. I could have let myself out and secured it easily, but instead do you know what I did?"

"Please tell me."

"I went out the way I entered. Through the porthole, through the dog door on the floor." He reddened and stopped abruptly.

"You what?"

"I did!"

"You went out through the dog door; why?" I asked him, also chuckling softly.

"I'm just plain stupid, that's my guess. I pushed out once again feet first."

I laughed aloud with him then for an instant, realizing that an avalanche of ideas was soon to crash upon us. Should I interrrupt his laughter? Would he need my prodding? Had my patient at this point the acumen, the objectivity to analyze the rest? I started nondirectively:

"The way you're feeling now seems quite the opposite of the depression, wouldn't you say?"

"I'm feeling wonderful this minute, grand! If only we could package this and save it, and draw from it whenever we need to! I'm so relieved. I feel released."

"I'm glad. Do you know why?"

"I acted like a baby. On the floor. I feel relieved. Released! I got down on all fours, went through that dog door like a baby coming out, like getting born!"

"You're absolutely right!" I shouted. "Good for you. Now keep on going, please."

"The birth canal," he managed. Ho! Ha! She was going to the hospital. Of course!"

"That's why you felt so anxious," I proposed. "Just like your mother. You would be abandoned once again and have to *move*. Into the city. That's precisely what you said."

"I see it. I really see it. Only help me. Help me, please."

We had at least a dozen different options. Which to pick up first? How to rank order them? How to keep accessible this portion of Joel's mind? In all honesty, I didn't know the wisest choice. "You went back to the 'scene of the crime,' eh?" I suggested, "Back to an early trauma, but did I understand that you went through the dog door twice?"

"I did."

"Know why?"

"Of course, I have *two sisters*! I was abreacting Martha's pregnancy *with both*."

"Even in your pushing through feet first!"

"Like Loomis through the coal chute!"

"Absolutely right! And what about red 'F?'"

"That's Dr. Fred. I see it. I can see the reason that I loved him. I feel I almost understand. In fact, I can. The reason that I sucked him. He was Martha nursing!"

"Is there more?"

"Of course."

"Then say it."

"I'm flashing onto Hawker, Dr. Hawker. He mothered me when I moved down to school."

"He 'babied' you?" I asked.

"Most certainly! In every way."

What else? The whole of it. Like logs that had been damning up a stream. Like the last precipitous expulsion that delivers us a baby to this world. The dikes had ruptured. Out the torrent flowed.

His subway "game": the squeezing out two times. Two births. Both Grace and Mary. I resurrected my exhibits "A" and "B." His signal markers dropped there in the heat of action, now returned to with the smoke blown off—how a "culture" has to "abreact gestation" and the act of childbirth and his urgency to suck and need to phone A.A. Recall?

Then confrontation with his catastrophic suicide attempt with Hawker's pledged allegiance to a sib, instead of him. Could

Joel deny his terrible excess of feeling? Did he see, with me, displacement at its core?

He did.

All of it was dropping into place. How dreadful though the limitations of our vocal instrument: that it confines us so to uttering our starbursts of ideas in single file. One pair of lungs, one windpipe, and one tongue!

We had to play Lysander, he and I, and chop their heads off, singly, as they wriggled through the pass.

It crossed my mind that feelings such as mine might well have been the basis of the cryptic allegory of the camel's passing through the needle's eye.

So.

Open thus Pandora's Box. All about emerging the monsters of his Hell. His ghouls: abandonment by Martha, Grace's birth. His infantile perceptions and fantasies of her nursing. The rejections. Hungers, loneliness. His ricochet off Sam, to whom he tried to turn. The fading warmth of his eccentric Grandma, then her death. His having once again to move. Don't forget Miss Bleek, his peers, and Hawker, nor Bruce, nor all the useless shoddy substitutes for nurture—love from fingers, cigarettes, or drink. Or drugs! Then crawling twice through Mistress Buffum's door.

Like cypress roots, arching downward into brackish, fetid, swampy waters. Whatever showed above was built upon decay. A slough. His basis was a slimy insubstantial bog. How clear the perils of those structures on it. How facile flowed (in retrospect) a prophecy for likes of Joel!

Was there yet a resurrection for this man? Salvation? Would he, could he, with his insight, shape his life anew?

For five months, together, he and I repeated, rediscovered. Yes, re-discovered. Confirmations cropping up. His wish to suckle and be loved, instead of Grace (and Mary). No nook or

cranny nor symbol could hide it. Naked, standing, sunlit, bright
as day!

But what to do with such new wisdom? Penthouse keys, if
Joel should wish to use them. Did he though? To saunter into
virgin byways? Pick up options long since spurned?

That is not for me to know, it seems.

I had fulfilled the terms as written in our contract. He had
been lifted out of his depression. He never had petitioned more,
of therapy or of analysis. His choice: the "gay" life, or the
"straight." So too if he should opt for drink or drugs. *Free
choice* and all that such connotes.

I spoke those words to him the day he took his departure.
I shook his hand, lingering a little sad myself to watch his
ancient car go wending down the hill. Then, in my empty office,
for a silent hour or so, I stoked his fading trace.

To sit in "analytic judgment." Who should be indicted? In
that cast of villains was there one who had played a leading role?
One prima ballerina? At last I closed the book, unsure.

Joint guilt?

Do you remember how the ancient Scottish courts brought
in at length their verdicts of *non liquet* when the issue wouldn't
solve as neatly as one wished? Clear "Ay" or "Nay?"

I knew I should settle Joel's precisely in such ambiguity of
terms. Lengthy trial. Plenty of evidence, and facts, and even, it
was hoped his "cure." Without a resolution of the nagging
central issue—on whom to pin the blame, or whom to "penal-
ize" *in fine.*

Full circle to our title question of
"Whodonit?"
Who, indeed?

DATE DUE